THINKING OTHERWISE

THINKING OTHERWISE

HOW WALTER LAFEBER EXPLAINED THE
HISTORY OF US FOREIGN RELATIONS

EDITED BY SUSAN A. BREWER,
RICHARD H. IMMERMAN, AND
DOUGLAS LITTLE

CORNELL UNIVERSITY PRESS
Ithaca and London

Thanks to generous funding from the LaFeber-Silbey American History Fund, the ebook editions of this book are available as open access volumes through the Cornell Open initiative.

Copyright © 2024 by Cornell University

The text of this book is licensed under a Creative Commons Attribution-NonCommercial-NoDerivatives 4.0 International License: https://creativecommons.org/licenses/by-nc-nd/4.0/. To use this book, or parts of this book, in any way not covered by the license, please contact Cornell University Press, Sage House, 512 East State Street, Ithaca, New York 14850. Visit our website at cornellpress.cornell.edu.

First published 2024 by Cornell University Press

Library of Congress Cataloging-in-Publication Data

Names: Brewer, Susan A. (Susan Ann), 1958– editor. | Immerman, Richard H., editor. | Little, Douglas, 1950– editor.
Title: Thinking otherwise : how Walter LaFeber explained the history of US foreign relations / edited by Susan A. Brewer, Richard H. Immerman, and Douglas Little.
Description: Ithaca : Cornell University Press, 2024. | Includes bibliographical references and index.
Identifiers: LCCN 2024018052 (print) | LCCN 2024018053 (ebook) | ISBN 9781501777561 (hardcover) | ISBN 9781501777578 (paperback) | ISBN 9781501777592 (epub) | ISBN 9781501777585 (pdf)
Subjects: LCSH: LaFeber, Walter—Influence. | LaFeber, Walter—Knowledge and learning. | United States—Foreign relations. | United States—Foreign relations—Study and teaching.
Classification: LCC E183.7 .T45 2024 (print) | LCC E183.7 (ebook) | DDC 327.73—dc23/eng/20240513
LC record available at https://lccn.loc.gov/2024018052
LC ebook record available at https://lccn.loc.gov/2024018053

For Walter LaFeber
Teacher, Scholar, and Inspiration

History has to be rewritten by each generation. Even if the facts are the same, the slant on the facts will be different.
   —Cornell historian Carl Becker answering the question: What is the good of history?

A professor is someone who thinks otherwise.
   —Walter LaFeber praising Carl Becker

Contents

Acknowledgments ix

Introduction: Thinking Otherwise
SUSAN A. BREWER, RICHARD H. IMMERMAN,
AND DOUGLAS LITTLE   1

1. Remembering Walt: From the Arts Quad to the Beacon Theatre
   DAVID GREEN AND DOUGLAS LITTLE   12

2. Walter LaFeber: The Making of a Wisconsin School Revisionist
   LLOYD C. GARDNER AND THOMAS J. MCCORMICK   32

3. Finding Walter LaFeber in the Records
   DAVID A. LANGBART   46

4. Extending the Sphere: *The New Empire*
   SUSAN A. BREWER AND ROBERT E. HANNIGAN   62

5. Reconstructing the Backstory: *America, Russia, and the Cold War*
   FRANK COSTIGLIOLA AND JEFFREY A. ENGEL   82

6. Thinking about Democracy: *Inevitable Revolutions*
   LORENA OROPEZA AND JAMES F. SIEKMEIER   104

7. Turning to Asia: *The Clash*
   ANNE L. FOSTER AND ANDREW ROTTER   132

8. Demystifying Globalization and US Power: *Michael Jordan and the New Global Capitalism*
   SAYURI GUTHRIE-SHIMIZU AND JESSICA WANG   153

9. Confronting the Tocqueville Problem:
   The Deadly Bet
   ERIC ALTERMAN AND RICHARD H. IMMERMAN   176

Coda: With a Bow to Walter LaFeber,
"What Then Can We Say in Conclusion?"
SUSAN A. BREWER, RICHARD H. IMMERMAN,
AND DOUGLAS LITTLE   200

*Bibliography of Walter LaFeber's Works:
How Did He Ever Find the Time?*   207

Index   213

About the Contributors   223

Acknowledgments

It is unorthodox to begin acknowledgments in an edited volume by thanking one of the contributors. But this book is unorthodox for multiple reasons, and as editors we must direct our first thank-you to Frank Costigliola and Diann Bertucci. Not long after Walter LaFeber passed away in March 2021, a cohort of his former students started to bat around ideas about how to pay him tribute. What would be appropriate for someone who taught us, who mentored us, who inspired us, and who literally changed our lives? To drill down into the question, Frank and Diann hosted more than a half-dozen of us at their farm in Connecticut. Even as they fed us scrumptious meals, giving real meaning to the "farm-to-table" concept, they gave us free rein over their house and deck to talk about Walt and formulate a strategy for honoring him. That discussion gave rise to this book, and for this reason we can't exaggerate the value of Frank and Diann's hospitality.

In this same vein, we must thank Sandy LaFeber, Suzanne Kahl, and Scott LaFeber, who drove down from Boston to join us. They not only provided us with insights about Walt that inform this book, but they also encouraged us to undertake the project. That was vitally important, because we all knew that Walt would have called it a waste of our time. Sandy, Suzanne, and Scott's endorsement of the project—and beyond that, their manifest enthusiasm for it—removed our hesitancy to violate Walt's wishes. They continued to offer us their collective support and wisdom throughout, ensuring that the project was truly a family affair.

The same can be said for Lloyd Gardner, who drove up from New Jersey with Nancy to share with us his stories about and understandings of Walt that date back to their time as graduate students together at the University of Wisconsin in the 1950s. That Lloyd and Nancy would make this effort confirmed to us that by producing a book, a tribute that made a scholarly contribution as well as honored our favorite professor, we were doing right by Walt. Lloyd subsequently underscored that confirmation by allowing us to include an article that he and Tom McCormick published in *Diplomatic History* back in 2004 about Walt and the Wisconsin School. And like the LaFeber family, Lloyd was always available to answer our questions and correct our mistakes.

We held that Connecticut "retreat" in September 2021 and hit the ground running immediately afterward. Within weeks we contacted Cornell University Press (CUP) to explore its interest in publishing a book that exposed and explained Walt's understanding of the history of US foreign relations. CUP was, of course, the appropriate press. Yet the framework for the book remained undeveloped, we had yet to invite all the contributors, and we had not even begun to draft a proposal. Michael McGandy nevertheless offered us a contract after but one phone call. For that we are so very grateful. And we are even more grateful to Sarah Grossman, who took over the project after Michael left the press. As our editor, Sarah went well beyond the call of duty, which we will further elaborate on in a moment.

But first we need to express our profound thanks to Andrew Tisch, without whom this project might never have gotten off the ground and would almost certainly never have reached fruition in all its dimensions. For decades Andrew had demonstrated his respect and affection for Walt. He and his brother had established the Andrew H. and James S. Tisch Distinguished University Professorship, which Walt held during his final years at Cornell. (After Walt's death, Andrew established the Walter LaFeber chair.) Fifteen years earlier, in 2006, Andrew had organized the event at the Beacon Theatre, in New York City, where Walt delivered his "Farewell Address" to an audience of well over 2,000. So even as we were preparing our book proposal for Cornell University Press, Andrew offered to help fund and organize a conference to mark the book's completion. In fact, it was Andrew who suggested that we hold the conference at the new Cornell Tech campus on Roosevelt Island in New York City, and then he immediately agreed with our suggestion to plan a get-together in Ithaca to workshop the chapters in October 2022, a year prior to the estimated completion date of the manuscript and the Roosevelt Island conference. Andrew's generosity and his "cheerleading" added to the project's momentum that the Connecticut retreat in 2021 had generated.

By the time we held the workshop on Cornell's Ithaca campus, we had arrived at a title: *Thinking Otherwise: How Walter LaFeber Explained the History of US Foreign Relations*. The title reflected Walt's commitment always to question the historical record and received wisdom. That attribute was essential to his scholarship and to the excitement he instilled in his students. We had already decided that six of the chapters would each be based on one of Walt's six major monographs, and in order to include more of Walt's students in the book, we decided that each chapter would be coauthored. This decision added a significant wrinkle to the project. Many of us had never coauthored any

ACKNOWLEDGMENTS　　xi

publications, and some of the selected co-authors didn't even know each other. Yet somehow, perhaps due to Walt's influence, by October 2022, less than a year after we launched the project, the authors were able to present complete drafts of their assigned chapters, which every one of us read, and read carefully.

As a consequence, the workshop improved the book manuscript immeasurably. We all agreed that none of us had experienced more productive or constructive critiques of our work. Andrew helped fund the workshop and attended throughout. So did David Maisel, a student whom Walt had influenced as much as any contributor to the book. David donated his own money, helped arrange for funding through Cornell's Department of History, and made available to us his personal archive of correspondence with Walt (as did Andrew!). With regard to funding and other support for the workshop, we received vital assistance from Tamara Loos, the chair of the history department. Tamara made possible what we thought was impossible. No less vital was the assistance of Michael Duane Williamson, the history department's administrative manager. Michael supervised the financial intricacies and single-handedly orchestrated the complicated logistics. Tamara was on leave when we held the workshop, so she passed the baton to the interim chair, Lawrence Glickman. Going beyond his administrative role, Larry attended the workshop sessions and offered us terrific advice. So, too, did Ruth Lawlor, who had just joined the department as the historian of the "US in the World." Ruth became so integral to the project during the Ithaca workshop that we anointed her an honorary member of the "LaFeber posse," the name by which the contributors came to be known.

Acknowledging how much we benefited from Larry's and Ruth's input at the workshop brings us back to Sarah Grossman. Sarah likewise attended throughout, and as one of Walt's former students herself, regularly intervened in the discussions with substantive and stylistic advice. And she was there to answer our questions: about audience, about the relationship among the chapters, even about diction and terminology. Sarah was the kind of hands-on editor that a book such as this really needs, pushing us to add this or subtract that, but always gently. And when, over the subsequent months, Sarah was not available, and even when she was, Jacqulyn Teoh, also a CUP acquisitions editor, was equally hands-on. There were many moving parts to this manuscript, and Jackie made sure each one of them stayed on track so the production process never missed a beat. Our copy-editing team—Mary Ribesky and Wendy Nelson—did great work with a careful eye and a light touch. And we give special thanks to Evan Earle, the Cornell University archivist, and his staff, including Grace Bichler and Julia Gardner, for tracking down and digitizing many of the photos in the book. And we must also thank the two anonymous reviewers who provided helpful advice in addition to their thumbs up.

Because the evolution of *Thinking Otherwise* and the conference at New York City's Cornell Tech campus in October 2023 that marked its culmination were so intertwined from the project's inception, we would be remiss if we did not express in these acknowledgments our appreciation for those who made the conference not only possible but also such a success. Again, we start with Andrew Tisch, who provided funding, masterminded the fundraising, and even conceived of and then produced memorable "swag"—a hockey puck that featured a photograph of Walt. And talk about hands-on! Andrew was in contact on virtually a weekly basis with a liaison for the posse, offering every kind of advice and suggestion imaginable (even on the swag!). In this he was ably assisted by Patricia Peters, on whom we came to depend for so many of the organizational matters and who also contributed to our planning.

It was in large part because of Andrew and Trish that Cornell's exceptionally capable Office of Alumni Affairs, primarily but not exclusively the Office of Northeast Corridor Engagement, came to shoulder the bulk of the burden for organizing and publicizing the conference—thereby promoting *Thinking Otherwise* in advance of its publication. We can't even begin to itemize all of their efforts on our behalf. But we can list each of those who enthusiastically and cheerfully came to our aid, not by titles but in alphabetical order so that we signal that, from our perspective, rank had nothing to do with their contributions. Thank you Erika Axe, Andrew Gossen, Casey Lucier, Kevin Mahaney, Veronica McFall, Lizeth Jaimez Mendoza, Michael O'Neill, Michelle Jennifer Vaeth, Arienne Watson, and Stephanie Watt. Also deserving our thanks are Monica Yant Kinney, Cornell's associate vice president for communications; Beth Saulnier, the editor in chief of *Cornellians*; and Joe Wilensky, senior editor and writer for *Cornellians* whose columns about our project (and derivative one on campus dogs) excited us as well as the Cornell community. We also want to express our deep gratitude to Kathy Mendall, the assistant director of events at Cornell Tech; Joycelyn Baddoo, the conference service manager for the Graduate New York hotel on the Cornell Tech campus; and Christian Comacho, Beatriz Ramos, and Bradley Esquea of the Constellation Culinary Group.

Among the highlights of the conference were two roundtables composed of some of Walt's former students who have made their marks in the worlds of policy making, business, industry, law, and education. We hoped to include snippets from these discussions in the book, but the timing of the publication made that impossible. Videotapes will be available online to the public at large. We take this opportunity to thank the roundtable chairs, Tom Pepinksy,

ACKNOWLEDGMENTS

Cornell's Walter F. LaFeber Professor of Government, and Andrew Tisch (again!), and all the participants: Jeffrey Bialos, Eric Edelman, Robert Einhorn, Stephen Hadley, Paul Jones, Shannon Smith, Stephen Arbogast, Alison Dreizen, LizAnn Rogovoy Eisen, David Maisel, Peter Schuck, C. Evan Stewart, and David Zalaznick. Jeff Engel directs the Center for Presidential History at Southern Methodist University, and exploiting the CPH's experience and expertise, he organized an oral history project that built on the roundtables' foundations. The transcripts will also be available to the public online—specifically on a website constructed and hosted by the CPH. So thank you Jeff, Brian Franklin, Zachary Conn, Augusta Dell'Omo, Lai Yee Leong, Jonathan Ng, Greta Swain, and the invaluable Ronna Spitz.

These acknowledgments would be incomplete without our thanking those Cornell officers who provided advice, support, and, not insignificantly, funding. These include President Martha Pollack, Provost Michael Kotlikoff, Dean Colleen Barry of the Brooks School of Public Policy, and Derk Pereboom, Senior Associate Dean for Arts and Humanities.

Finally, coming full circle, we must end these acknowledgments on the same unorthodox note we began with. Although perhaps they should, editors rarely thank the contributors to an edited volume. In the case of *Thinking Otherwise*, however, it would be criminal for us not to do so. Despite working with a tight deadline and requiring frequent consultation, the co-authors (and in one case the sole author) of each chapter made our responsibilities as editors not only easier but literally also joyful. They accepted our suggestions graciously, they rejected them respectfully (and, with a nod to Walt, diplomatically), and they responded promptly. Indeed, we wonder how many editors can boast that they turned in a manuscript that included this many chapters written by this many authors by a deadline that, frankly, seemed unrealistically ambitious. And we achieved this feat without a single case of heartburn. So thank you, again in alphabetical order, Eric Alterman, Frank Costigliola, Jeff Engel, Anne Foster, Lloyd Gardner, David Green, Sayuri Guthrie-Shimizu, Bob Hannigan, David Langbart, Lorena Oropeza, Andy Rotter, Jim Siekmeier, and Jessica Wang. And finally, thanks to you, Walt. All of the contributors acknowledge that you deserve primary credit for our evolving into the scholars, professionals, and colleagues that we are today. We are proud to call ourselves your students.

Introduction
Thinking Otherwise

SUSAN A. BREWER, RICHARD H. IMMERMAN, AND DOUGLAS LITTLE

Walter LaFeber, one of the most distinguished US historians, wowed generations of Cornellians from the moment he arrived in Ithaca in 1959 through his death in March 2021. He was a legendary and revered teacher whose lectures on the history of US foreign policy drew hundreds of students every semester during the 1960s, 1970s, and 1980s. He was a prize-winning scholar whose insightful accounts of US relations with Russia (and the Soviet Union), Central America, and Japan and best-selling textbook, *The American Age*, became "must-reads" in history courses across the country and around the globe. He was a devoted mentor to dozens of undergraduate and graduate students who pursued careers in college teaching, US government service, the law, the fine arts, philanthropy, and business and industry. And perhaps most important, in his lectures, his scholarship, and his dealings with the contributors to this book, he made a habit of thinking otherwise.

On a sun-dappled Saturday afternoon in September 2021, eight of us converged on Frank Costigliola's house nestled in the Connecticut woods to reminisce and celebrate Walt's life. Out of that informal gathering came plans for a book honoring him. The idea had emerged in the wake of a glowing tribute that had taken place at a meeting of the Society for Historians of American Foreign Relations (SHAFR) a few months earlier. Walt's wife Sandy, his daughter Suzanne, and his son Scott also drove down from Boston for the day. Over white wine and craft beer, we shared our favorite stories about Walt, both

LaFeber was an extraordinarily approachable teacher, a brilliant historian, and the kindest and wisest mentor the contributors to this volume have ever known. Courtesy of the Cornell University Archives.

personal and professional, and reached consensus on several things. He was the greatest teacher and wisest mentor that anyone present had ever encountered. His days must have lasted more than twenty-four hours for him to have written so many iconic books and articles while still managing to stay in touch with students, friends, and colleagues. He preferred dogs to cats. Although he often lost faith in the Chicago Cubs, he never lost his love for them. And if Walt were to learn that a project such as this was in the works, he surely would have asked: "Don't you all have something more productive to do with your time?"

At a literal farm-to-table dinner that night and brunch the following morning, this self-styled "LaFeber posse"—five former undergraduates, two former PhD students, and a lifelong friend—came up with an idea for an unconventional tribute designed to showcase not their own research but Walt's scholarly work and his profound impact on the profession. The LaFeber posse would eventually double in size (evenly split between undergraduate and graduate alums who spanned some four decades of study with Walt at Cornell) and begin meeting regularly over Zoom to plan the collection of chapters that follows. Over Halloween weekend in October 2022, the Cornell history department, with notable support from Andrew Tisch, David Maisel, and the LaFeber family, hosted a workshop in Ithaca that brought the entire posse together for the first time in the flesh. It was an experience unlike any academic gathering any of the posse members could remember. After a presentation of each chapter, there was a freewheeling discussion about how best to ensure that the whole was greater than the sum of the parts. Posse members criticized and complimented one another. They told stories. Mostly strangers previously, they bonded over Walt.

What has emerged is a tribute divided into two sections. Chapters 1 to 3 profile "Walt the person" by charting his career at Cornell, recalling his formative years in graduate school, and showing how he literally made his way into the archival records, where he did so much scholarly research. Chapters 4 to 9 celebrate "LaFeber the great historian" and demonstrate his enduring influence on the field of US diplomatic history by linking six of his monographs and related writings to his abiding concern about the fate of the US experiment from the eighteenth century to the present. Neither biography, nor historiography, nor hagiography, this book is a testament to a teacher-scholar who managed to inspire thousands of students and publish more than a dozen books while still finding time to attend baseball games, even when his beloved Cubs were not playing, and to catch Tony Award–winning performances on Broadway.

Walter LaFeber arrived at Cornell University a few weeks shy of his twenty-sixth birthday and would spend his entire career teaching there. Cornell is an Ivy League school but also a land-grant institution, a place that, when Walt arrived, combined the intimacy of tiny Hanover College, where he had earned his BA, and the high-powered research environment of the University of Wisconsin–Madison, where he had earned his PhD. Ithaca, the city Walt came to call home, had a population of just under 30,000 in August 1959, twenty times the size of Walkerton, Indiana, where he had grown up, but much smaller than Boston or New Haven. In short, Cornell was a perfect fit, and Ithaca was a perfect setting, for a rising academic star who, as David Green and Douglas Little confirm in chapter 1, soon became the archetypal teacher-scholar on campus.

During the late 1950s, Cornell could already boast a cadre of world-famous faculty—including Hans Bethe in physics, Clinton Rossiter in government, and Vladimir Nabokov in comparative literature—who set a high standard for engaged teaching. In no time at all, Walt would join their ranks, thanks mainly to his two-semester lecture course on US foreign policy but also his seminars on Cold War diplomacy and, occasionally, his rendition of the US survey pitched to first-year students. The secret to his success in the classroom was not very complicated. Walt kept his lectures focused on the forest rather than the trees, he never wavered in setting high expectations for his students, and he radiated a kindness and a humility that made him extraordinarily approachable.

Undergraduates and PhD students were not the only Cornellians enthralled by Walt LaFeber. As early as the mid-1960s, faculty colleagues across campus admired his leadership and respected his commitment to principle. From the 1970s through the 1990s and beyond, deans, provosts, and presidents sought his counsel, and trustees were astonished by his commitment to the university. Yet although Walt was hopelessly devoted to Cornell, he remained, first and foremost, a historian who had no interest whatsoever in becoming an administrator, as he once made very clear with his trademark sense of humor. "When Dale Corson became President in 1969, . . . I told someone I thought so highly of Dale that I'd help collect the garbage at Cornell if he asked me," Walt recalled long afterward. "Several years later, Dale asked me to be Dean of the Arts College. I immediately said no." Then came the punchline: "He said he had heard I'd collect garbage for him. I said that yes I would, but I would not be Dean."[1]

In chapter 2, Lloyd Gardner and Thomas McCormick reveal how Walt LaFeber came to be that historian. After earning his MA at Stanford, he entered the PhD program at the University of Wisconsin—then, as now, a hotbed of progressivism in a state where the ghost of Robert ("Fighting Bob") LaFollette shadow-boxed with the country's leading right-wing demagogue, Joseph ("Tail Gunner Joe") McCarthy. Madison, the state capital, was riven by a town and gown divide, with many locals convinced that graduate students in the humanities and social sciences, and the professors who taught them, were at best parlor pinks and at worst card-carrying communists. The reality, however, was a bit different. After all, this was the Midwest in the 1950s. Like Gardner and McCormick, his good friends from his renowned graduate student cohort, Walt was a disenchanted member of the "Silent Generation" who liked to sip lime Cokes at Rennebohm's drugstore in the afternoon. But often in the evenings, all three of them would eagerly attend bull sessions hosted by William Appleman Williams, where they traded ideas with him and other young UW faculty.

Walt came to challenge Cold War orthodoxy while writing a dissertation on the roots of US expansion in the nineteenth century and discovering how, as another historian would put it several decades later, the United States had managed to hide an empire.[2] To be sure, Bill Williams and Walt's (and Bill's) mentor, Fred Harvey Harrington, always asked: Where's the economics? But the "Wisconsin School revisionists" took their cues from Charles A. Beard, not Karl Marx, and those who later claimed that Walt and his comrades were "economic determinists" or, even worse, apologists for the Kremlin, either misunderstood or misrepresented the nature of their critique of US foreign policy. Rather than endorsing Soviet premier Nikita Khrushchev's attacks on US imperialism, Walt LaFeber shared President Dwight Eisenhower's fear that the exigencies of the Cold War abroad were putting democracy at risk at home. "We must guard against the acquisition of unwarranted influence, whether sought or unsought, by the military-industrial complex," Ike warned in a farewell address not long after Walt left Madison for Ithaca. "The potential for the disastrous rise of misplaced power exists and will persist."[3] Two decades later Walt would succinctly describe his place on the political spectrum. "I'm hardly a radical revisionist, as people who are (and are also good friends, such as Lloyd Gardner) keep reminding me," he told one of the contributors to this book in September 1980. "It is difficult to hold a chair at Cornell and be a radical—at least some times. On the other hand, I'm not about to go into a monastery to prove a point."[4]

As David Langbart makes clear in chapter 3, few historians at Cornell or anywhere else have been more committed than Walt LaFeber to archival research or as determined to promote preservation of records and scholarly access to classified material. Walt's books utilize a broad array of US documentary sources ranging from the Library of Congress and the National Archives to presidential libraries and state historical societies. He recognized the importance of multi-archival research, frequently visiting the British Public Record Office and utilizing Latin American, Russian, and Japanese documents in translation. And as chair of the State Department's Historical Advisory Committee during the Nixon and Ford administrations, Walt was a persistent, though not always successful, advocate for more rapid declassification of government secrets that were essential for the accuracy of the *Foreign Relations of the United States* series.

The archives reveal that not long after the fall of Saigon, the United States Information Agency invited Walt to deliver a series of lectures in the Far East. In late 1975 Walt visited universities in Singapore, Japan, and Thailand, where he recapped the history of the US emergence as a Pacific power and ruminated on the likely fallout from the debacle in Vietnam. Walt's candid appraisal of the US predicament in Asia reflected a sincere, but critical, patriotism. This was consistent with the values he embraced during graduate school at Wisconsin and throughout his career at Cornell: the resolve necessary to make the past come alive in the lecture hall, faith that scholarly integrity would set the historical record straight, a belief in the importance of an educated citizenry, and the hope that, under the right circumstances, US policy makers might learn from their mistakes.

Chapters 4–9 highlight our second goal: to address Walter LaFeber's wide-ranging contributions to the field of diplomatic history and the broader public conversation about US foreign policy. His scholarship has had a profound impact on our understanding of the history of US foreign relations. Some of his writings became master narratives for the important matters he explored, while others nudged the field in new directions. Examined collectively, chapters 4–9 reveal the common denominators of LaFeber's scholarship: the implication of the admonition to "extend the sphere," the synergies between domestic dynamics and foreign imperatives, and the interplay of structural forces and individual agency. At the same time, these chapters reveal LaFeber's remarkable range. His monographs spanned geography and chronology, addressing economics, race, political culture, and technological advances, sometimes alone but often in combination.

These chapters are written to stand alone, but they are best understood together. By focusing on six of LaFeber's most important books and linking them to contemporary issues, we, the contributors to this book, examine the broad spectrum of his concerns, his arguments, and his enduring influence. These considerations, in turn, have led us to expand and extrapolate from what we have learned. Put differently, LaFeber's writings have provoked us to think otherwise.

Like most freshly minted historians, Walter LaFeber revised and expanded his dissertation into his first book. And as Susan Brewer and Robert Hannigan detail in chapter 4, oh, what a book it was! In *The New Empire*, LaFeber outlined the intellectual, strategic, and economic underpinnings of an outward thrust that culminated in war with Spain in 1898 and the emergence of the United States as a great power. He showed that far from being an aberration, the US acquisition of colonies in the Caribbean and the Far East during the late 1890s signaled the US transition from continental to transoceanic expansion, a compelling new interpretive framework that in 1963 earned him the American Historical Association's Albert J. Beveridge Prize.

In his lectures and in his writings on the antebellum period, LaFeber traced this expansionist impulse back several generations to James Madison, the

"Father of the Constitution," who argued in the 1780s that the most effective solution to the political challenges facing the new republic was to "extend the sphere." Then LaFeber turned the spotlight on his hero, John Quincy Adams, who as secretary of state in 1823 persuaded the president he served to promulgate the Monroe Doctrine, a geopolitical blueprint for a rising US empire that would take on increasingly theological overtones from the 1890s to the 1940s and beyond. "I've not been able to discover how doctrine became a term in US foreign policy, but it is clear that it has an overweight religious component that makes it central to understanding US foreign policy—and why Americans support it," LaFeber confessed four decades after the publication of *The New Empire*. "It began when doctrine first appeared during the 2nd Great Awakening and took off from there—until now, every President has to be certified American by having a doctrine."[5]

Having reframed the traditional narrative of the US collision with Spain during the 1890s, LaFeber turned his attention to the US collision with the Soviet Union on Harry Truman's watch. In chapter 5, Frank Costigliola and Jeffrey Engel not only reveal how LaFeber came to write *America, Russia, and the Cold War*, his most widely read book, but also uncover the evolution of a great historian's thinking in response to the shifting relationship and intensifying rivalry between the superpowers. Juggling the relativism of Carl Becker, the realism of George Kennan, and the revisionism of his mentors at Wisconsin, LaFeber sought to solve a riddle posed by Reinhold Niebuhr: Was the Cold War a Greek tragedy of inevitability or a Christian tragedy of possibility? Through ten editions, LaFeber would spend forty years refining his answer, adding new research, while preserving a crisp, concise analysis of the evolving Soviet-US rivalry that would be read by thousands and thousands of students. Dismissing those who framed the Cold War as "a long peace" that never saw the United States and Russia fire shots in anger at each other, he emphasized the terrible human costs that the superpowers inflicted on ordinary men, women, and children after the Cold War spilled over into Asia, Africa, the Middle East, and Latin America.[6]

A year after the sixth edition of *America, Russia, and the Cold War* appeared in 1988, LaFeber reiterated that both Washington and Moscow had a responsibility to end the decades-old conflict peacefully. "I cared less about who was the good and who was the bad guy," he said, explaining that he was "much more interested in pointing out how both the Soviet and US systems, not just the Soviet, had their backs against the wall by the mid-1980s and had to make some compromises in the Cold War to survive intact, or relatively intact."[7]

The rise of Mikhail Gorbachev and the soft landing at the end of the Cold War would have surprised Niebuhr, and LaFeber gave George H. W. Bush high marks in 1989 for not dancing on the Berlin Wall. Yet the next three decades would bring a series of missed opportunities that seemed to confirm that, even after the fall of communism, conflict between the United States and Russia would remain a chronic condition. The 1990s brought neither "the end of history" nor a massive "peace dividend." Rather, emerging from the post–Cold War decade were failed states from Somalia to Haiti, the sudden collapse of the Kremlin's empire, and the rise of Islamic extremism—problems that could not be solved by relying on military alliances, covert operations, economic leverage, or other gadgets that had been in the US tool kit during the Cold War. By the early twenty-first century, LaFeber feared that a new cold war with Russia was inevitable, not only because of Vladimir Putin's determination to reverse what the Russian autocrat saw as the greatest tragedy of the twentieth century—the demise of the Soviet Union—but also because of US arrogance and ignorance in expanding the NATO military alliance into former Soviet domains.

Readers of chapter 6, by Lorena Oropeza and James Siekmeier, will not be surprised to learn that inevitability was also the central theme of LaFeber's most controversial book. *Inevitable Revolutions* was published in 1983, just as Washington was escalating its not-so-secret covert war against left-wing insurgents in Central America, whom the Reagan administration claimed were Cuban-inspired and Soviet-controlled. Vigorously rejecting that claim, LaFeber argued that the turmoil in Nicaragua, El Salvador, and their neighbors was merely the latest episode in the centuries-old US quest for hegemony over its Latin neighbors. Driven by security concerns in the Caribbean, economic interests ranging from Guatemala to Chile, and reflexive anticommunism, US policies and actions had produced not democracy but "neo dependency," a brutal and exploitative system that would cost thousands of lives in Central America during the 1980s.

In many ways, *Inevitable Revolutions* was a bookend to the story LaFeber had begun to tell in *The New Empire*. Race figured much more prominently in his analysis of the 1980s than in his account of the 1890s, something that reflected a field in transition, with diplomatic historians focusing less on the white men who controlled US foreign policy and more on the people of color who were on the receiving end of US hegemony. Because *Inevitable Revolutions* sold well and was widely adopted for classroom use, LaFeber became a lightning rod for supporters of Reagan's anticommunist crusade in Central America, transforming him briefly into an embattled public intellectual, a role in which he was never comfortable. His abiding faith in democracy, however, never wavered, notwithstanding right-wing critics erroneously branding him a Marxist.

Even as he was chronicling the carnage in Central America, LaFeber was turning his attention to Asia, where, as Anne Foster and Andrew Rotter highlight in chapter 7, he prophesied that deepening rivalries across the Pacific would preoccupy US policy makers well into the new millennium. *The Clash*, which won the 1998 Bancroft Prize, is much more than an overview of US relations with Japan from the 1850s through the 1990s. As with his past work, LaFeber adopted a state-centered approach, but he examined tensions between Washington and Tokyo through a transnational lens and utilized many Japanese-language sources to tell his story from both ends of the telescope. The book also reflects an acute sense of place, with the geographic distance between LaFeber's native Midwest and the Far East shrinking geopolitically, like objects in a side-view mirror that are actually closer than they appear.

Once again, race figured prominently in *The Clash*, not only in LaFeber's analysis of the xenophobic mutual demonization that led the United States and Japan to engage in a "war without mercy" during the 1940s, but also in his description of the striking differences in how the two countries approached economic matters during the 1970s and 1980s. With a bow to the cultural turn in diplomatic history, LaFeber argued that Japanese-style capitalism—hierarchical, government-directed, and oligopolistic—had deep roots in the island nation's past that ran counter to US practice and tradition, which featured the open door, a faith in the magic of the marketplace, and a ferocious individualism that had enabled nineteenth-century statesmen to extend the sphere. At a time when the Clinton administration was preoccupied with crises in the Balkans and the Middle East, *The Clash* made a prescient case that, sooner rather than later, the United States would need to pivot to Asia.

In chapter 8, Sayuri Guthrie-Shimizu and Jessica Wang underscore LaFeber's abiding mistrust of centralized economic power; his lifelong enthusiasm for baseball, basketball, and other sports; and, hovering above both, his fondness for state-centered diplomatic history and his ambivalence about "the cultural turn." *Michael Jordan and the New Global Capitalism* could only have been written by a Wisconsin School revisionist who grew up shooting hoops in high school, rooting for the Notre Dame Fighting Irish, and shuttling regularly between Walkerton, Indiana, and Wrigley Field. At the dawn of what LaFeber suspected would become the Asian Century, baseball had emerged as the national pastime in Japan, and Michael Jordan, aka "His Airness," who had been acclaimed the greatest player in NBA history, was more popular in China than Mao Zedong.

Thanks to ESPN and other media giants, professional sports became one of the most potent instruments of US "soft power" in the post–Cold War era, while US multinational corporations like Nike, Michael Jordan's sponsor, became force multipliers. Equally important, as LaFeber pointed out in his SHAFR presidential address in 1999, was innovative US technology, which served as the third leg of this soft-power tripod during a short-lived "unipolar moment" after the Cold War, when policy makers in Washington struggled to prevent Japan from surpassing the United States economically and to prepare for China's emergence as a military superpower. Yet despite LaFeber's cogent critique of Nike, Microsoft, and the "Coca-colonization" of the world, his model failed to recognize the resilience of non-US folkways or the ability of local peoples around the world to forge new meanings from US cultural exports. Nevertheless, his warning that, by concentrating too much financial power in a handful of multinational conglomerates, globalization was more likely to bring corporate autocracy than universal prosperity, would ring true by the third decade of the twenty-first century.

In chapter 9, Eric Alterman and Richard Immerman address Walter LaFeber's career-long preoccupation with the durability of the US experiment. They discuss his final book, *The Deadly Bet*, as a timeless but underappreciated political allegory featuring heroes and villains during the *annus horribilis* 1968. *The Deadly Bet* was published in 2005 at the very moment when the United States was sinking ever deeper into quicksand on the Euphrates as a result of a disastrous policy that evoked memories of an earlier quagmire on the Mekong. This succinct book is LaFeber's most explicit commentary on US racism, political opportunism, and other domestic pathologies. The teacher and citizen-scholar shared Alexis de Tocqueville's conviction that democracy was not compatible with empire, and he feared that the fallout from the 9/11 attacks might be worse than the legacy of the Vietnam War.

Donald Trump's four years in the White House heightened LaFeber's fears, and his preferred outcome in the 2020 election was never in doubt. "Biden can go to sleep after his inauguration and remain comatose until 2025," LaFeber quipped two months before voters went to the polls, and "he'll still be more constructive than Trump has been or ever will be."[8] He lived long enough to watch right-wing insurrectionists storm the US Capitol, a chilling reminder that the people of the United States should not take anything for granted. LaFeber was always careful not to read too much into the lessons of the past, but he agreed with Mark Twain's witticism: "History never repeats itself, but it does often rhyme."

The Deadly Bet evokes a series of questions about the past and future of the United States that were implicit in everything Walter LaFeber had ever written, beginning with *The New Empire*. What happens when "extending the sphere" is no longer an option, let alone a solution? Is the challenge posed by post–Cold War Russia any less dangerous than that posed by the Soviet Union? Did Reagan's misguided policies in Central America create an unsolvable problem along the southern border, where thousands of refugees continue to flee political violence dating from the 1980s? Can the United States pivot to Asia without triggering another clash, this time not with Japan but with China? Can US policy makers find ways to harness neoliberal globalization fueled by technological innovation and prevent the free-market mantra from triggering trade wars, financial instability, and an anti-US backlash? Will 2024 bring another *annus horribilis* far worse than the one in 1968? Is an empire for liberty an oxymoron?

Throughout a lifetime of historical inquiry, Walter LaFeber returned to these profound questions again and again because he was convinced that the fate of the US experiment hung in the balance. Like our teacher and mentor, we recognize that the answers remain elusive. Nevertheless, we have chosen to pay homage to him and his scholarship here by revisiting his questions, enhancing the conversation, and heeding his advice always to think otherwise.

Notes

1. Walter LaFeber email to Douglas Little, May 9, 2002, in the authors' possession.
2. Daniel Immerwahr, *How to Hide an Empire: A History of the Greater United States* (New York: Farrar, Straus and Giroux, 2019).
3. Dwight Eisenhower, "Address to the American People," January 17, 1961, https://www.archives.gov/milestone-documents/president-dwight-d-eisenhowers-farewell-address.
4. Walter LaFeber letter to David Langbart, January 2, 1980, in authors' possession.
5. Walter LaFeber email to Douglas Little, June 5, 2003, in authors' possession.
6. See, for example, John Lewis Gaddis, *The Long Peace: Inquiries into the History of the Cold War* (New York: Oxford University Press, 1987).
7. Walter LaFeber letter to Douglas Little, September 24, 1989, in authors' possession.
8. Walter LaFeber email to Susan Brewer, August 2020, in authors' possession.

Chapter 1

Remembering Walt
From the Arts Quad to the Beacon Theatre

David Green and Douglas Little

The vibe inside Broadway's Beacon Theatre on April 25, 2006, felt like an opening night, but the evening actually marked the curtain call for Walter LaFeber's remarkable forty-seven-year run teaching US diplomatic history far above Cayuga's waters.[1] The setting was familiar to anyone who had heard Walt lecture over the years—a table, a podium, and a blackboard with a brief outline chalked in his distinctive scrawl. More than 2,500 friends, colleagues, and former students had gathered in the Beacon (which looked like a jumbo version of Bailey Hall, the largest auditorium on the Cornell campus) to hear their favorite teacher's long goodbye, delivered as always without notes. Walt did not disappoint. Calling his valedictory lecture "Half a Century of Friends, Foreign Policy, and Great Losers," he provided a primer on the perils facing US policymakers early in the new millennium while prompting his listeners to reminisce about the moment when they first crossed paths with the man who changed their lives.[2]

Walter LaFeber arrived on Cornell's Arts Quad with little fanfare in the autumn of 1959. He was a midwesterner, unfailingly polite, unassuming, and a little aloof, a grocer's son who hailed from Walkerton, Indiana, a small town not far from South Bend. After graduating from tiny Hanover College, thirty-five miles upstream from Louisville, Kentucky, on the Hoosier side of the Ohio River, Walt headed west to Stanford for his MA before returning home to the heartland to complete his PhD at the University of Wisconsin in Madison. He joined a Cornell history department in transition, a junior replacement for Dexter Perkins, a former president of the American Historical Association and the country's leading expert on the Monroe Doctrine.[3] Before long Walt held the Marie Underhill Noll endowed chair and was the leader of an all-star cast of US historians—including Michael Kammen, Joel Silbey, Richard Polenberg, Mary Beth Norton, R. Laurence Moore, and Stuart Blumin—that by the early 1970s would make Cornell a top-ten place to undertake graduate study in US history.[4]

Although Walt was fond of Dexter Perkins, he regarded himself as the intellectual heir of Carl Becker, an equally distinguished historian who taught at Cornell from 1917 to 1941. Like Walt, Becker was a midwesterner, born in Waterloo, Iowa; and, also like Walt, Becker earned his PhD at the University of Wisconsin, where he studied with Frederick Jackson Turner, whose "frontier thesis" would be repurposed and applied to foreign policy by what came to be known as "the Wisconsin School" of diplomatic history. Becker's most gifted student at Cornell was Fred Harvey Harrington, who subsequently spent half a century at Wisconsin as history department chair, university president, and Walt's teacher, mentor, and role model. Becker had taught Harrington to question conventional wisdom and to explore the synergy between political and economic power, and Harrington passed these lessons along to Walt. When Walt arrived in Ithaca fresh out of graduate school, he was completing an arc that Becker had begun to lay out on the Arts Quad a generation earlier. Through Harrington, Walt absorbed and enthusiastically embraced Becker's most important message about academic life: "A professor is someone who thinks otherwise."[5]

Thanks to Fred Harvey Harrington, "thinking otherwise" was in the intellectual DNA of all the historians he trained during the 1950s at the University of Wisconsin, where some swore they could hear Becker's ghost wandering through Bascom Hall. Lloyd Gardner and Thomas McCormick have captured the electric atmosphere that they and Walt experienced in graduate seminars and in the lectures of William Appleman Williams, then Harrington's most famous protégé. All four were midwesterners—Gardner and McCormick from Ohio, Williams from Iowa, and Walt from Indiana—who were skeptical of the East Coast foreign policy establishment and critical of the financial power wielded by Wall Street.[6] Self-styled "revisionists," they challenged anticommunist orthodoxy in Eisenhower's America. Yet unlike three of their equally controversial contemporaries—Eugene Genovese, Gabriel Kolko, and Howard Zinn—Walt and his Wisconsin School comrades were influenced more by Charles Beard than by Karl Marx. Walt saw himself as a social democrat and worried that "the loose, if not cynical, use of democracy to justify certain foreign policies" favored by US business interests was making democratic processes like free elections "meaningless and indeed dangerous."[7]

All of Walt's books, from *The New Empire* (1963) through *The Deadly Bet* (2005), reflect the influence of Carl Becker, Charles Beard, and two other public intellectuals—Henry Adams and Reinhold Niebuhr. Walt was especially fond of Becker's answer to that perennial question: What is the good of history? "The facts may be determined with accuracy, but the 'interpretation' will always be shaped by the prejudices, biases, [and] needs of the individual and these in turn will depend on the age in which he lives," Becker had explained in 1932. "Hence history has to be re-written by each generation. Even if the facts are the same, the slant on the facts will be different."[8]

Walt had a particular soft spot in his heart for his fellow Hoosier and "friend of Becker," Charles Beard, whose *Economic Interpretation of the Constitution* was an "ur-text" for most members of the Wisconsin School. Beard did not get everything right, of course, as when he implied that FDR had opened "the back door to war" by purposely exposing the US Pacific Fleet to Japanese attack on December 7, 1941.[9] One of the few times Walt ever grew visibly angry, however, was when he recalled the nasty screed written by Harvard's Samuel Eliot Morison for the August 1948 issue of *The Atlantic* with the catchy subtitle "History through a Beard." One might question another historian's interpretation, but never his patriotism or his scholarly integrity.

A Harvard man whom Walt admired, on the other hand, was Henry Adams, the grandson and great-grandson of presidents. Adams was a snob and a curmudgeon, but he was also a brilliant historian who conducted multi-archival research and thought systematically about both the past and the power of the United States. Some of Adams's writings, like his use of the laws of thermodynamics to explain civilizational decline, bordered on nonsense, and Adams had a huge ax to grind with Thomas Jefferson, whom he regarded as a demagogue and a usurper. Nevertheless, Walt was quick to point out that Henry Adams provided a prophetic warning for twentieth-century US policymakers when he "pointedly spelled out how war and organizing for war undermined many Jeffersonian principles (especially the hatred of debt, centralized government, and investment of scarce resources in the military)."[10]

Another Ivy Leaguer who influenced Walt's thinking was Reinhold Niebuhr, a Missouri-born graduate of Yale Divinity School. A social democrat and a staunch friend of labor, Niebuhr preached liberalism at home and interventionism abroad during the early 1940s but developed ambivalent feelings about the looming confrontation with the Soviet Union at the end of that decade. In *The Irony of American History*, a book that was required reading for all of Walt's undergraduates and graduate students, Niebuhr worried that US Cold

LaFeber was a tie-and-jacket man and a gifted storyteller who chalked an outline on the blackboard in his distinctive scrawl before lecturing to hundreds without notes. Cornell University Library Division of Rare and Manuscript Collections.

Warriors would inadvertently adopt the authoritarian tactics of their adversaries in the Kremlin.[11] With Becker, Beard, Adams, and Niebuhr accounted for, Walt added two final ingredients to his recipe for writing good history: a dash of cynicism, often drawn from Lord Acton, the nineteenth-century Cambridge don who once famously quipped that "the strong man with the dagger is followed by the weak man with the sponge"; and a profound anxiety, based on the early warnings of the French aristocrat Alexis de Tocqueville regarding the corrosive effect of war on US democracy.[12]

All six of these figures made appearances in Walt's legendary survey of US foreign relations at Cornell. The class met on Tuesday, Thursday, and, yes, Saturday mornings, first in the Goldwin Smith auditorium and later, at the height of the Vietnam War, in Bailey Hall, which seated close to 1,600. A big part of the attraction was Walt's persona: a modest fellow who delivered extraordinary lectures without notes, without props, and without raising his voice. His teaching style was indelibly influenced by his mentor at Wisconsin. Fred Harvey Harrington had "strode up and down restlessly before undergraduate classes," Walt recalled, "rapidly laying out the evolution of American global power and doing so without any notes before 450 students at one time."[13] Walt was more laid back. A lanky "tie and jacket" man, he would arrive for class precisely at 11:15, scrawl an outline on the blackboard, speak for exactly fifty minutes, and then draw things to a close by asking, "What, then, can we say in conclusion?"

Walt was a gifted storyteller. Anthony Fels (class of 1971) remembered that "each lecture was truly a work of narrative art, constructed with a provocative beginning, middle sections of development, and crystal-clear conclusions."[14] History majors would frequently bring their boyfriends or girlfriends, and sometimes even their parents, on Saturday mornings, and the final lecture always received a standing ovation. Nonmajors were just as impressed as majors. "Walt LaFeber," hotel school alumnus Andrew Tisch recalled, "was the professor you never forgot."[15] It did not matter whether a student's politics leaned left or right. James Doub (class of 1969) reminded one of the contributors to this book: "You and I were on polar ends of the political spectrum back in our days together, . . . [yet] we shared a fondness and awe of a professor, who was well beyond any of the many learned and talented scholars [on campus]."[16] Other Cornell undergraduates who later became distinguished historians, including Nancy Cott, Mark Lytle, and Drew McCoy, were similarly inspired by Walt's teaching. David Maisel (class of 1968), who pursued a career in finance, struck up a personal correspondence with Walt that would last a lifetime. "Those of us who took that course enjoyed a learning experience that we can probably never adequately describe or praise," Richard Immerman recalled many years later. "In a number of specific cases, like my own, it changed lives."[17]

That Walt's approach appealed to Cornell students of differing political persuasions provides a sharp contrast to early reactions of some more-established academics outside the Cornell community. The decline of McCarthyism during the late 1950s had made it unacceptable to apply such slurs as "communist" to the new generation of revisionist historians. However, another more "respectable" label—"economic determinist"—quickly emerged as a means of accomplishing the same purpose, and it soon became the epithet of choice for many of the Wisconsin School's early critics, who claimed that because of their political biases, these young historians ignored noneconomic factors and thereby seriously distorted the historical record.

What was particularly striking about the label was its use in an effort to discredit Marxists and revisionists alike. That the Wisconsin historians had learned from Williams, who in turn had profound respect for Beard's economic interpretation of the US Constitution, gave the "economic determinist" label a superficial credibility. Yet in reality the label merely provided a convenient excuse for establishment academics to evade embarrassing economic issues. After Walt's first book, *The New Empire*, won the American Historical Association's Albert J. Beveridge Prize in 1963, establishment critics found it harder to apply the label to him with any credibility. Even so, as late as 1966, when one of the coauthors of this chapter was applying for his own first teaching position, an interviewer, knowing the applicant's academic lineage, explicitly asked if he was "an economic determinist." His answer—"If you'll tell me what it is, I'll tell you if I am one"—elicited an approving laugh from Walt when he learned about it afterward; it also sufficiently disarmed the search committee so that he got the job. Nevertheless, the very emergence of the phrase as a pejorative of choice underlines the insecurity and defensiveness of establishment historians that generations of Cornell students happily did not share.

Walt's Jimmy Stewart–like "Mr. LaFeber Goes to Bailey Hall" demeanor was not the only reason his survey of foreign policy was so successful. The topics he covered were exceptionally diverse. For starters, Walt incorporated a crash course in Cornell history into his panoramic narrative. Students learned that Andrew Dickson White was not only the university's first president but also Ulysses Grant's commissioner to Santo Domingo and Grover Cleveland's minister to Russia, and that one of White's successors, Jacob Gould Schurman, was ambassador to China and Weimar Germany during the 1920s. Willard Straight (class of 1901) served as US consul-general in Mukden, China, where he helped prevent the open door from slamming shut during the Taft administration, and later he accompanied Woodrow Wilson's peace planners to Paris, where he died of complications from "the Spanish flu" in December 1918. Edward M. House (class of 1881), Wilson's de facto national security adviser and Straight's boss, drafted key portions of the Versailles Treaty. During World War I, Walter Teagle (class of 1900) became president of Standard Oil of New Jersey and broke Britain's monopoly over Persian Gulf petroleum a decade later. Walt pointed out that William Rogers, Eisenhower's second attorney general and Nixon's first secretary of state, and Sol Linowitz, Jimmy Carter's point man during negotiations with Panama over the canal, both held Cornell law degrees. And as neoconservatives climbed ever higher up the policy-making pyramid in Washington during the 1990s, Walt reminded students that it was Allan Bloom, a big man on the Arts Quad who had taught political philosophy during the late 1960s and loomed large at the residential community of Telluride House, who convinced Paul Wolfowitz and a posse of Cornell classmates that they could and should change the world.

Walt's most memorable lectures, however, featured riveting and sometimes revisionist portraits of more important historical figures. He made visionaries like James Madison and empire builders like William Henry Seward come to life. He dazzled students with the stories of "great losers" like Aaron Burr, whose conspiratorial machinations in the trans-Appalachian West during Jefferson's second term were right out of a screenplay for a Hollywood blockbuster, and

Henry Wallace, another midwesterner who questioned the wisdom of the East Coast elite and was run out of Harry Truman's Washington on a rail. Walt called out liars like James K. Polk and demagogues like Joseph McCarthy. And he praised those rare souls who dared to speak truth to power, including Daniel Webster, who fought Jacksonian expansionism during the 1840s, and George Kennan, who cautioned against "imperial overstretch" in Southeast Asia in the 1960s and again in the Middle East early in the new millennium.

Perhaps the most remarkable historical figure to make an appearance in the course was Brooks Adams, Henry's eccentric brother and the author of *The New Empire*, a title that Walt would borrow for his own Beveridge Prize–winning first book. Brooks had urged policymakers such as Henry Cabot Lodge and Theodore Roosevelt to make the United States a world power as the nineteenth century drew to a close, Walt explained, and his vision of a "new empire" helped inspire TR and others to seize the opportunity for global economic and strategic expansion provided by the breakdown of the Spanish Empire in early 1898. At the same time, Walt was quick to point out that many years later, Brooks came to have serious second thoughts about the policy course that he had so confidently advocated in the late 1890s. The universe, Brooks wrote in 1919, "far from being an expression of law originating in a single primary cause, is a chaos which admits of reaching no equilibrium, and with which man is doomed eternally and hopelessly to contend."[18] To the delight of his students, Walt ended the lecture by singing Brooks's late-in-life shaving song, which went, "Goddamn, goddamn, goddamn, goddamn, goddamn, goddamn, goddamn." By the third "goddamn" the lecture hall was usually convulsed with laughter.

Walt did not leave everyone laughing. Without access to her transcript, one cannot be certain that Ann Coulter (class of 1984), the founding editor of the conservative *Cornell Review* who would later become a far-right flamethrower, ever took his class, but "Frenchy LaFeber" was clearly not her favorite teacher. "Professor Walter LaFeber said Reagan's Latin American policy was 'the diplomatic counterpart of trying to use gasoline to extinguish a gasoline fire,'" Coulter complained in *Treason*, her 2003 diatribe against liberalism. "The Creative Writing Department's loss was the History Department's gain!" Claiming that Walt had been "proved spectacularly wrong in everything he ever said about the Cold War," she sneered that his won/loss record had not improved after 9/11 because, like most academics, he tried "to make simple ideas sound complex," as when he "referred to American intervention abroad to make the world safe for democracy as 'Wilsonianism.'"[19] One can only imagine Ann Coulter's dismay upon learning that Walt had been the first recipient of Cornell's John M. Clark Award for excellence in teaching back in 1966, when she was still in kindergarten.

LaFeber's office door was always open, and he made a point of getting to know all of his students and encouraging them to pursue careers in the ivory tower and government service. Courtesy of the Cornell University Archives.

Walt regarded Coulter's hatchet job as a badge of honor, and his students had no difficulty recognizing who was the spectacularly wrong simpleton. One undergraduate summed up the impact of Walt's teaching this way on ratemyprofessors.com in 2005: "This guy is the best prof. that I have had at Cornell. His lectures are literally works of art. . . . You must have him before he retires."[20] Walt's PhD students echoed this high praise. "His brilliant lectures on American foreign relations at Cornell persuaded me to specialize in diplomatic history as a graduate student," Susan Brewer recalled long afterward. "Along with the Monroe Doctrine and the Yalta Conference, there was room for Herman Melville, Jane Addams and John Wayne."[21] Anyone wishing to recapture the spirit of Walt's amazing courses should skip *Treason* and have a look instead at his best-selling textbook, *The American Age*.[22]

Walt was well aware of how effective he was in the lecture hall, but he probably did his best teaching inside his office, first in Sibley Hall and then on the fourth floor of McGraw Tower. Walt's office décor put students at ease. A long-suffering fan of the Chicago Cubs, he kept an autographed photo of their Hall of Fame shortstop Ernie Banks on his desk with the inscription "Keep going Walt," and he always reminded visitors that "anyone can have a bad century."[23] The inside of his office door featured two distinctive items. There was George Santayana's famous dictum, as updated by Walt LaFeber: "Those who don't know the past are doomed to repeat it, but those who do know the past are doomed to repeat it anyway." And there was a magazine ad for "Big Wally," a household cleaner from the 1970s.

The line outside Walt's office on Tuesday and Thursday afternoons always snaked down the hall, but he did not head home until he had spoken with everyone, undergraduates first and then graduate students. Jeffrey Engel remembers walking into 432 McGraw Hall as a freshman and being greeted warmly. Walt "gave me a chance though he did not know me at all. He gave everyone a chance," Engel said. "He also gave willingly of his time, to an extent that I now, as a professor myself, find almost incomprehensible."[24] Eric Alterman tells a similar story about how writing an honors thesis with Walt changed his life. "Students would line up for hours to speak to him during office hours, trading slots in the queue the way others exchanged beers and joints back at the dorm," Alterman smiled years later. It was well worth the wait, however, because as he put the finishing touches on his latest book, Alterman found himself "using some of the same notes, which I saved because they remind me of how hard Walt made me work to live up to his demanding expectations."[25] Jessica Wang, who began as a biology and chemistry double major, recalls that Walt was not only a superb teacher but also a remarkable mentor "who knew how to match his students' experiences with their evolving academic identities." As she pursued a senior thesis on nuclear-age politics, Walt suggested trying MIT as the right place to combine a science background with graduate studies in history. She confesses, however, that after working with Walt, "any PhD program other than Cornell was bound to be anti-climactic."[26]

Walt's graduate seminars were modeled on Harrington's, with heavy doses of reading (sometimes five books a week), lots of papers, and scintillating conversation. Because Walt was "old school" and could not abide sloppy writing, years later the historians he trained still think twice before splitting an infinitive or ending a sentence with a preposition. Indeed, many still refuse to do either. He emphasized the importance of archival research, but he was not the sort of scholar who would cross an ocean to check a comma, and when dissertation work dragged on too long, he would remind his weary graduate students that the perfect was the enemy of the good. Anne Foster, who worked with Walt during the 1990s, could not imagine a better mentor. "We always had to listen well to hear praise. Not that he withheld it. But he was not effusive," she recalled. "One day, though, he said to me [and] Shannon Smith, Lorena Oropeza, Sayuri Shimizu and Susan Brewer that he benefited by the prejudice of Harvard and Yale, which at that point still rarely to never accepted women for PhDs in foreign relations history.... That felt odd to us when we were of course the ones who benefited."[27]

Some of Walt's undergraduates and PhD students pursued careers in government service rather than the ivory tower. "Many of us became LaFeber addicts, taking his classes, becoming history majors—of American foreign policy, that is," John Wolff (class of 1990) told a reporter in 2006. "We'd pester him to mentor our honors theses, name our fish 'Wally' and hope one day that we'd be the ones calling on him for advice from our future perches in the State Department, White House, Pentagon, CIA, NSA or from wherever it was we were going to change the world."[28] Several Cornell alums would actually make those calls. Samuel "Sandy" Berger, who graduated in 1967 and went on to serve as Bill Clinton's NSC adviser, remembered that "Cornell had a great government department at that time, with Clinton Rossiter, Andrew Hacker, Walter LaFeber, and George Kahin." In Walt's case, of course, Berger got the department wrong, but he got the experience right. More important, he kept in touch with Walt over the years.[29]

Stephen Hadley, who graduated two years after Berger, served as NSC adviser during George W. Bush's second term. "When I was at Cornell, I took Walter LaFeber's course in diplomatic history," Hadley recalled five decades later. "He was a wonderful diplomatic historian, and there are a whole group of people, Paul Wolfowitz, Eric Edelman, Dan Fried, ... who came to Washington and did foreign policy because they were inspired by his course. I was one of those people."[30] Walt crossed paths with Paul Wolfowitz at Cornell's Telluride House in the 1960s but had little contact with him thereafter.[31] Eric Edelman, who wrote his honors thesis with LaFeber before migrating rightward and finding his way into Dick Cheney's inner circle, remarked that although Walt was "one of the leading members of the Wisconsin School of revisionist diplomatic history," he was "also culturally actually sort of a conservative person."[32] Dan Fried, who became a career ambassador at the State Department, always cherished his time at Cornell. "Walt LaFeber was an intellectual guide and mentor for a generation of foreign policy officials, myself included," he tweeted in March 2021. "He nailed the combination of circumstance, ideas, and people that drives history. A great person. And a good one."[33]

When it came to direct political involvement, on the other hand, Walt had a natural skepticism toward academic self-righteousness. He well understood the difference between knowledge, or the accumulation of information, and wisdom, which was about the use one made of whatever information one chose to acquire. In a world marked by growing complexity and increasingly rapid global change, it was all too easy to amass enormous knowledge, and power, without demonstrating any discernible wisdom. The most dangerous situations were when policymakers, and their academic advisors, allowed their belief in their own virtue to dictate which information they chose to accumulate and which to ignore. Thus, Walt had no time for "action intellectuals" like Arthur Schlesinger Jr., whose role as JFK's court historian had made him complicit in the Bay of Pigs invasion. "Well, they did it, they really did it," he told one of the authors of this chapter on April 17, 1961. The most appalling aspect of the entire episode was the combination of arrogant self-righteousness and willful ignorance of Cuban history on the part of both Schlesinger and a president who had always considered himself a historian.

Even with respect to on-campus events such as the anti–Vietnam War teach-ins, which began at Cornell in 1965, Walt held back for almost a year before agreeing to participate. He regarded the teach-ins as more political than academic events, and he was reluctant to cross the line. When in early 1966 word got out that Walt was speaking at the next teach-in, the Memorial Auditorium in Willard Straight Hall filled to capacity an hour in advance. After a student asked Walt a question, he began his response with the words, "As I said in the paper . . ." In short, Walt treated his participation in the teach-in with the same seriousness he showed in his presentations at academic conferences. For those in attendance, this was the moment when teach-ins went mainstream at Cornell and helped fuel the nationwide antiwar movement that ultimately led Lyndon Johnson to refuse to seek reelection. Neither Walt nor the other Cornell teach-in participants were delighted with Johnson's replacement, of course, yet the moment stands as striking evidence of Walt's insistence upon scholarly integrity in his teaching, not only in the classroom and but also in more informal settings.

Although Lloyd Gardner later joked that Walt must have done something terribly wrong to have trained two NSC advisors, his old friends and Cornell colleagues recognized him for the master teacher that he was. Joel Silbey, whose San Francisco Giants won three World Series while Walt's Cubs were winning just one, had high praise for his office mate's teaching. "I've always been impressed by the extraordinary devotion of his students," Silbey marveled. "We all strive for that; he achieves it. We've always considered him to be our leader and model of what we'd like to be." Glenn Altschuler, a professor of American Studies and himself a Cornell PhD, agreed wholeheartedly.

"Justly celebrated for his teaching and scholarship, Walt is great, truly great, in my judgment, because of the way he lives each day, unfailingly attentive to students, staff and colleagues," Altschuler explained. "He is Midwestern *mensch*—the best thing that's happened to Cornell in the last half century."[34] Tim Borstelmann, who joined the Cornell faculty as LaFeber's "heir apparent" in 1991 and temporarily camped out in his office, recalled many years later how Walt had "freely shared his superb book collection, a mini-library of our discipline at the time."[35] Fred Logevall, who replaced Borstelmann in 2004, remembers Walt as "a distinguished scholar, a true gentleman, and, most of all, a deeply humane and generous person."[36] Mary Beth Norton, the first female historian to win tenure at Cornell, agreed that Walt was one of a kind. "No other member of the department has commanded the same respect as Walt in the 35 years I have known him," she exclaimed shortly after he retired. "His integrity, humaneness and commitment to principle mean that his comments always carry much weight in department meetings."[37]

These qualities had come into sharp focus four decades earlier during a crisis that put Cornell in the headlines around the world. On April 18, 1969, African American students protesting racist incidents on campus occupied Willard Straight Hall, issued a set of nonnegotiable demands, and smuggled fifteen rifles and ammunition into the basement. Racial tensions had been building for months, but most faculty and students were in a state of shock. "Oh my God, look at those goddamned guns," Steve Starr of the Associated Press gasped as he snapped a Pulitzer Prize–winning photo of Thomas W. Jones and a half-dozen Black undergraduates carrying rifles and draped with bandoliers as they exited the Straight and marched across campus to the newly established Africana Studies Center. The crisis grew even more ominous after Jones told a radio interviewer two days later that both the faculty and the administration were racist and that "Cornell University has three hours to live."[38]

Walt, who had just become chair of the history department, was horrified by these developments. He had been deeply troubled by the events of 1968—the assassinations of Martin Luther King Jr. and Robert Kennedy and the race riots in Washington, D.C., and elsewhere—and he supported Cornell's plans to recruit more African American students and to establish a Black Studies program. He balked at the creation of a separate "Black College," however, and was appalled by the armed occupation of the Straight. When President James Perkins (no relation to Dexter) agreed to reverse course and nullify sanctions that had been imposed on Jones and his comrades, Walt stepped down as department chair and flew to New York City with a group of senior faculty to meet with the executive committee of the Cornell board of trustees. The fallout was swift; President Perkins was forced out and replaced by his provost, Dale Corson.

The Straight takeover shook the university to its very core. Several prominent faculty, most notably Allan Bloom, resigned, and a year later many on campus attributed the suicide of Bloom's Government Department colleague, Clinton Rossiter, in part to his deep despair over the events of April 1969. Walt briefly considered moving to the University of Maryland, but in the end he chose to stay at Cornell, where he remained an outspoken champion of academic freedom. "What a university is all about is rational discourse," Walt long afterward told Donald Downs, a University of Wisconsin political scientist and Cornell alumnus who had taken Walt's survey of US foreign relations the spring semester following the Straight takeover. "Once you introduce any kind of element of force into the university, you compromise the institution." For Walt, this was totally unforgivable. "We have to make a distinction between procedure and politics," he explained. "I'm a relativist in terms of object and conclusion. I don't think I am necessarily right. What I am absolutist about is the procedure you use to get there."[39]

By the mid-1970s Walt was widely regarded as the most distinguished and most respected member of the Cornell faculty. His lecture courses had begun to shrink, and he now taught back in Goldwin Smith auditorium rather than Bailey Hall. Still, his books on the Cold War and the Panama Canal received rave reviews and his op-eds appeared in the *New York Times* and the *Washington Post*. As always, his teaching and his research were inextricably intertwined. As part of Cornell's celebration of the US bicentennial, President Corson invited Walt to do something that no other faculty member had ever done—deliver the university's commencement address. For Corson, who had worked closely with Walt to quell the Straight crisis, this was a no-brainer. "It was the bicentennial," he explained many years later. "I felt that something significant should be said by someone who could say it with authority."[40] True to form, Walt delivered. A university must assume the role of "midwife when revolutionary ideas enter an un-revolutionary society," he told the graduates in May 1976. "The founders of this nation and the founders of Cornell shared a common commitment, indeed a common passion, a belief in the power of ideas to transform individual lives and improve human society."[41] This was exactly what Walt's teaching had done over the years for hundreds of his students.

Having witnessed the university nearly implode due to what he regarded as bureaucratic incompetence, Walt had a jaded view of administrative work. He revered Dale Corson and respected his successors, Frank H. T. Rhodes and Hunter Rawlings. Nevertheless, although offered the opportunity twice, he was not interested in serving as dean of the College of Arts and Sciences. When former students sought his advice about whether to become administrators, he would chuckle and recall what Alfred Kahn, a Cornell dean who had picked up

LaFeber became the only Cornell faculty member ever to deliver the university's commencement address in May 1976, when he celebrated America's bicentennial. Courtesy of the Cornell University Archives.

the pieces after the Straight takeover, told him: "You'll spend 85 percent of your time holding the hands of the 15 percent of the faculty you don't respect, but it will only *seem* like an eternity." Walt's message was clear. Choosing a career in administration would likely mean abandoning life as a teacher-scholar.

Walt never became an administrator, but as his career drew to a close he was recognized as the avatar of the university. In the aftermath of the 9/11 attacks in 2001, President Rawlings invited him to address the Cornell community on a day of national remembrance. Standing before 12,000 students, faculty, and staff gathered on the Arts Quad, Walt mourned the dead but warned the living about the likely consequences of "a new war—the first war, as it is being called, of the 21st century." Twenty-one Cornell alumni died on 9/11, along with nearly 3,000 other Americans. "Their deaths will have been in vain," Walt sighed, "if they result in a war, which will necessarily be long and costly, in which we do not remember the fundamental values of our individual rights, and our individual obligations to a larger community."[42]

Five years later, with the United States mired in a long and costly war in Iraq that called into question fundamental US values, Walt delivered his valedictory lecture at the Beacon Theatre in Manhattan. By then he had been named Cornell's first Andrew and James S. Tisch Distinguished University Professor. Cornell had originally planned to hold the event uptown at the American Museum of Natural History, but the response from alumni was so overwhelming that the university opted for a bigger venue on Broadway. The 2,500 Cornellians lucky enough to be there on April 25, 2006, were treated to one last magical tour through 200 years of US foreign policy conducted by the maestro they first encountered in the Goldwin Smith auditorium or Bailey Hall.

In the beginning, there was John Quincy Adams, whom Walt always referred to as "JQA" and regarded as the greatest US secretary of state. (This may be the only point on which Walt and Yale's Samuel "Wave the Flagg" Bemis agreed.) JQA was great not just because he loved opera and swam nude in the Potomac, but also because he was committed to the US national interest while appreciating both the limits of power and the power of ideas. "America, with the same voice which spoke herself into existence as a nation, proclaimed to mankind the inextinguishable rights of human nature," Adams had remarked in 1821. Following this statement of faith, JQA issued a warning that by the time of Walt's valedictory lecture had proved prescient several times over: "But she goes not abroad in search of monsters to destroy," because "she well knows that by once enlisting under other banners than her own, were they even the banners of foreign independence, she would involve herself beyond the power of extrication." Adams emphasized that the consequences of such a US misstep would be dire. "She might become the dictatress of the world. She would be no longer the ruler of her spirit."[43] In not so many words, John Quincy Adams was saying that exporting democracy was a risky business in places like Latin America, where wars of independence had unleashed radical social forces that were proving difficult to control; it was even riskier in terms of what it would do to the United States itself.

Had Woodrow Wilson heeded JQA's warning, Walt suggested, he might not have been so quick to try to make the world safe for democracy a century later. Perhaps because Wilson was a political scientist rather than a historian (or perhaps because he attended Princeton rather than Cornell), he never fully understood that democracy doesn't travel well. Wilson's famous prescription for bringing order to revolutionary Mexico—"We must teach the South Americans to elect good men"—might have been a nice sound bite back in 1914, but his decision to send Black Jack Pershing and 6,000 US troops south of the Rio Grande two years later led many Mexicans to charge that the United States was exporting democracy at gunpoint. When left-wing radicals translated national self-determination into revolutionary nationalism in China, Russia, and parts of Europe during and after World War I, Wilson was not amused, and he aligned himself with some decidedly undemocratic forces to combat Bolshevism, which he came to regard as the biggest threat to US-style democracy. The self-righteous Wilson, of course, failed to see the irony in employing undemocratic means to promote democracy, but his pragmatic secretary of state, Robert Lansing, was very well aware that the Presbyterian in the White House was "playing with dynamite" by preaching self-determination to peoples whose political and economic objectives were very different from those of the United States.

Nowhere, Walt emphasized, was the gap between the rhetoric and the reality of self-determination greater than in the Middle East, where Wilson's Fourteen Points publicly promised democracy to Arabs, Kurds, and other subject peoples liberated from Ottoman rule while France and Britain, with the blessing of the United States, secretly carved out spheres of influence at Versailles. Over the strong objections of Arab nationalists, the French established protectorates over Lebanon and Syria while the British made similar arrangements in Palestine and Transjordan. Then, having already occupied oil-rich Mesopotamia, Britain fused three Ottoman provinces—Kurdish Mosul in the north, Sunni Baghdad in the center, and Shiite Basra in the south—into Iraq, an artificial nation-state headed by a king whose vocabulary did not include terms like "democracy" or "free elections." In short, having set out to make the world safe *for* democracy in 1917, Woodrow Wilson helped make Iraq safe *from* democracy three years later.

Walt closed the lecture by retelling a story that most of his audience had heard in one form or another in his unforgettable survey of US foreign relations. One of the young progressives who accompanied Wilson to Versailles was William Christian Bullitt, a Yale-educated action intellectual from a Main Line Philadelphia family who was deeply committed to exporting democracy to the world. Thoroughly disillusioned by what he regarded as Wilson's betrayal of US principles at the conference table, Bullitt and several of his friends very publicly resigned from the US delegation. When a startled reporter asked, "Now what are you going to do?," Bullitt replied: "I'm going to lie in the sands of the Riviera and watch the world go to hell." Walt brought the house down with his own laconic conclusion: "He went, and it did." The "great losers" were not only Woodrow Wilson and William Bullitt, but more important, the Arabs, Asians, and Africans who were foolish enough to believe that US leaders meant what they said about self-determination.

Although Walt did not mention the relevance of all this for the contemporary Middle East that evening, everyone knew he regarded George W. Bush's invasion of Iraq as a fool's errand. "The Bush administration trying to act like Woodrow Wilson abroad," he had wisecracked privately eighteen months earlier, "resembles Al Capone trying to proselytize converts to Christianity at a Bingo party."[44] Being a good historian frequently entailed speaking truth to power. "Academic freedom means the freedom, indeed means the

LaFeber delivered a valedictory lecture at Broadway's Beacon Theatre in April 2006 and received a standing ovation from 2,500 Cornellians. Courtesy of the Cornell University Archives.

requirement," Walt had reminded another contributor to this tribute at about the same time, "to criticize American society when evidence accumulates that society has gone off in the wrong direction."[45]

Walt's final lecture was not a Jonathan Edwards–style fire-and-brimstone sermon, however, but instead a Reinhold Niebuhr–style meditation on the irony of American history. This came as no surprise to his former students, who knew that Walt had always been a teacher, not a preacher. Of the two Cornell alumni of Walt's foreign relations survey who went on to become NSC advisors, one, Sandy Berger, was seated in the front row at the Beacon. Like the rest of the crowd, he gave Walt a standing ovation. The other was a last-minute no-show. The pressure of making policy in the Persian Gulf and elsewhere prevented Stephen Hadley from making the trip from Washington to New York City. Had Hadley been able to attend Walt's curtain call on Broadway, however, he surely would have recognized that the realism of John Quincy Adams, the irony of Reinhold Niebuhr, and the gentle wisdom of his old teacher made quite a compelling case for rethinking the Bush administration's approach to the war in Iraq.

After retiring, Walt continued to shake his head about current US foreign policy while serving as Cornell's ambassador emeritus at alumni events around the country. Walt's final scholarly article appeared in 2009 in the *Political Science Quarterly*, where he applied the lessons from his valedictory lecture explicitly to

US intervention in the Middle East early in the twenty-first century.[46] That article, like everything else he ever wrote, emphasized that the United States cannot meet the challenges facing the world today unless US citizens become more aware of the past. "The message of LaFeber's scholarship is that US history cannot be written from the inside only," Andrew Rotter and Frank Costigliola explained in their 2004 tribute to Walt. "Each one of LaFeber's books is cosmopolitan, in that it undercuts ethnocentrism, solipsism, and a cranky isolationism by situating the United States in an international system, wherein people in other countries are at least to some extent agents of their own fates."[47]

Nor has Walt's impact upon Cornell students ceased with his death. One of the coauthors of this remembrance, who earned a BA and PhD under Walt's supervision during the 1960s and who shared his fascination with Latin America, has taught a regular summer session course at Cornell since 2019.[48] Ever since Walt's passing, on the first day of class he tells the students about LaFeber's impact upon Cornell and upon his own career. He emphasizes his own responsibility to pass along the research skills Walt taught him, so that these newest Cornellians, too, will become part of Walt's enduring legacy.

Alison Dreizen (class of 1974), a LaFeber enthusiast who serves as general counsel for the American Historical Association, summed up the scholar, the teacher, and the man quite well: "When I arrived at Cornell in 1970, LaFeber was already a campus legend," she wrote a few months after Walt's death. "His lectures were mesmerizing. . . . He seamlessly wove together the influences of decision makers, domestic politics, intellectual theory, popular culture, and historical relationships in both the United States and other nations." The standing ovation that she and thousands of others delivered at the Beacon Theatre was proof of all that, but there was also something larger at work. "Walter LaFeber was a mentor to me and countless others in the truest sense of the word: an adviser, a consultant, a cheerleader, and a friend," Dreizen explained. "He cared about his students not just academically but as people. He proved that you could be a brilliant innovative thinker, a mesmerizing speaker, and a prolific writer and still be a wonderful human being."[49] The contributors to this book and scores of other Cornell alumni could not agree more.

Notes

1. An earlier and briefer version of this chapter appeared in the August 2006 issue of *Passport*, the SHAFR newsletter.

2. Readers can find a video of LaFeber's valedictory lecture at https://www.cornell.edu/video/walter-lafeber-beacon-theatre-2006. For those who never had the pleasure

of seeing him in action, this is a great way to get a glimpse of his inimitable delivery and his remarkable storytelling ability.

3. Perkins's successor as John L. Senior Professor of American Civilization was Clinton Rossiter, a political scientist, but it was Walt who was hired to teach diplomatic history. Glenn Altschuler and Isaac Kramnick, *Cornell: A History, 1940–2015* (Ithaca, NY: Cornell University Press, 2014), 92–93.

4. For more on LaFeber's background and its significance, see especially chapters 2, 5, and 7 in this book.

5. Jenny Proctor, "One Role of a Professor Is to 'Think Otherwise,' Says LaFeber," *Cornell Chronicle*, October 18, 2010, https://news.cornell.edu/stories/2010/10/renowned-professor-talks-being-professor.

6. See chapter 2, originally published as Lloyd C. Gardner and Thomas J. McCormick, "Walter LaFeber: The Making of a Wisconsin School Revisionist," *Diplomatic History* 28 (November 2004): 612–24.

7. Walter LaFeber, "The Tension between Democracy and Capitalism during the American Century," *Diplomatic History* 23 (Spring 1999): 263n1.

8. Letter from Carl Becker to William Dodd, January 27, 1932, in *What Is the Good of History? Selected Letters of Carl L. Becker, 1900–1945*, ed. Michael Kammen (Ithaca, NY: Cornell University Press, 1973).

9. On Beard, see Walter LaFeber, "The World and the United States," *American Historical Review* 100, no. 4 (October 1995): 1024–26.

10. LaFeber, "The World and the United States," 1019.

11. On Niebuhr, see Walter LaFeber, *America, Russia, and the Cold War, 1945–2006* (New York: McGraw Hill, 2008), 52–54, 450.

12. See, for example, Walter LaFeber, "The Last War, the Next War, and the New Revisionists," *Democracy* 1 (January 1981): 93.

13. Walter LaFeber, "Fred Harvey Harrington: Teacher and Friend," in *Behind the Throne: Servants of Power to Imperial Presidents*, ed. Thomas McCormick and Walter LaFeber (Madison: University of Wisconsin Press, 1993), 11.

14. Fels quoted in Andrew Rotter and Frank Costigliola, "Walter LaFeber: Scholar, Teacher, Intellectual," *Diplomatic History* 28, no. 5 (November 2004): 629.

15. Tisch quoted in Blaine Friedlander, "Walter LaFeber, Revered History Professor, Dies," *Cornell Chronicle*, March 10, 2021, https://news.cornell.edu/stories/2021/03/walter-lafeber-revered-history-professor-dies.

16. Doub email to Richard Immerman, December 20, 2022, in authors' possession.

17. Immerman quoted in Rotter and Costigliola, "Walter LaFeber," 630.

18. Brooks Adams quoted in Walter LaFeber, *The New Empire: An Interpretation of American Expansion, 1860–1898* (Ithaca, NY: Cornell University Press, 1963), 95.

19. Ann Coulter, *Treason: Liberal Treachery from the Cold War to the War on Terrorism* (New York: Crown Forum, 2003), 175, 188.

20. Posted March, 12, 2005, https://www.ratemyprofessors.com/professor/161645.

21. Brewer quoted in Sam Roberts, "Walter LaFeber, Historian Who Dissected Diplomacy, Dies at 87," *New York Times*, March 10, 2021.

22. Walter LaFeber, *The American Age: United States Foreign Policy at Home and Abroad since 1750* (New York: W. W. Norton, 1989).

23. Franklin Crawford, "'Keep Going Walt': An Old-School Historian Who Inspired a Generation of LaFeber Addicts," *Cornell Chronicle*, April 26, 2006.

24. Engel quoted in Rotter and Costigliola, "Walter LaFeber," 628.
25. Eric Alterman, "The Remarkable Influence of Walter LaFeber," *The Nation*, March 17, 2021.
26. Jessica Wang emails to Douglas Little, June 22 and August 19, 2022, in authors' possession.
27. Anne Foster email to Douglas Little, March 21, 2021, in authors' possession.
28. Wolff quoted in Crawford, "'Keep Going Walt.'"
29. Berger Oral History interview, March 24, 2005, https://millercenter.org/the-presidency/presidential-oral-histories/samuel-r-berger-oral-history; LaFeber letter to Douglas Little, June 5, 2003, in authors' possession.
30. Hadley quoted in "State of Play: An Interview with Steve Hadley," *Asia Chess Board Podcast*, October 21, 2019, https://www.csis.org/analysis/state-play-interview-steve-hadley.
31. David Dudley, "Paul's Choice," *Cornell Alumni Magazine*, July/August 2004, 54.
32. Edelman Oral History, June 2, 2017, https://millercenter.org/the-presidency/presidential-oral-histories/eric-edelman-oral-history.
33. Fried tweet, March 13, 2021, https://twitter.com/ambdanfried?lang=en.
34. Silbey and Altschuler quoted in Crawford, "'Keep Going Walt.'"
35. Thomas Borstelmann, "A Drive-By Tour of US Foreign Policy," *Diplomatic History* 43 (April 2019): 391.
36. Fredrik Logevall, "In Memoriam: Walter LaFeber," *Passport*, September 2021, 58.
37. Norton quoted in Crawford, "'Keep Going Walt.'"
38. Starr and Jones quoted in Ian Wilhelm, "Ripples from a Protest Past," *Chronicle of Higher Education*, April 17, 2016.
39. Quoted in Donald A. Downs, *Cornell '69: Liberalism and the Crisis of the American University* (Ithaca, NY: Cornell University Press, 1999), 18.
40. Corson quoted in Crawford, "'Keep Going Walt.'"
41. LaFeber, "Cornell and the Bicentennial," 28 May 1976. The authors are grateful to Skip Newman (class of 1976) for sharing his autographed copy of Walt's commencement address. See also Altschuler and Kramnick, *Cornell*, 153–54.
42. LaFeber remarks, September 14, 2001, https://news.cornell.edu/stories/2001/09/lafeber-gives-remarks-national-day-prayer-and-remembrance; Altschuler and Kramnick, *Cornell*, 449.
43. John Quincy Adams, "Address on July 4, 1821," in *John Quincy Adams and the American Continental Empire*, ed. Walter LaFeber (Chicago: Quadrangle, 1965), 45.
44. LaFeber email to David Langbart, October 16, 2004, in authors' possession.
45. LaFeber quoted in Rotter and Costigliola, "Walter LaFeber," 631.
46. Walter LaFeber, "The Rise and Fall of Colin Powell and the Powell Doctrine," *Political Science Quarterly* 124, no. 1 (Spring 2009): 71–93.
47. Rotter and Costigliola, "Walter LaFeber," 617.
48. See David Green, *The Containment of Latin America: A History of the Myths and Realities of the Good Neighbor Policy* (Chicago: Quadrangle Books, 1971).
49. Alison Dreizen, "In Memoriam: Walter F. LaFeber," *AHA Perspectives*, September 2021.

CHAPTER 2

Walter LaFeber
The Making of a Wisconsin School Revisionist

LLOYD C. GARDNER AND THOMAS J. MCCORMICK

We first met Walt LaFeber in the fall of 1956 in Fred Harvey Harrington's seminar at the University of Wisconsin. At that time, the prevailing critique of American foreign policy in the academy was the Realist commentary most effectively presented in George Frost Kennan's *American Diplomacy, 1900–1950*.[1] With the "fall" of China in 1949 to the Communists, the State Department and the Truman administration had been put on the defensive by Republican charges that the Nationalists had been abandoned by the United States—largely because the Government had either acted out of a tragically mistaken belief that the Communists were simply "agrarian reformers," or, in a more sinister interpretation, because leftist New Dealers had betrayed the nation. Kennan had himself proposed, while still in government, that someone undertake to respond to these accusations. The result was the series of lectures he delivered at the University of Chicago that became the book.

"Realism" appeared to posit two critiques, however, that were (and are) sometimes at odds with one another—this was increasingly evident as the century went on. On the one hand, realists cautioned against overextension, arguing that a major problem for Americans was to fit their ambitions and goals to the limitations upon power (even a power as awesome as that possessed by a nuclear-armed United States). On the other, realists argued that Americans—Wilsonian moralists to the core—tried too hard to "do the right thing" in foreign policy, leaving them at a disadvantage in a world where an unscrupulous enemy would break any treaty, pursue any chicanery, trample on any nation's independence. In short, what was needed was an unblinking look at moral man's responsibility in an immoral world, to paraphrase another of the realist founding fathers, theologian Reinhold Niebuhr.

The University of Wisconsin in this era remained something of an anachronism, or, looked at the other way around, ahead of its time in not taking the prevailing realist critique(s) as seriously as they were at other places where graduate students learned their history and methodology. On the contrary, categories like "realism" and "moralism-idealism" seemed a bit suspect—perhaps too contrived and vacuous to be analytically useful. Wisconsin was the bastion of progressivism, of course, and had a long tradition of excellence; it stood out as a university dedicated to public service as well as scholarship, and had a famed history department that stretched back to the days of Frederick Jackson Turner. The "older" generation of historians in Madison in the late 1950s included Merle Curti, Howard K. Beale, William B. Hesseltine, and Merrill Jensen. The coursework in American foreign policy was provided by Fred Harvey Harrington, already launched on a career path that would soon take him to the presidency of the university. At a time when most of the profession had turned away from the works of Charles A. Beard, these Americanists nevertheless remained Beardians. Even Curti and Beale, who often stressed the role of ideas in their work, insisted, following Beard, upon grounding those ideas in the material reality that helped produce them.

Fred Harrington had not had a great number of graduate students in previous years, but until the mid-1950s American diplomatic history did not draw nearly so well as Curti's courses in intellectual history or Hesseltine's in Civil War history. Harrington's seminar of 1956–1957, however, was to produce a bumper crop of future historians, including Walter LaFeber. Walt arrived in the fall of 1956 with a master's degree from Stanford, where he had studied with Thomas A. Bailey. All graduate students in that era, and for many years afterwards, were at least acquainted with Bailey's text, *A Diplomatic History of the American People*. It was by far the most popular text for undergraduates—and with good reason. Bailey's genius was to make history readable, and to encourage the student to understand that diplomatic history was not just one clerk talking to another. Walt learned well that if one wished to be heard, one must be read; and to be read, one must be lively; and his books have all reflected that Bailey influence, even as his interpretations have gone in a variety of directions other than Bailey's emphasis upon the role of public opinion.

Harrington's seminar in American diplomatic history that fall was quite large—the beginning of the "boom" in diplomatic history. In addition to the three of us, there were a number who would have distinguished careers, among them Carl Parrini (later of Northern Illinois University), David Healy (University of Wisconsin-Milwaukee), and Bernie Wax (American Jewish Historical Society). Barbara Welter (Hunter College), who was to make her mark in women's history, joined us second semester. Harrington himself proved to be a physically imposing (6'4" with a powerful voice and manner) and intellectually awesome presence. Deeply cynical about human nature and motives, he nonetheless nurtured an abiding faith in democracy, one he carried over into his decade-long presidency of the university in the 1960s and to his directorship of the Ford Foundation in India in the 1970s. He reconciled those contrary tendencies of cynicism and democratic idealism with a heavy sense of irony that permeated his sharp, dry humor, his scholarship, and his seminar stewardship. (Walt himself once wrote in his inscription to Tom's copy of *The New Empire*: "To Tom—who shares a love for," among other things, "irony" and "Fred Harrington." Walt's own abiding sense of irony in his writings, teaching, and persona are quite reminiscent of Fred.)

In the first week, Fred read off a huge list of books we were to read for the next week's discussion. Graduate school was quite a shock, until one realized that "reading," in the sense we were used to, meant something else at this level. It meant "extracting" the thesis of any book assigned, not starting at the first page and going straight through to the end. The books included a whole variety of approaches and subjects, but Harrington never told us beforehand, or after the discussion, what books were good or bad, which ones were especially useful. For all that, we were on our own. Among that first batch was Kennan's *American Diplomacy, 1900–1950*, Hans Morgenthau's *In Defense of the National Interest*, Robert Osgood's *Ideals and Self-Interests in American Foreign Relations*, Frank Tannenbaum's *The American Tradition in Foreign Policy*, and Charles Beard's *The Idea of National Interest*.[2] If a question came up during discussions, Harrington, a consummate bibliophile, always had another book to suggest. We covered various special subjects, such as ethnicity, interest groups, and the differences between political science and history. Harrington himself seemed indifferent throughout to the underlying theories of our readings. His methodology was inductive rather than theory-driven. (Yet, when the time came, he would call back to Wisconsin William Appleman Williams, still the most stimulating and provocative theory-man who has ever written on U.S. foreign policy.) The seminar students, however, were excited about the theories and, especially, the realist perspective of Morgenthau and Kennan. Only Carl Parrini, the sole seminar member with economics as an outside field, mentioned Beard. Our collective failure to engage Beard's arguments led Harrington to suggest, at seminar's end, that we reread Beard's *The Idea of National Interest* and make him the focus for our next meeting. Harrington often ended seminars in that fashion. After saying little, "smoking" paperclips (was he a reformed chain smoker?), and constantly taking notes on slips of paper (were those criticisms of us or merely doodles?), he would saw off whatever tree limbs we had crawled out on in the previous two hours.

The second half of the semester was given over to student critiques of papers presented. Harrington assigned two students to lead each critique and we quickly understood that he was less interested in assessing the paper's author than he was in judging the thoroughness of the two critics in demonstrating their mastery of internal and external criticism. On occasion he brought in more advanced students who were already at the dissertation stage and used them to further demonstrate the fine art of taking apart and critiquing a work. One of those was Robert Freeman Smith. Our presentations were largely based on prior MA or senior theses: Walt's on Secretary of State Bainbridge Colby, Lloyd's on FDR and colonialism, and Tom's on Arthur S. Vandenberg and bipartisanship—all written from a conventional realist and internationalist perspective. Since Walt and Tom already had their MAs, Lloyd's new work for his master's degree received more detailed attention. Lloyd's first seminar presentation, on Franklin D. Roosevelt's policies toward European colonialism in World War II, was realist to the core. He recalls, however, that as he worked on FDR, Harrington made a point of asking, "What about economics?" At first, Lloyd simply didn't get it, and added some pages on Lend-Lease, without really grasping what Harrington was trying to suggest—that maybe the United States had some interests in the fate of the colonies that went beyond balance of power.

That year with Harrington gave us "words to live by." "Most books should have been articles and most articles should not have been published." "Most of us have only three good books in us"—the rest is just fluff and career-building (and implicitly a waste of good ink and paper). "Most books have only one idea, if that; only the rare good ones have more." In an effort to wean us from an excessive reliance on the *New York Times* as the paper of record, he tweaked it with the usual "All the news that fits, we print"; "The *Chicago Tribune* has better international coverage than the *New York Times*"; and "The *Times* is as useful as any other newspaper in wrapping trash." More positively, and repeatedly, Harrington over time imbued us with the Wisconsin Idea, rooted in LaFollette Progressivism, that suggested that scholarship was as important as teaching: scholarship that was not afraid to question conventional wisdom and accepted truths; scholarship that produced new ways to think about and address the social, economic, and political ills of the State and of the Nation. In a sense, the University and the State were to be joined through the nexus of citizen-scholars. Yet he also made clear that the Wisconsin Idea had its dangers to be guarded against—that it could easily degenerate into boosterism and transform the University into a servant of large corporate interests in the name of serving the whole community. Harrington's principles presciently warned against "activist" intellectuals and the notion of the "Best and Brightest," whose egos have shadowed the history of the nation since the arrival of the New Frontiersmen on the Potomac.

Inside and outside the seminar, both Lloyd and Tom quickly became good friends with Walt and with each other. That may be because all three of us brought with us much of the same personal baggage. We all grew up in small, midwestern towns, Walt in Walkerton, Indiana, population 2,000, near South Bend. We were all Protestants raised in a tradition of suspicion of centralized power. Lloyd, for example, went to Ohio Wesleyan University, a Methodist-related school; Walt went to Hanover College, a Presbyterian school in southern Indiana, while Tom graduated from the University of Cincinnati. We were all fraternity men in college. We were political moderates—Adlai Stevenson Democrats except for Tom, who liked Ike. We all married our college sweethearts and remain married to them today. In short, save for our sophistication in choosing our spouses, we were pretty conventional raw material of the sort produced by the 1950s, and yet somehow readier than we realized for Wisconsin to work with and shape.

Propinquity helped to speed up those friendships. Our individual carrels were in the same wing and floor of the magnificent Wisconsin State Historical Society, so we would visit back and forth when we were not disturbing other folks or, more often, just take casual breaks together in the society's lobby. (Lloyd remembers a fierce debate over the relative merits of Federalists and Antifederalists that left a passing librarian shaking his head at the ability of graduate students to feel passionate about such things.) Over time, these meetings became more serious encounters at our apartments and outdoor outings, and our wives became an integral part of growing relationships. It was at our first session together, a picnic featuring Sandy LaFeber's barbecued chicken, that Walt somehow managed to endear himself to Nancy Gardner and Jeri McCormick despite insisting—much to their irritation—that boxing was an art form and Ernest Hemingway our finest writer. And it was at one of our apartment dinners that Walt confessed that he had given serious thought to abandoning graduate school for the life of novelist, thinking that political novels like *The Last Hurrah* might be a better way than academic monographs to reach a broader audience. Happily for all of us, his history has had a far longer and more enduring reach than the work of most novelists.

One source of Walt's ennui was Harrington's decision to leave teaching for the administrative post of vice president for academic affairs. Not wanting to leave us in the lurch, Harrington had given us the option of staying with him as dissertators, but none of us were certain if he would really have the time for us. At the end of the day, Walt and Tom took Harrington up on his option, while Lloyd chose William Appleman Williams as his dissertation director. (As it played out, all three of us had equal access to both Harrington and Williams. So we were all Harrington students and we were all Williams students, and our essays are to be found in the *Festschrifts* for both.)

Although Harrington had mentioned Williams in seminar a few times, none of us knew much about him. Walt owned a copy of *American-Russian Relations* and had read parts of it for his master's thesis.[3] Now we all read it and found ourselves shaking our heads in disbelief at the book's provocative "Coda" on the early Cold War, subtitled "The Sophistry of Super-Realism." We were made to feel even more anxious about Williams's impending arrival by the accounts of older students who had known Williams before and described him as "a socialist Socrates who got out on the wrong side of the bed." We soon had occasion to form our own opinions when all three of us found ourselves working as T.A.'s for Williams, either in his Foreign Relations class or in his general U.S. history survey.

Williams's impact was immediate and electrifying. Tom remembers sitting next to Walt in the very back row, listening to Williams's first lecture on the topic of—what else?—the Open Door paradigm in American foreign policy. After it was over, Tom turned to Walt and said: "There is a Thomistic logic to everything this guy says, and if we ever accept his first premises, we are dead in the water." The shock we felt soon turned to fascination and a determination to find out what made this man tick. Part of that learning process, beyond hearing the lectures, was to observe what Williams read. Every Thursday afternoon, without fail, Williams walked into the periodical room of Memorial Library, notebook in hand, and spent the rest of the day working his way through all the new arrivals from A through Z, and not just history journals, but those in political science, sociology, anthropology, psychology, economics, literature and American Studies. And the books in his office reflected a similar span of inquiry. On one wall were books by the likes of Gunnar Myrdal, Wilhelm Dilthey, G. D. H. Cole, E.H. Carr, Isaac Deutscher, and Erich Fromn. On the other were *all* the volumes of *Papers Relating to the Foreign Relations of the United States* published to that point (which Williams had literally read word for word) as well as a miscellaneous collection of committee hearings.

Wanting a more hands-on opportunity for understanding Williams, we finally worked up our courage to invite Williams and his wife to dinner at Walt's apartment, a couple of blocks off campus on the second floor over Lou's Tobacco Shop. (Williams, who smoked small cigars the way Harrington "smoked" paperclips, was perhaps Lou's best customer.) The Williams charisma, evident in

LaFeber earned his PhD in 1959 at the University of Wisconsin, where he was inspired by the teaching and research of Fred Harvey Harrington (left) and William Appleman Williams (right). Courtesy of the University of Wisconsin Archives.

his lectures, turned out even stronger in close proximity. Part of the evening was pure gossip and storytelling, at which Williams excelled. And the history faculty members—once his professors and now his colleagues—were prime targets. It was all wonderfully titillating for second-year graduate students like ourselves, who could feel like we were being let in on the family secrets—and even a few skeletons in the closet. The major part of the evening, however, was conversation, at once serious but lively, about historical topics. Like countless similar discussions with Williams over the next thirty years, this first one lasted until the wee hours of the morning. Lloyd remembers one of us asking him where the New Deal fit into his interpretation. His extended reply was a précis of a later review he would write for *The Nation* of Arthur M. Schlesinger, Jr.'s *The Crisis of the Old Order*.[4] Williams's essay, entitled "Right Crisis, Wrong Order," argued that the depression was a crisis of the *new order*, an order that dated back to the late nineteenth century and had demonstrated more continuity than change in a line that ran from Mark Hanna to Woodrow Wilson to Herbert Hoover to FDR. Much of Williams's argument anticipated its fuller development four years later in the last section of his *Contours of American History*, entitled "The Age of Corporation Capitalism," which has since become known variously as liberal corporatism, corporate liberalism, and American neocorporatism.[5]

That late night exercise in thinking outside the box became a common experience for us in the next several years. The settings were usually informal—bull sessions in Williams's office after class, late afternoon coffee at Rennebohm's Drug Store, late afternoon beer at the Brathaus, and occasional dinners at Williams's house. The topics were wide-ranging: Marx and Freud, Beard and neo-Beardians, Hamilton and Jefferson, Madison and John Quincy Adams, internationalism and isolationism, Faulkner and Hemingway, Count Basie and Duke Ellington, Melville and Hawthorne, democratic socialists and social democrats and so forth and so on—and on. What was common to all was the search for underlying assumptions—that is, the imperative for a true intellectual to strip away and discover the assumptions and premises, usually unstated, that underlay the categories and constructs that scholars used. And the place to begin, we learned, was to discover the underlying assumptions of one's own *Weltanschauung* and to subject them to critical questioning—a process of self-examination (the "examined life," if you will) that had to be an ongoing, life-long enterprise. There was ample opportunity for that self-criticism when, in the course of time, we began our dissertations; and when Bill was putting the finishing touches on *The Tragedy of American Diplomacy* and the beginning strokes on *Contours of American History*.[6] (Tom's wife, Jeri, typed the manuscript, so Tom got to see it hot off the press.) Over the course of these encounters, "Professor Williams" morphed into simply "Bill," as we all began the long and wondrous process of building friendships that endured. (Managing such informality with Harrington's awesome persona was a more difficult matter for some of us. Tom confesses that he was probably fifty years old before he could squeeze out the first "Fred" of his life.)

Harrington and Williams, while central to our intellectual metamorphosis, were not our sole influences. Other members of that neo-Beardian department played roles for some or all of us, as did an array of fellow graduate students. Consider some of the faculty influences—auditing Merrill Jensen's lectures on early American history, where he emphasized domestic social-economic conflict and took implicit issue with Williams's emphasis on empire-building; doing research papers for Merle Curti's intellectual history course, where we developed a fascination with John Q. Adams and Reinhold Niebuhr even before Williams' arrival; and having lunches with Howard Beale, whose study of Theodore Roosevelt led him to challenge our economic interpretations of America's rise to world power. For Walt and Lloyd, Philip Curtin was especially influential. All the Americanists were required to take two non-American history fields, one in medieval or ancient, the other in modern history. Professor Curtin had developed a field called the British Empire. (Later, he would transform it into the Atlantic World and then to the even larger Third World.) Walt chose imperial Britain as his outside modern field. Curtin's study of the British Empire sharpened Walt's conceptualization of empire and encouraged him to think comparatively. So his scholarship on the American empire has always been implicitly informed by his understanding of an earlier British empire, both formal and informal. (Apparently, Walt could also project those concepts further back in time: he and Don Kagan once taught a comparative course on the Roman and American empires at Cornell in the summer of 1968.)

Also influential were other grad students. Almost too numerous to mention, any list certainly would include our seminar mate, Carl Parrini, who brought his broad command of international economics to a dissertation that would eventually become his brilliant *Heir to Empire*, a study of U.S. economic diplomacy during World War I and after; Marty Sklar, already embarked on his pioneering studies in American corporatism and progressivism that would result in his complex and sophisticated analysis of the law and the market in his *Corporate Reconstruction of American Capitalism*;[7] and Saul Landau, who combined his political activism and his research skills to produce a bevy of provocative books on U.S. policies in Latin America. One might also note that even Wisconsin's undergraduates had their indirect impact in providing a kind of progressive milieu that required you to take notice of it even when you did not directly participate in it: a Socialist Club that was both large and active, well-attended and well-covered protest rallies and demonstrations against the Eisenhower Doctrine and the U.S. invasion of Lebanon in 1958, and the decidedly left-wing tilt of the undergraduate student newspaper, the *Daily Cardinal*. When that dominant progressivism was challenged by activist students on the Right, Center, and even the Left, the competition of ideas and ideology rubbing up against each other only added to the excitement.

In 1959, the three of us went our separate ways. Lloyd and Tom were still a year away from finishing up, but Lloyd took a teaching job at Lake Forest College and Tom stayed behind at Wisconsin as a research fellow. Walt, the workaholic embodiment of the Calvinist ethic, had already finished his dissertation by then and accepted the job-of-a-lifetime (literally, as it turned out) at Cornell University, where Dexter Perkins, the great scholar of the Monroe Doctrine, was moving toward retirement. Before we parted ways, we all did considerable soul-searching about our teaching careers. In particular, we debated whether we had an obligation to state our own assumptions to our future students or, fearing that our Wisconsin revisionism might turn students off before they engaged us, whether we should keep them to ourselves. However we each resolved that conundrum, all of us already understood what Bill Williams would later tell a legislative investigating committee on the prowl for subversives. Asked what he taught, he said, "I teach people how to think." Not *what* to think, mind you, but *how* to think. So it seemed to us that our job was not to propagandize and make fledgling revisionists out of our students. Our job was to teach them to think *critically*—and the place to start was how to discover and question underlying assumptions. And what better place than to let them start on us—in the hope that they would eventually question the assumptions of all their teachers, all their books, all their governmental authority figures, and eventually—most importantly—all their own assumptions. We wanted students to get outside the mental boxes that they had inhabited before they entered the university.

In the decades since graduate school, we have both stayed close to Walt—in three different ways. First, we stayed connected because we were imaginative and energetic in finding ways to see each other in varying combinations of twos and threes (or, when we were lucky and our wives could join us, in fours or sixes). And however social these encounters were, they always ended up in the same passionate, intellectual discussions that helped keep all of us grounded in the enthusiasms of that graduate school experience. Nancy Gardner noted one time that the conversation almost seemed to pick up at exactly the same point where it had left off six months or a year earlier. Second, we stayed close because we often worked together as collaborators. In 1973, the three of us wrote a

LaFeber and his lifelong friends Lloyd Gardner (left) and Tom McCormick (right) met during graduate school at the University of Wisconsin, where they became the Three Musketeers. Photo by Duane Hopp, October 17, 1962, University of Wisconsin–Madison Archives, General Photo Collection, box 63, folder 3/1 Harrington, Fred Harvey. Courtesy of Sandra LaFeber

textbook in U.S. foreign relations called *Creation of the American Empire*.[8] It proved to have a short shelf life, largely because it tried to be both a textbook and an analytical think-piece and fell between the two stools, which was unfortunate because much of it was original and first-rate. A decade later, the three of us joined Bill Williams in turning out *America in Vietnam: A Documentary History*, and a year later, Lloyd edited a *Festschrift* for Williams called *Redefining the Past* to which all of us contributed essays.[9] Seven years on, in 1993, Walt and Tom coedited another *Festschrift*, honoring Fred Harrington. It was entitled *Behind the Throne: Servants of Power to Imperial Presidents*, and once more, all three of us wrote essays for it.[10]

Finally, each of us remained linked to Walt because he was so generous with his time in reading and critiquing our works-in-progress. Whether it was a complete book manuscript, a shorter think-piece journal article, or a pending conference paper, Walt has been there for each of us. Moreover, the critique was unfailingly brilliant and on-the-money. (One must note that Walt was, and is, rather more reticent about his own work; one usually knows what Walt is working on about the same time his autographed copy of the finished product arrives at the doorstep.)

While we lack the disinterested distance to assess Walt's work over the last forty years, we do feel secure in saying a few things about both the contemporary character and the literate quality of that work. When Walt's dissertation on Grover Cleveland's Latin American policy was revised and immensely expanded to become *The New Empire*, and to win the Beveridge Prize in 1963, it was apparent that all of his books would have "contemporary" themes.[11] The forces he identifies as shaping the outlook of American policymakers in the late nineteenth century can easily be seen at work today as a later generation of leaders pursues its objectives. The average life of a scholarly book is probably twenty years or less. *The New Empire* is as popular today as when it was first published, precisely because it does speak to issues not fixed in one place, at one time. Whether these issues include the exceptionalism of American ideology, or the more easily identified economic interests behind specific policies, LaFeber takes us to the heart of the matter.

Consider some of the works that followed *New Empire*. *The Panama Canal* (1978) put the 1974–77 treaty negotiations in historical perspective, educating an uninformed American public, and some of its leaders as well, to the historical realities at a time when the 1977 treaty had become a political hot potato.[12] His *Inevitable Revolutions* (1983) similarly attempted to educate the American public at the time of the Sandinista regime in Nicaragua on why it was that the peoples of the Caribbean and Central America did not look at world events in the same way that leaders in Washington did, by placing the unrest in historical context.[13] In the process, he reminded his readers of the relevance of dependency theory more than a decade before antiglobalization forces would revive it. His 1993 book in the Cambridge History series, *The Search for Opportunity*, made imaginative use of Joseph Schumpeter's concept of "creative destruction" to recast how we (and perhaps Walt himself) viewed the era between the end of the Civil War and World War I.[14] The prize-winning *The Clash* (1997) provided the same stimulus for understanding Japanese-American relations, offering up "the clash" over China and the "clash" of competing forms of capitalism as compelling categories for a very complex set of relations.[15] And finally, LaFeber's *Michael Jordan*, surveying the career of one of America's greatest sports heroes of the twentieth century, highlighted the dynamics underlying both "globalization" and the attacks of 11 September 2001.[16]

Besides their contemporary feel, Walt's work is noted for a lively and literate style that delights and engages university students and scholars alike. That quality is nowhere more evident than in his two immensely popular textbooks, *America, Russia, and the Cold War* and *The American Age*.[17] Both contain the same themes that he established in his monographs; indeed, he puts them forth quite clearly in the introductions and opening chapters of each textbook.

(In that sense, Walt was immodest or merely wrong when he inscribed Tom's first edition copy of the Cold War book. "Here it is, Tom," he wrote, "a thousand-and-one facts in search of a thesis.") But it is the magical ability to subtly weave those themes in and out of a narrative story line that really propels those books along and keeps the reader engaged. They read like a John Dos Passos novel, yet rest on a lifetime of intense historical research.

The success of Walt's books has been of great significance to the profession of foreign relations historians. The ups and downs of the Wisconsin School's reputation in that profession read like a Hegelian dialectic. At its height in the Vietnam era of the 1960s and early 1970s, in relative decline in the Thermidorian reaction of the late 1970s and refired Cold War 1980s, it enjoyed a modest resurgence in the 1990s when American foreign policy continued to act in much the same ways and for much the same reasons even though the Cold War was over—suggesting that with or without a Communist menace (and by extension, with or without the menace of terrorism), the dynamics of American foreign policy continue to be much the same as they were a century ago when "the new empire" was launched upon the global scene. It is more than a little ironic, of course, that many of the critiques of state-centered history (to use the broadest term about current attitudes in academia) actually have their source in works produced by scholars working in the Wisconsin tradition, turning the "consensus" notion on its end to examine the assumptions of policymakers and historians both steeped in the Grand Narrative.

Throughout those ups and downs of the Wisconsin School, no one has been more influential than Walt in both refining and keeping alive the arguments that Williams and Harrington first set forth in the 1940s and 1950s. And whether those arguments are embraced, rejected, or modified is less important than the essential fact that they be engaged and considered. That this is clearly the case in so much of our current scholarship speaks, of course, to the power of the arguments themselves; but it also speaks to the ability of Walt to be read, and read widely, both in the best of times and in the worst of times.

Probably no other historian of American foreign relations has given his profession and his readership quite the same sense that history really matters, that where we have been will indeed determine where we are going unless we understand the past—not as a template for the future, or the future as an extension of a useful past—but as a record of successes and follies. All through his career Walt LaFeber has taken seriously the Wisconsin injunction that scholarship and publication exist not simply to achieve an upward trajectory in the world of academic fame and fortune, but to serve a public interest as well.

Notes

This chapter was originally published as Lloyd C. Gardner and Thomas J. McCormick, "Walter LaFeber: The Making of a Wisconsin School Revisionist," *Diplomatic History* 28, no. 5 (November 2004), 613–624, https://doi.org/10.1111/j.1467-7709.2004.00443.x. Printed by permission.

1. George F. Kennan, *American Diplomacy, 1900–1950* (New York: New American Library, 1951).
2. Kennan, *American Diplomacy, 1900–1950*; Hans Morgenthau, *In Defense of the National Interest* (New York: Knopf, 1951); Robert Osgood, *Ideals and Self-Interest in American Foreign Relations* (Chicago: University of Chicago Press, 1953); Frank Tannenbaum, *The American Tradition in Foreign Policy* (Norman: University of Oklahoma Press, 1955); Charles A. Beard, *The Idea of National Interest* (New York: Macmillan, 1934).
3. William Appleman Williams, *American-Russian Relations, 1781–1947* (New York: Rinehart, 1952).
4. Arthur M. Schlesinger, Jr., *The Crisis of the Old Order, 1919–1933* (Boston: Houghton Mifflin, 1957).
5. William Appleman Williams, *The Contours of American History* (Cleveland: World Publishing, 1961).
6. William Appleman Williams, *The Tragedy of American Diplomacy* (New York: Dell, 1972).
7. Carl P. Parrini, *Heir to Empire* (Pittsburgh: University of Pittsburgh Press, 1969); Martin J. Sklar, *The Corporate Reconstruction of American Capitalism, 1890–1916* (New York: Cambridge University Press, 1988).
8. Lloyd C. Gardner, Walter F. LaFeber, and Thomas J. McCormick, *Creation of the American Empire: U.S. Diplomatic History* (Chicago: Rand McNally, 1973).
9. William Appleman Williams, et al., ed., *America in Vietnam: A Documentary History* (Garden City, NY: Anchor Books, 1985); Lloyd C. Gardner, ed., *Redefining the Past: Essays in Honor of William Appleman Williams* (Corvallis: Oregon State University Press, 1986).
10. Thomas J. McCormick and Walter LaFeber, eds., *Behind the Throne: Servants of Power to Imperial Presidents, 1898–1968* (Madison: University of Wisconsin Press, 1993).
11. Walter LaFeber, *The New Empire: An Interpretation of American Expansion, 1860–1898* (Ithaca, NY: Cornell University Press, 1963).
12. Walter LaFeber, *The Panama Canal: The Crisis in Historical Perspective* (New York: Oxford University Press, 1979).
13. Walter LaFeber, *Inevitable Revolutions: The United States in Central America* (New York: W. W. Norton, 1983).
14. Walter LaFeber, *The American Search for Opportunity, 1865–1913* (New York: Cambridge University Press, 1993).
15. Walter LaFeber, *The Clash: A History of U.S.-Japan Relations* (New York: W. W. Norton, 1997).
16. Walter LaFeber, *Michael Jordan and the New Global Capitalism* (New York: W. W. Norton, 1999, 2002).
17. Walter LaFeber, *America, Russia, and the Cold War, 1945–1966* (New York: McGraw-Hill,, 1967); LaFeber, *The American Age: United States Foreign Policy at Home and Abroad since 1750* (New York: W. W. Norton, 1989).

Chapter 3

Finding Walter LaFeber in the Records

David A. Langbart

During the fall of 1975, Walter LaFeber taught a freshman seminar on presidential power and US foreign policy since 1940. I was one of the fortunate fifteen new Cornellians admitted into that class. While we were busy with our research papers in late October and November, LaFeber was traveling in Asia as a speaker for the United States Information Agency (USIA). Four decades later, while working as an archivist at the National Archives, I discovered in USIA files the reports about LaFeber's visit that had been sent back to Washington by US diplomats in Tokyo, Bangkok, and Singapore.

Walter LaFeber was a committed and energetic historian. Not only did he use the records and materials in the National Archives, the presidential libraries, and other manuscript collections, but he also literally came to be *in* the files. He was a creator and subject of significant US government records as a result of his membership on the Department of State's Advisory Committee on Foreign Relations of the United States and his role as a speaker for the USIA. To both of these endeavors, LaFeber brought his characteristic wit, erudition, and humility, as well as his expertise and intellect. Records on both activities either already are or will eventually be in the National Archives.

As with any good historian, Walter LaFeber grounded his scholarship in a broad range of archival and manuscript holdings. A review of the citations and bibliographies to *The New Empire, Inevitable Revolutions* and *The Clash*, as well as the other books and articles discussed elsewhere in this book, reflect long hours of research in the primary sources. Even *America, Russia, and the Cold War*, which is more a synthesis than a research tome, reflects time spent researching in the records.

An inveterate user of government records working on subjects for which most of the documents start out as classified, LaFeber recognized that access to the documents was imperative in order to learn what policymakers thought and did and how policy was implemented. He was, therefore, very concerned about government secrecy and worked both publicly and behind the scenes for openness and access to the records, which he believed was vital to the writing of good history. And he fully appreciated that good history was vital to creating an informed public, which was the very foundation for good citizenship as well as essential to holding government officials accountable for their behavior.

LaFeber's commitment to those beliefs inspired his service on various committees, which benefited the larger historical community and by extension the general public. He served on the Advisory Committee on Foreign Relations of the United States (known today as the Advisory Committee on Historical Diplomatic Documentation, or more commonly, the HAC) from 1971 to 1974, as chair in 1974. He represented the American Historical Association and was the first of the so-called New Left, or revisionist, foreign policy historians appointed to the committee.[1] He brought to the committee different historical perspectives just as the Historical Office was beginning to deal with significant new problems in compiling and printing the series *Foreign Relations of the United States* (FRUS), the official documentary record of US foreign policy.[2] One of the most notable of these problems was how to include in the *FRUS* series documents from the other agencies that were increasingly involved in the making of US foreign policy in the early years of the Cold War, especially the National Security Council (NSC), the Department of Defense (DOD), and the Central Intelligence Agency (CIA). Minutes of the committee's meetings demonstrate that LaFeber actively participated in those meetings.[3]

On July 20, 1971, on behalf of the secretary of state, Acting Assistant Secretary of State for Public Affairs William D. Blair Jr., under whose purview the Historical Office fell at that time, sent letters inviting three scholars to join the committee for four-year terms, replacing others whose appointment had expired. Walter LaFeber was one of those invitees.[4] At the time, the committee met once a year on the first Friday in November. LaFeber accepted and began his term by attending his first meeting on November 6, 1971, the fifteenth annual meeting of the committee. That he accepted indicates the importance of the work, as LaFeber did not relish such committee duties. The discussion covered a variety of topics relating to the work of the Department of State's Office of the Historian, then referred to as "HO" but now as "OH," primarily the compilation and publication of *FRUS* volumes. Among them were the implications of the recent announcement by the White House of its interest in special documentary projects on the Korean War, the 1958 Lebanon crisis, and the Cuban Missile Crisis. The committee also discussed the discontinuance of publication of *Current Documents*, clearance/declassification issues, and staffing levels for the Historical Office.[5]

The timing of LaFeber's service on HAC was auspicious. *FRUS* volumes appeared more than two decades after the events they documented, which meant that the early 1970s saw the review and publication of records regarding the dawn of the Cold War. In addition, LaFeber had just published the second edition of *America, Russia, and the Cold War* (1971) and therefore attended these meetings with both a wealth of knowledge and a load of questions about US policy. In a number of cases, these were questions about the increasing role of US military and intelligence operations that he would address in his own scholarship in subsequent years. For example, the committee's discussion about declassification of documents relating to covert US interference in the 1948 Italian elections was perhaps LaFeber's first opportunity to advocate transparency.[6] Other clearance issues involved the unresponsiveness of the Department of State's desk officers and other agencies, especially the Department of Defense; the new involvement of the White House and National Security Council as the compilations moved into the late 1940s after establishment of the NSC; and the problem of incorporating CIA documents. LaFeber understood that the integrity of *FRUS* depended on the official historians having unhindered access to the underlying sources.

Throughout LaFeber's tenure on the committee, those same issues persisted even as new ones arose and intensified. The new matters included access to materials at the presidential libraries, the pace of publication of the *FRUS* volumes, and the inclusion of documents relating to covert activities. Continuing issues included the executive order on declassification of US government records, the HO's deteriorating relationship with the NSC, the growth and increasing complexity of the volume of records to be searched and edited, records management, office budget, and technical editing.[7]

LaFeber's service on the committee culminated in 1974, when he served as chair. He was unanimously elected for that position by his fellow committee members. During his year at the head of the table, the committee dealt with many of the same problems as in prior years and new issues expanded the list. Among those continuing problems, the issue of NSC documentation proved especially vexing. A major new subject of discussion was related to an effort

LaFeber (third from left, with head in hand) chaired the State Department's Historical Advisory Committee from 1974 to 1976, pressing the Ford administration to expedite the declassification process. National Archives Photo 59-N-VS-1065-2-74.

to meet the presidentially mandated goal of publication no more than twenty years after the date of the documents chosen for inclusion. The Historical Office proposed a major reconception of the series under which the volumes would be compiled in trienniums, rather than the traditional annual approach that dated back to the first volume covering 1861. This change was supposed to gain time, reduce duplication of effort, improve efficiency, and lead to more focused compilations.

LaFeber took a keen interest in this proposal, expressing serious reservations. He noted that it would lead to fewer overall pages (and thus fewer documents) being published and had the potential of slowing rather than expediting access to the records themselves. To make up for the decrease in the number of documents printed, the Historical Office was considering the issuance of microform supplements containing additional, unedited documents. Ultimately the office adopted both the triennium approach and the issuance of microfiche supplements.[8] Another issue that came up was the revival of *Current Documents*, something LaFeber went on record as favoring.

One matter that came up only incidentally was the major change in the Department of State's central recordkeeping system instituted between 1973 and 1974. Because the *FRUS* compilers worked on records that were twenty to twenty-five years old, the new records system did not yet affect their work. Still, at least one historian in State's Office of the Historian worried about the potential consequences of the coming change. Later that new system would create myriad problems and headaches for the Department of State's historians, the committee, and the recordkeepers at the National Archives.

In 1974 Carol Laise served as the assistant secretary of state for public affairs and oversaw OH. She was one of relatively few women in the Foreign Service and at the time was the highest-ranking woman in the Department of State, the first ever to serve at the assistant secretary level. Through his work on the committee, LaFeber struck up a friendship with her. She sensitized him to the lowly position of women in the Department of State. Even though their contact did not continue, he later noted that "she pioneered the trail that other women began to fill in the Foreign Service."[9]

LaFeber sent the committee's annual report to Secretary of State Henry Kissinger on December 26, 1974. Given his later criticism of Kissinger, the irony of LaFeber corresponding with him is profound. In his cover letter LaFeber called FRUS "unsurpassed by any other governmental series for its importance and distinction," but he noted that the series was "at a crucial turning-point." Hitting the most important issue, he stated that if declassification problems were "not immediately solved," the series "will be severely damaged and lose the proud position and influence it now enjoys within the world academic community."[10]

The report, largely written by LaFeber, went into more detail and adopted some alarming language. After noting that FRUS "has been distinguished for its thoroughness and honesty in presenting the record of American diplomacy," the report warned that the "series is now in grave danger." Rather than shrinking the gap from the date of the creation of the documents to the date of publication in FRUS to the presidentially mandated twenty years, the gap was growing and stood at twenty-six years. Making matters worse, this delay stood in the way of scholarly access to the records themselves, as the opening of the files to researchers was then tied to publication of FRUS. Additionally, the declassification of documents was growing more difficult and plans were afoot that could lead to a significant decrease in the number of documents published.

To mitigate the problems, the report made eight recommendations, the most important of which were:

- Because the "fundamental problem is the failure of governmental agencies, and especially the National Security Council, to declassify documents," the "Secretary of State must intervene if necessary to ensure that other government agencies, and the National Security Council in particular, expedite the release of documents" to meet the deadlines for publication.

- The bureaucratic mechanisms for oversight of the classification and declassification of records should be revised, including strengthening the role of the Interagency Classification Review Committee, establishing a formal advisory committee composed of representatives of several academic organization, much like the *FRUS* committee.
- The essence of chosen documents not cleared for publication should be incorporated using other documents, and the omitted documents should be identified for ease of later access.
- The *FRUS* volumes should be compiled in trienniums, but at the then-current level of seven volumes per year; in other words, twenty-one volumes per triennium.
- The committee should hold a second meeting each year in April.[11]

Assistant Secretary Laise forwarded the committee's report to Secretary of State Kissinger, echoing the concerns of the committee in her cover memorandum. She noted that the delay in publication "is contrary to our commitment to enlarge public understanding . . . ; it affects our credibility with the nongovernmental foreign affairs community, academia, and the Congress; and it adds to our burdens under the Freedom of Information Act." She stated bluntly that "the prime reason for this deteriorating situation is our inability to obtain timely declassification action" from other agencies, especially the NSC, and that Secretary Kissinger's "personal intervention" was required. Laise wrote that there was need for a "new attitude" and improved machinery for declassification. The latter could be solved by empowering the Department of State's Council on Classification Policy. She attached a draft response to LaFeber and recommended authorizing the Council on Classification Policy to "decide" internal conflicts on classification/declassification matters. Kissinger agreed, scribbling "except for NSC material" next to his approval.[12]

Two and a half months after receipt of the committee's report, Kissinger sent LaFeber a letter that the Historical Office had prepared for Kissinger to sign, which can only be considered a pro-forma response. Still, it is significant that at this time matters such as the committee's annual report were addressed to the secretary of state, whose staff prepared a personal reply. Today the chairman submits the annual report to the Office of the Historian, which manages distribution and follow-up. Kissinger thanked LaFeber for a "thoughtful report" and agreed that publication of *FRUS* must be sped up. He had, therefore, directed that steps be taken to increase the pace of declassification, including conveying his concerns to the other agencies involved through the assistant secretary for public affairs. Kissinger noted that other recommendations required further study. He did not inform LaFeber of his refusal relating to NSC materials.[13]

At the time, LaFeber was satisfied with his committee experience. Years later, however, he noted that the "top people" at the Historical Office "blew much smoke (read: misled us)" and confessed that not a lot of progress had been made solving the problems faced in compiling *FRUS*. He noted in particular that there were still clearance problems and that the delay between the dates of the documents and the date of publication continued to grow.[14] Those issues persist to this day. Indeed, the target date for publication of *FRUS* volumes is now set at thirty years after the date of the document's issue, and largely due to clearance problems, that target is virtually never met.

Richard Immerman, another contributor to this book, served on the committee, by then commonly referred to as the HAC, from 2009 to 2021 and as chair from 2010 to 2021. He noted the following about LaFeber's work on the committee:

> Both the HAC and *FRUS* underwent dramatic transformations following Walt's tenure. The HAC grew in size and representation, and the number of its meetings increased to four times a year. Likewise, the number of *FRUS* volumes more than doubled for each presidential subseries, and as did the scope of the volumes. In 1991, moreover, Congress enacted the Foreign Relations Authorization Act, thereby statutorily empowering the HAC and mandating that *FRUS* provide a "thorough, accurate, and reliable" history of the United States foreign relations. OH compilers, consequently, gained access to a broader range of federal records. Yet the challenges the HAC has continued to confront are the same that Walt identified and anticipated, most notably the interagency review process, standardization of the declassification guidelines among the departments and agencies, and the timeliness of publication. Walt helped establish the precedents that we followed.[15]

Even after leaving the committee, LaFeber's concern with records, declassification, and the National Archives continued. Much of that work took place out of public view in various academic and other meetings. In 1980, however, he publicly criticized plans for the National Archives, then a component of the General Services Administration (GSA). Admiral Rowland G. Freeman, head of GSA, proposed a scheme to disperse many records housed in the Washington, D.C., area to National Archives facilities around the country. Among other things, Freeman described those plans as an effort to bring the records to citizens. The plan led to both internal rebellion and outside pressure.

The proposal and professional reaction to it were reported in a *Washington Post* article in late December 1979. LaFeber responded with a letter to the editor published under the heading "Leave the Archives Alone." "[The] policy will make it impossible to do historical research in many subjects," he pointed out, "unless the researcher has the funds to travel around the country."[16] In a line cut from the letter by the *Post* before publication, LaFeber referred to Admiral Freeman's plan "as one of idiocy." He added that at a recent meeting of the American Historical Association, many of the historians in attendance agreed with that characterization and no one objected or dissented.[17] Privately he joked, "If a battleship steams down Lake Cayuga to zero in on" his home, the author of this chapter would know the full story.[18]

In the fall of 1975, shortly after his term on the advisory committee ended, LaFeber once again found himself in service to a US government agency, this time on a trip for the USIA as part of its "Volunteer Speakers" program. Under that program, US experts from a wide range of fields traveled abroad to share their expertise with foreign audiences. Speakers included musicians, artists, actors, writers, scientists, anthropologists, mathematicians, historians, government officials, and others. Coming so soon after the fall of Saigon, it is not clear what motivated USIA to choose LaFeber, a noted critic of US foreign policy, for this trip, although it is important to note that the agency chose speakers who reflected a wide range of opinions. Indeed, LaFeber's motivations for undertaking the tour are perhaps even less clear. The primary purpose of the trip to Japan was to participate in an academic symposium on post–World War II Asia.[19]

This trip explains why the Freshman Seminar I was taking doubled up on sessions early in the semester and then had a long period without meeting to work on our major research papers. The course, on the relationship between presidential power and US foreign policy, focused on the period since 1940, but also looked back to earlier events that illustrated issues that continued to resonate in US foreign policy. The fifteen students allowed into the course knew they were in the big leagues when they received a significant reading assignment to complete for the first seminar session.

LaFeber was one of the least pretentious people I had ever met. During the first class he made it clear that although addressing him as "Professor LaFeber" was acceptable, he preferred "Mr. LaFeber." "Dr. LaFeber" was definitely out. The seminar (History 203), which met once a week for two hours, was the setting for the first of many times I would hear LaFeber discuss John Quincy Adams or Willard Straight when explaining more modern aspects of US foreign policy. In addition to our readings, there were several writing assignments, including a major research paper based on original research in primary sources. Grammar, syntax, and style counted, too. To aid in our writing, LaFeber directed us to familiarize ourselves with the guidance in *The Elements of Style* by

William Strunk Jr. and E. B. White. My copy of that small book from that seminar has traveled with me ever since and sits on my desk to this day. That he would undertake this class for freshmen, with its emphasis on writing, was just one more example of LaFeber's commitment to teaching. Despite having a teaching assistant, LaFeber graded the multiple papers each student wrote, providing copious comments about content and style. Whatever skill I have as a writer stems largely from what I learned in that seminar.[20]

Only later did I learn the real reason for the hiatus in seminar meetings from reading a file of USIA records in the National Archives: LaFeber had been on a trip to East and Southeast Asia sponsored by that agency. The texts of his talks are not available, but the reports by his official hosts indicate that he discussed US foreign policy in the 1920s and the 1970s. His class lectures from the time covered those topics, too, albeit for a different audience.

In the class lectures LaFeber countered the idea that the United States was disengaged and isolationist during the 1920s. Indeed, the title of his primary lecture on the 1920s was "Interventionism Called Isolationism."[21] He explained that even though the United States was not as active a participant as it had been during World War I, it was certainly more involved internationally than it had been before the war. Rather than relying on its political position, let alone its military might, the US used its economic and financial power to change the world; the flag followed commerce. While that may not have been involvement in a conventional foreign policy sense, the US was nevertheless an engaged and influential actor on the international scene.

As for the 1970s, that was more current events than history, but LaFeber still brought his critical thinking to the subject. He explained that US policymakers were adjusting to the US position in a post–Vietnam War world. Despite the breakup of the domestic consensus on foreign policy, even in a diffuse world the United States was still a, if not the, major player. With the rise of nationalism, US power was declining, but the United States still wanted to maintain political and economic stability in order to contain Soviet expansionism and deal with new political and economic blocs. With the end of the war in Vietnam, US relations with other nations in Southeast Asia took on more importance.

LaFeber's first stop was Thailand. In Bangkok, LaFeber spoke at the universities of Chulalongkorn and Chiang Mai. Several months later, the USIS (United States Information Service) post in Bangkok provided this summary of LaFeber's November visit.[22]

> Dr. Walter La Feber [sic], Noll Professor of History at Cornell University, lectured on foreign policy before members of the political science

and history faculties. . . . In his lectures, he contrasted U.S. foreign policy during the immediate post World War I period with the 1970's. He portrayed the United States as a responsible world power adjusting to the new political realities in Indochina and interested in the maintenance of friendly relations with Thailand. In his formal presentations and in social gatherings, Dr. La Feber [sic] served to support the post's first and third objectives regarding the resiliency of current U.S. foreign policy and future relations with Thailand.[23]

The Bangkok Post had invited him to speak to support its work demonstrating US interest in maintaining a mutually beneficial relationship with Thailand and to explain the US ability to "formulate positive and responsible foreign policies" in the current international environment.[24] The reporting officer wrote that LaFeber predicted that the US would not revert to isolationism. Rather, it would continue its engagement in the world, including Southeast Asia after the debacle of Vietnam. LaFeber received pointed questions from his audiences on the latter point, to which he responded by citing "several examples of recent US foreign policy moves in Europe, Latin America and S.E. Asia which reflected . . . the ability of American foreign policymakers to formulate new policies in response to world developments." An earlier message indicated that LaFeber was particularly "effective in the discussion period following his presentation. He handled tough questions candidly and sincerely."[25]

Following Bangkok, LaFeber visited Singapore. During his stay there, he met with Ministry of Foreign Affairs officials to discuss current US foreign policy and lectured and discussed analogies of US foreign policy in the 1920s and 1970s at the University of Singapore history department and with a group of career officers in the Singapore Armed Forces. He met with the ministry officials on a Saturday. The USIS post there sent the following summary:

> Cornell historian Walter La Feber [sic] spent two days in Singapore cogently explaining—through historical comparisons—basis and backing for American foreign policy. He stressed in precise, persuasive, and confident manner that U.S. is bound to continue involvement in world affairs and that broad consensus between executive, legislative, and public applies to most major foreign policy issues. His sometimes skeptical but always keenly interested audiences—composed of government officials, academics and military officers—responded extremely well to Dr. La Feber [sic], who is first-rate volunteer speaker.[26]

In the more detailed report, the embassy's public affairs officer (PAO) noted that "few speakers have so precisely supported [post] objectives." He reported that LaFeber explained that the United States was so involved in the world that it could not withdraw even if it wanted to and that on major foreign policy issues there was "remarkable consensus" among the administration, Congress, and the public. The report also noted that audiences respected LaFeber's candor, noting that he was "articulate, persuasive, and very well prepared," "impressive in his formal remarks and the discussions that followed," and "never evaded a question." The PAO closed his report stating "The speaker was extremely effective, the subject was interesting, and the audience responded well—what more could we ask for? La Feber [sic] would be welcome back to Singapore any time."[27]

LaFeber concluded his November trip with a visit to Tokyo. While there, he spoke primarily to other academics but also to some businessmen and professionals. The USIS post in Tokyo reported the visit this way:

> LaFeber evaluation mailed January 19. Evaluation reads: "Dr. LaFeber is an extremely good speaker. Articulate, concise, and provocative, he set forth stimulating analogies between US foreign policy of the 20's and the 70's. While maintaining his credible academic position, he was very supportive of US foreign policy, particularly with the US-Japan relationship. Audience response was excellent. The discussion session was lively and right on the objectives."[28]

As any student who took a class with LaFeber can attest, the high praise of his expertise, presentation, and demeanor in the USIA reports is not an exaggeration. The reports may even understate the reality. His genius as a lecturer was his ability to convey to a big audience large amounts of important information in a manner that made it feel like he was speaking only to you in an intimate conversation. Given his public criticism of contemporary US foreign policy, some of the assessments of his talks are perplexing. It is difficult to square LaFeber's stated positions with comments such as he believed that a "broad consensus between executive, legislative, and public applies to most major foreign policy issues"; that "he was very supportive of US foreign policy"; or that he believed the US was a "responsible world power." LaFeber seldom pulled his punches; perhaps this was his polite midwestern way of avoiding embarrassment for his hosts.

Many years later LaFeber still had pleasant memories of this trip to the Far East. He especially remembered that the audience in Singapore was particularly sharp. LaFeber's work for USIA did not end there. In 1987, for example, he did some work for the Voice of America, which was then a part of USIA.[29]

LaFeber's move into scholarship on the Cold War and other topics more current than those covered by *The New Empire* forced him to confront the broader issues of records in general and the specific matter of classification/ declassification of documents. He received an insider's firsthand view of those issues while serving on the *FRUS* committee, when submitting his own Freedom of Information Act requests, and when working on academic committees concerned with the issue. Strongly believing that citizen access to records of their government was important for the survival of democracy, he was one of the scholars who pressed government agencies to be more open.

Unlike the other contributors to this book, all of whom are academics, I have spent my entire professional career in government service at the National Archives, for most of those years working in one way or another with foreign affairs records. While I always planned to major in history, my thoughts about a post-college career took me away from that field. Long before he gently ordered me to stop calling him "Mr. LaFeber," Walt helped me chart my journey into archival work. That freshman seminar and another seminar I took the next year with political historian (and Walt's close friend) Joel Silbey were major catalysts. Those classes, additional LaFeber and Silbey classes, and those with other professors in the history department opened up history in a way I had never before anticipated, let alone experienced, and set the stage for a major change.

Landing a Federal Summer Internship at the National Archives was the final catalyst. I was not working with foreign affairs files, but the attraction of working with the original records was visceral and immediate. After that interest became manifest, Walt made clear how important archives, archival work, and knowledgeable archivists are to the success of historians and other users of the records, clearly stating the value of such work. After I secured a permanent position at the National Archives upon graduation, I relied on Walt as a sounding board for the next forty-one years, and he unfailingly provided support, encouragement, assistance, and feedback. We corresponded regularly and I benefited from those exchanges. That said, what I learned in his classes was particularly important to my two decades directly involved with the archival appraisal and scheduling of foreign affairs and intelligence records and continues to be so in my subsequent archival work.[30] In turn, over the years, I was able to assist Walt, and his students, with their research in the records, assistance Walt was always kind enough to acknowledge in his publications.

Notwithstanding his critiques of US international behavior and reputation for speaking truth to power, LaFeber maintained contacts with senior policymakers who held opposing views, some of whom were his former students. In one case his connection with a very senior official on the staff of Secretary of State George Shultz was instrumental to the success of a major project involving the scheduling of the records of the principal officers of the Department of State. Without the involvement of that official (not a Cornellian), the project would not have gone forward. Walt's willingness to involve himself in such behind-the-scenes actions helped to nurture my career, but also reflected his understanding of the importance of the records and the archives.

Coincidentally, just as I began full-time work at the National Archives, *Prologue*, the journal of that agency, published an article by LaFeber titled "'Ah, If We Had Studied It More Carefully': The Fortunes of American Diplomatic History," a historiographical overview of the development of the field of diplomatic history in the United States up to that point. He noted at the time, "I wrote the essay as sort of 'old home week'—it gave me an opportunity to say some things about my old teachers—Bailey and Harrington—that I had long wanted to say."[31]

As might be expected for an article published in a journal sponsored by an archival organization, embedded in his essay LaFeber commented on the importance of records-based research. He noted how the opening of new records and manuscript collections led to new perspectives on events that previously had been portrayed only by the media and the memoirs of participants. The use of new records helped to create a "robust" field of study. He noted years later, "Everything we do is really based on the records."[32] That statement is "eye candy" to an archivist and the best kind of affirmation.

Beginning with the then-widespread assessment that the field of diplomatic history as moribund, LaFeber sketched out in his inimitable way the development of the field of US foreign relations. The message that he delivered was that obituaries proclaiming the death of diplomatic history as a field of study were premature.[33] Rather than being a field marking time and past its prime, since the 1960s there had been significant developments. There was a new interest in the relationship of domestic and foreign policies, especially regarding the questions of executive power, economics, civil rights, and social conditions.[34] There was an understanding that the examination of US overseas interests requires the examination of more than just the formal diplomatic exchanges and treaties between countries. There was the use of social science methods. There was a realization that US foreign policy had to be understood as it developed as part of the world system. Those and additional developments in the study of US foreign relations since then have proved him correct. The field of diplomatic history was (and is) alive and well and continues to change. Walter LaFeber was at the heart of that, as the coauthors of the following chapters make crystal clear.

Notes

Opinions are those of the author and do not reflect those of the National Archives and Records Administration or any other agency of the US government. Portions of this chapter originally appeared in the author's National Archives Text Message blog post "Historian in the Records," https://text-message.blogs.archives.gov/2021/03/22/historian-in-the-records/.

1. By 1970 there was a recognition that the members of the advisory committee were not representative of the historical profession. See Richard W. Leopold, "A Crisis of Confidence: Foreign Policy Research and the Federal Government," *American Archivist* 34 (April 1971): 139–55. This article is Leopold's presidential address to the Society for Historians of American Foreign Relations (SHAFR) in December 1970.

2. *FRUS* is the official documentary record of US foreign policy. It is a selection of documents from the files of the Department of State, the White House, and other agencies compiled by the State Department's Office of the Historian. Besides providing the text of important foreign policy documents, it also includes source citations that indicate the location of the original documents. In this way, *FRUS* serves as a guide to the location of additional documents on the same and related subjects not selected for publication.

3. Discussion of the committee's work comes from its minutes, which will eventually be deposited in the National Archives. See the Office of the Historian website at https://history.state.gov/historicaldocuments/frus-history/documents. See also the official history of the Office of the Historian: William B. McAllister, Joshua Botts, Peter Cozzens, and Aaron W. Marrs, *Toward "Thorough, Accurate and Reliable": A History of the Foreign Relations of the United States Series* (Washington, DC: US Department of State, Office of the Historian, Bureau of Public Affairs, 2015), 177–208.

4. Letter from Acting Assistant Secretary of State William D. Blair Jr. to Walter LaFeber, July 20, 1971, file PR 10 Foreign Relations of US, 1970–73 Subject-Numeric Files, RG 59: General Records of the Department of State, US National Archives (USNA). The HAC now meets four times a year.

5. The *Current Documents* series, published under various titles, presented, on a near-contemporary basis, public foreign policy messages, addresses, statements, interviews, press briefings and conferences, and congressional testimony. The series began in 1950 with *A Decade of American Foreign Policy: Basic Documents, 1941–1949*. In 1957 the Department of State published *American Foreign Policy, 1950–1955*. Thereafter, it issued annual volumes titled *American Foreign Policy: Current Documents* for the years 1956 through 1967. The Department of State resumed the series in 1983 with the publication of *American Foreign Policy: Basic Documents, 1977–1980*. In 1984 the annual volumes resumed with the publication of *American Foreign Policy: Current Documents 1981*. The last published volume covered 1991, at which time publication ceased.

6. For the significance of the 1948 Italian elections, see Walter LaFeber, *The American Age: United States Policy at Home and Abroad since 1750* (New York: W. W. Norton, 1989), 459.

7. Successive presidents have issued executive orders governing the declassification of federal records. At the time of writing, the current one, issued by President Barack Obama on December 29, 2009, is Executive Order (EO) 13526.

8. The first triennium covered the years 1952 to 1954. That structure eventually gave way to compilations based largely on presidential administrations; the microfiche supplements gave way to electronic-only volumes.

9. Walter LaFeber email to David Langbart, December 14, 2019. All communications from LaFeber to the author are in the author's possession.

10. Walter LaFeber to Henry Kissinger, December 26, 1974, P750062-1407, Central Foreign Policy Files, 1973-79/P-Reel Printouts, RG 59: General Records of the Department of State, USNA.

11. Annual Report (1974) of Advisory Committee on "Foreign Relations of the United States," P750062-1408, Central Foreign Policy Files, 1973-79/P-Reel Printouts, RG 59: General Records of the Department of State, USNA. When reconstituted by legislation in 1991, the committee was mandated to meet four times a year in recognition that once was not enough.

12. Assistant Secretary of State for Public Affairs to the Secretary of State, March 4, 1975, P750062-1412, Central Foreign Policy Files, 1973-79/P-Reel Printouts, RG 59: General Records of the Department of State, USNA.

13. Henry Kissinger to Walter LaFeber, March 8, 1975, P750062-1404, Central Foreign Policy Files, 1973-79/P-Reel Printouts, RG 59: General Records of the Department of State, USNA.

14. Walter LaFeber letter to David Langbart, January 29, 1989.

15. Richard Immerman email to David Langbart, September 21, 2022, in author's possession.

16. Thomas Grubisich, "GSA Chief Gives Archivists a Geography Lesson," *Washington Post*, December 22, 1979, A5; Walter LaFeber to the Editor, *Washington Post*, January 19, 1980, A14.

17. Walter LaFeber to the Editor, *Washington Post*, January 1, 1980. Copy in author's possession.

18. Walter LaFeber letter to David Langbart, January 20, 1980.

19. USIA to USIS Tokyo, Telegram 21221, September 2, 1975, file: LaFeber, Walter 1976, Entry P-73: Volunteer Speakers Files, 1968–81, Office of the Associate Directorate for Programs, Office of Program Coordination and Development, RG 306: Records of the USIA, USNA. Other scholars who were considered but were unavailable included John L. Gaddis, Akira Iriye, and Ernest May. LaFeber's seminal article on early 1940s policy toward Indochina was about to be published. See Walter LaFeber, "Roosevelt, Churchill, and Indochina, 1942–1945," *American Historical Review* 80 (December 1975): 1277–95.

20. Years later LaFeber commented that the seminar "remains one of the most satisfying I have taught. It was a good class and there were indeed great arguments in that class." Walter LaFeber letter to David Langbart, September 18, 1993.

21. History 314 Syllabus, spring 1977. Discussion of the class lectures is based on spring 1977 History 314 lecture notes in the author's possession.

22. USIS posts were the USIA's field operations offices.

23. USIS Bangkok to USIA, Message No. 16, April 12, 1976, Volunteer Speaker—Dr. Walter LaFeber, file: LaFeber, Walter 1976, Entry P-73: Volunteer Speakers Files, 1968–81, Office of the Associate Directorate for Programs, Office of Program Coordination and Development, RG 306: Records of the USIA, USNA.

24. The English-language newspaper *Bangkok Post* carried a notice for LaFeber's talk at Chulalongkorn University on November 13, 1975 (p. 5). The notice said he was conducting a seminar organized by the faculty of political science titled "Historical Analogies: American Foreign Policy in World Politics—A Comparison of the So-Called 'Multipolar World' of the 1920's and 1970's." My thanks to Professor Tamara Loos for locating this notice.

25. USIS Bangkok to USIA, Message No. 16, April 12, 1976, Volunteer Speaker—Dr. Walter LaFeber and US Embassy Bangkok to USIA, Telegram 1916, file: LaFeber, Walter 1976, Entry P-73: Volunteer Speakers Files, 1968–81, Office of the Associate Directorate for Programs, Office of Program Coordination and Development, RG 306: Records of the USIA, USNA.

26. USIS Singapore to USIA Washington, Message No. 42, November 24, 1975, Program Evaluation of Volspkr Dr. Walter La Feber [sic], file: LaFeber, Walter 1976, Entry P-73: Volunteer Speakers Files, 1968–81, Office of the Associate Directorate for Programs, Office of Program Coordination and Development, RG 306: Records of the USIA, USNA.

27. USIS Singapore to USIA Washington, Message No. 42, November 24, 1975, file: LaFeber, Walter 1976, Entry P-73, RG 306: Records of the USIA, USNA.

28. Embassy Tokyo to USIA, Telegram 1139, January 29, 1976, and "Speaker Evaluation Sheet," January 19, 1976, file: LaFeber, Walter 1976, Entry P-73: Volunteer Speakers Files, 1968–81, Office of the Associate Directorate for Programs, Office of Program Coordination and Development, RG 306: Records of the USIA, USNA.

29. Walter LaFeber letter to David Langbart, October 9, 1987, and email August 31, 2016.

30. Only a very small percentage of all US government records are permanently preserved in the National Archives. The decisions on what to preserve and when the records will be transferred to the National Archives are made through the appraisal and scheduling process.

31. Walter LaFeber, "'Ah, If We Had Studied It More Carefully': The Fortunes of American Diplomatic History," *Prologue*, Summer 1979, 120–31. Thomas Bailey supervised Walt's MA at Stanford, and Fred Harvey Harrington directed his doctoral studies at the University of Wisconsin at Madison. Walt's comment that Bailey's lectures were "beautifully organized, spiced with telling anecdotes, well researched, and magnificently presented" (123) applied equally to his own. Walter LaFeber letter to David Langbart, October 28, 1979.

32. Walter LaFeber email to David Langbart, April 8, 2001.

33. The classic critique of the field at the time is Charles S. Maier, "Marking Time: The Historiography of International Relations," in *The Past before Us: Contemporary Historical Writing in the United States*, ed. Michael Kammen (Ithaca, NY: Cornell University Press, 1980), 355–82.

34. This was presaged in, of all places, a 1950 Department of State publication titled *Our Foreign Policy*. The first sentence reads, "There is no longer any real distinction between 'domestic' and 'foreign' affairs."

CHAPTER 4

Extending the Sphere
The New Empire

SUSAN A. BREWER AND ROBERT E. HANNIGAN

Legions of Cornell University undergraduates remember Professor Walter LaFeber's two-semester survey of the history of US foreign relations as a treasured part of their college education.[1] As a lecturer, LaFeber was not only eloquent and clear. His style also invited students to try to understand why exploring the past could be both exciting and important. That was likewise the aim of LaFeber's written work. What many students may not have realized is just how closely interwoven what they were learning in class was with his reading, research, and writing. LaFeber believed that good scholarship and good teaching go hand in hand. Depending on when they took his course, Cornell students were either hearing the firsthand results of a great historian's efforts to make sense of the past, or listening to his efforts to work through, *with them*, the ideas that would be in his next book.

"Extending the sphere," a quotation from James Madison's *Federalist No. 10*, is familiar to any Cornellian who took Professor LaFeber's undergraduate survey.[2] LaFeber would describe the ingenious notion proffered by the "Father of the Constitution" that a republican form of government, self-regulated by checks and balances, could succeed in a large territory. Throughout the course, LaFeber referred to "extending the sphere" as a cue for his students to consider how dilemmas over power and freedom were triggered by territorial, commercial, and overseas expansion. The question of the viability of republican institutions in the United States as it pursued its global ambitions would be fundamental to his interpretation of US history. In this chapter we begin by addressing LaFeber's prize-winning first book, *The New Empire: An Interpretation of American Expansion, 1860–1898*.[3] We then consider additional writings of his on Benjamin Franklin, James Madison, John Quincy Adams, and US policymakers between the Civil War and World War I that confirm expansion as a phenomenon with deep roots in, and serious consequences for, the republic in which he lived.

In the United States, the 1950s are still mostly remembered as a decade of self-satisfied celebration. That attitude was certainly evident in much of the US history taught during those years. Students, and others, learned that theirs was a country that over time had solved its serious domestic problems—if it had ever had any. (The historians who argued for this view are now generally referred to as members of the "consensus school.")[4] In terms of foreign affairs, meanwhile, the United States had recently overcome a tradition of disengagement to finally embrace its destiny as a—indeed, *the*—disinterested global champion of democracy and freedom. Comforting lessons of this ilk clearly appealed to a nation in the grip of a Cold War with the Soviet Union. But even in the 1950s there were those who thought otherwise, wondering whether such interpretations were particularly accurate or useful.

One, apparently, was Professor Robert E. Bowers, LaFeber's undergraduate mentor at Hanover College. By his own account, LaFeber decided to become a historian largely because of Bowers's thought-provoking courses on US foreign relations.[5] It was Bowers who advised LaFeber to pursue a master's degree at Stanford, where, under historian Thomas A. Bailey, he would learn to write in an accessible style. (LaFeber more than accomplished that.) But he ought then to move on to the University of Wisconsin for his doctorate. Madison, Bowers offered, was where the most significant reexaminations of the US past appeared to be under way.[6]

Indeed, they were. LaFeber later would recall that his graduate education at the University of Wisconsin was "a revelation." As Lloyd Gardner and Thomas McCormick explain in chapter 2 in this book, this was due largely to the teaching of Fred Harvey Harrington (who directed LaFeber's dissertation) and William Appleman Williams (one of Harrington's former students, for whom LaFeber was a teaching assistant). At Madison, a new generation of scholars was inspired by the progressive tradition of US historical inquiry, which called for the investigation of problems of economic and political inequality.

Years later LaFeber remembered both the demanding standards Harrington set and how much his graduate students admired and respected the kind of scholar and teacher he had been. For them, Harrington embodied what an intellectual's role was all about. They particularly appreciated his "willingness to . . . think the unconventional, to question the accepted, and . . . to deal with the roots, transformations, and effects of power" in a nation that had become "the most powerful in history."[7] It was a model that would guide LaFeber for the rest of his career. Harrington also shaped LaFeber's conviction that it was vitally important for Americans to examine the past in an honest and meaningful way.

Meanwhile, in his undergraduate lectures Williams was laying out themes that would be central to his soon-to-be published *The Tragedy of American Diplomacy*. Building on concepts derived from progressive historians like Charles Beard and the British scholars John Gallagher and Ronald Robinson, Williams suggested a decidedly new way of looking at past US interactions with other peoples. US diplomacy may have been explained in terms that sounded altruistic. Policy elites may have insisted that a leading global role had been forced upon them. But in Williams's view, the US government had, for most of its history, actively pursued a path of self-interested expansion and aggrandizement on the world stage. And that was something that its citizens now, during increasingly dangerous times, had to grasp and confront head-on. Otherwise the country would court disaster. As LaFeber correctly commented, *The Tragedy of American Diplomacy* "more than any other [book] influenced the next several generations of writers on American foreign relations."

Against what he later described as this "electric" backdrop, LaFeber decided to research the "pivotal" 1890s for his doctoral dissertation. Accepting Harrington's advice to carve out something manageable, he settled on the topic of US Latin American policy during the second Cleveland administration. As he related years later, however, he always intended to make of the project something more.[8] This he certainly did. By 1962 the dissertation had been expanded into a work of more than 400 pages, covering the entire late nineteenth century. While still in manuscript form, it won the Albert J. Beveridge Prize, bestowed annually by the American Historical Association on the most outstanding new work in American history. Not yet thirty, LaFeber had established himself as one of the most important historians of his generation.

Quite remarkably for a book that is now sixty years old, *The New Empire* remains today the place to start for anyone interested in studying the emergence of the United States as a world power. This is not because other influential investigations of the late nineteenth century have not been done. In fact, LaFeber, in the preface he wrote for the thirty-fifth anniversary edition of *The New Empire*, acknowledged, and celebrated, the "extraordinary amount of work" that had appeared on the book's subjects and themes since its publication.[9] Rather, it is because the fundamentals of the new interpretive framework it presented have never been set out more cogently and have only gained in acceptance.

The immediate critical response was overwhelmingly appreciative. Upon its publication, reviewers of *The New Empire* especially liked LaFeber's effort to illuminate "a shadowy corner of the American experience." J. C. Vinson, for example, writing in the *American Historical Review*, asserted, "The theory that America was thrust by events into a position of world power it never sought must now be re-examined."[10] Given that the book was overturning so much of the prevailing orthodoxy, this reception was perhaps unexpected. And in fact the author was himself surprised. In the preface noted above, LaFeber relates that at the meeting where the Beveridge Prize was awarded, he "saw a prominent senior American historian place his head in his hands . . . as if he wanted to exclaim, 'Say it isn't so!' From that moment," he continues, "I feared long unfavorable reviews and a short life for the book."[11]

One quite irate attack was mounted in 1978 by the naval historian James A. Field Jr. In an article titled "American Imperialism: The Worst Chapter in Almost Any Book," published in the *American Historical Review*, Field disparaged the idea that the United States had been pursuing any new, expansionist policy at all on the world stage in the nineteenth century, arguing instead that historians like LaFeber saw patterns and rationality where there was none. In Field's view, the United States may very well have been as "much or more the used" as the user in its international transactions."[12]

LaFeber did not believe that chapters on the 1890s were the worst in US diplomatic historiography. In response to this critique, he noted that Field echoed the analysis of Yale historian Samuel Flagg Bemis published forty years earlier. According to Bemis, LaFeber explained, "the grand story of American expansion rolls along until the narrative encounters 1898," which Bemis pronounced an "aberration." LaFeber pointed out, as did others, that Field made no serious effort himself even to explore, no less explain, why US policymakers took the specific steps they did during the momentous period leading up to and following the outbreak of war with Spain in 1898. For example, Field describes the explosion of the warship USS *Maine* as an accident of history—a claim that, LaFeber observes, begs "the central question of why the *Maine* was in Havana harbor in the first place."[13]

That the United States had expanded its control over territories in the Caribbean and the Pacific in the late 1890s had of course never been in dispute. Before the publication of *The New Empire*, most scholars had explicitly rejected the relevance of economic factors. The most commonly adduced explanations for the war with Spain, and the colonial expansion that followed, revolved around the impact of the sensationalizing "yellow press," the purported inability of President William McKinley to resist an outpouring of public outrage over Spain's brutal treatment of the people of Cuba, the fortuitous presence in key government positions of a cabal of "large policy" enthusiasts (led by Assistant Secretary of the Navy Theodore Roosevelt and Senator Henry Cabot Lodge of Massachusetts), the popularity of Social Darwinian ideas, and an alleged nationwide "psychic crisis," a mood of unease and frustration set off by the depression of that decade.[14]

The popular "yellow press" interpretation is succinctly captured in one sentence of Henry F. Pringle's Pulitzer Prize–winning *Theodore Roosevelt: A Biography*. "In all probability," Pringle argued, the war with Spain "never would have come had not Joseph Pulitzer and William Randolph Hearst been anxious to increase the circulation of their newspapers." As LaFeber notes in the 1998 preface, the *New York Times* continued to place a heavy emphasis on this argument in its commemoration of the war's centennial. It lives on in the classic film *Citizen Kane*, where the character Charles Foster Kane, a thinly veiled stand-in for Hearst, telegraphs his correspondent in Cuba, "You provide the prose poems, I'll provide the war."[15]

The notion that the 1890s were unrelated either to any prior developments in the nation's past or to US foreign policy in the twentieth century had appeared in the most recent treatment of the era. In *Imperial Democracy*, Harvard historian Ernest R. May concluded that the United States "had not sought a new role in world affairs" in the 1890s, but instead "had greatness thrust upon it."[16] By the 1990s historian Edward P. Crapol was noticing what remains the case today: scholars had come to agree that "the three decades prior to the Spanish-American War" of 1898 were "a crucial transitional phase leading to America's emergence as a major world power." Also, that the term "empire" was the correct one to describe that power.[17] These are the basic tenets of LaFeber's interpretation.

The New Empire argues that the expansion of the 1890s, which had roots in traditions dating back to the beginning of the country, was inspired by changes the United States had been undergoing as a result of its industrial revolution. US moves were not undertaken in a "fit of absent-mindedness."[18] They had not been driven by public opinion. McKinley was in control. He and his advisers acted with conscious intent. LaFeber refutes the waggish claim made by the Republican president that he was not even sure where the Philippine Islands were. He points out that McKinley months earlier had agreed to Naval Department orders directing Commodore George Dewey to attack the Philippines should war break out between the United States and Spain.[19] The book's title, finally, refers not only to the extracontinental islands acquired in the aftermath of the war with Spain, but also to what, in the author's view, would be a central preoccupation of twentieth-century US foreign policy—namely, the establishment and protection of a commercial empire overseas.

The approach LaFeber took in *The New Empire* would be echoed in most of his subsequent work. He did not believe an understanding of US foreign relations could be achieved simply by reading memoranda and diplomatic notes. A nation's approach to foreign affairs, he judged, had to be comprehended against the backdrop of its own internal affairs and development, its socioeconomic order, and its dominant culture. Thus, LaFeber stated in the very first sentence of the preface that his goal was "to examine the crucial incubation period of the American overseas empire by relating the development of that empire to the effects of the industrial revolution." What groups, organizations, ways of doing things, and values had come to predominate in the United States because of this transformation? What problems did the industrial revolution bring? What "solutions" to those problems were put forward? These were some of the questions he would address.

At the same time, LaFeber was unapologetic about studying carefully what historians today refer to as the "old white men" of the policymaking elite (all the better if those men had thought carefully about what they wanted to do and set down their thoughts on paper). They, after all, were the ones uniquely positioned to make key decisions about the nation's course (socioeconomic systems did not, in the abstract, do so). So, if war, conquest, empire, colonialism, and imperialism were important subjects to understand (and LaFeber certainly thought they were), it was futile to attempt to do so without thoroughly trying to understand the thoughts, values, and actions of such people. One thing he noted about the numerous policymakers he studied was how they often differed, one from the other, in their approaches, even while they generally shared basic goals and assumptions. Individuals, he was convinced, did matter.

Chapter 1, "Years of Preparation, 1860–1889," aimed to show, wrote LaFeber, that "the climactic decade of the 1890s can be properly understood only when placed in the context of the last half of the century." By the 1850s and 1860s, "the continental empire of which Madison, Jefferson, and John Quincy Adams had dreamed spanned North America." A "new empire," meanwhile, "had started to take form." Instead of "searching for farming, mineral, or grazing lands," Americans would now be looking for "foreign markets for agricultural staples or industrial goods." Not unlike the earlier continentalism, the chapter offers, this expansionism would also come to exact "a political and often a military price." The ensuing pages of the chapter trace the country's industrialization, the dramatic shifts of wealth and power (from southern planters to northern businessmen) that occurred after the Civil War, and the United States' growing interest in "new frontiers" in the form of foreign markets and raw materials. They looked for those, LaFeber notes, particularly throughout Latin America and in East Asia.

In LaFeber's view, William Henry Seward, secretary of state under Abraham Lincoln and Andrew Johnson, loomed over the entire late-nineteenth-century period, because "his vision of empire" foreshadowed subsequent policy. To Seward, a great nation required a transportation network of canals, railroads, and overseas bases; agriculture and manufacturing; exports; cheap labor; and public land at low prices. Even if his initiatives often failed (others, of course, like the acquisition of Alaska, did not), the influential New Yorker set the agenda for the diplomatists who followed him. Interest grew over the ensuing decades in such projects as the construction of a trans-isthmian canal and the acquisition of island bases that might facilitate US activity on the other side of the Pacific.

Each from a different angle, the next three chapters lay out how overseas expansion was being thought about, discussed, and acted upon by the 1890s. Chapter 2, "The Intellectual Formulation," looks at the writings of historian Frederick Jackson Turner; naval officer and historian Alfred Thayer Mahan; Protestant clergyman Josiah Strong, who advocated the spread of Christianity, "civilization," and US economic interests by what he believed to be the superior Anglo-Saxon race; and historian Brooks Adams, the grandson of John Quincy Adams and author of *The Law of Civilization and Decay* (1896), which argued that the westward movement of world power based on centers of commercial exchange put the United States in position to assume global dominance. The "writings of these men typified and, in some instances, directly influenced the thought of US policymakers who created the new empire," LaFeber writes. For example, Turner's emphasis on the salutary influence of the frontier in the US past and his concern that the frontier seemingly was now gone reinforced for many the belief that new opportunities would have to be found abroad. Mahan's widely read books and articles, meanwhile, made the case for the acquisition of bases, the construction of a canal, and the building of a navy so that a new empire might be brought into being.

In the next two chapters, LaFeber addresses the strategic and economic "formulations" of the era. He argues, in chapter 3, that "[President] Benjamin Harrison [1889–93] and his ambitious secretary of state, James G. Blaine, formulated the strategy the builders of the new empire followed during the remainder of the 1890s." This was reflected in efforts to acquire bases in the Caribbean and mid-Pacific, promote the trans-isthmian canal, draw the countries of South America into closer commercial relations with the United States, and, most successfully, boost construction of the sort of battleship fleet endorsed by Mahan.

Chapter 4, "The Economic Formulation," focuses especially on "the formation of a consensus by important political and business leaders on the necessity of a more expansive foreign policy." This, LaFeber argues, "resulted from the depression which struck the United States from 1893 to 1897." Most crucially, it reinforced in the minds of those leaders the desirability for the United States of access to markets abroad. Such outlets could even out the business cycle, thereby reducing the domestic social and political unrest that economic downturns had the capacity of generating.

The stage had been set for the United States to "extend the sphere" and pursue a much more active and assertive world role. Chapters 5 through 8 survey the events of the middle to late 1890s and demonstrate their connection to *The New Empire*'s principal thesis. LaFeber describes the Cleveland administration's confrontational approach to a dispute between Caracas and London over the boundary line between Venezuela and British Guiana. The president and Secretary of State Richard Olney were determined to demonstrate, not just to Britain but to all the other European powers, the continued attachment of the United States to the Monroe Doctrine. Washington would treat expansion in the Western Hemisphere by any of them as a threat to its security, its objective being to ensure that the region was under its own "commercial and political control."

Across the Pacific, concern grew that Imperial Russia might soon challenge access by other powers to markets in China. LaFeber traces how the McKinley administration closely monitored events there even as it became increasingly preoccupied by a revolution in nearby, strategically and economically valuable, Cuba. Indeed, he argues, McKinley's determination finally to eject Spain from the island, and end the disorder there, was in no small part motivated by his desire to be free to address East Asian events.

The upshot of such thinking, of course, was a victory over Spain that provided the United States not only with an enhanced position in the Caribbean but also with Spain's colonies of Guam and the Philippines. Congress, meanwhile, voted by joint resolution to annex Hawaii. LaFeber underscores, though, these acquisitions were not the ultimate goals. Contrary to what some previous historians believed, the islands were not taken to fulfill a colonial policy. Instead they were identified as strongpoints and stepping stones relevant to the pursuit of a new, and much broader, albeit less formal, commercial empire in the coming century.

In his essays and books that followed the publication of *The New Empire*, LaFeber explored the deliberate US commitment to expansion. For Americans, as he points out, expansion across the continent and overseas meant the pursuit of wealth, freedom, and opportunity. It also caused big problems, including war, corruption, exploitation, desolation, and the violation of republican ideals. In his analysis of eighteenth- and nineteenth-century US foreign relations, LaFeber examines the many predicaments that accompanied the extending of the sphere.

LaFeber traces the roots of US expansionism back to the colonial era. He spells this out explicitly in "Foreign Policies of a New Nation: Franklin, Madison, and the 'Dream of a New Land to Fulfill with People in Self-Control,' 1750–1804," an essay that appeared in *From Colony to Empire: Essays in the History of American Foreign Relations*, edited by William Appleman Williams. The subtitle comes from a poem by Robert Frost about James Madison's "dream of a new land" where people ruled themselves. It was a dream, to be sure, that did not include all the people on land that belonged to someone else. The concept of self-determination had a muddled history, as LaFeber often noted. Although it was a cardinal principle of the US republic, self-determination played an elusive role in US foreign relations. For example, in "Foreign Policies of a New Nation," LaFeber relates how the pursuit of a continental empire precipitated delusional invasions of Canada. When their northern neighbors refused to join the United States, the Americans tried to force them to do so.

The founders believed they could carry out expansion while also preserving republican virtue. The determination to expand came first. At the Albany Congress in 1754, Benjamin Franklin addressed, not the question whether the colonies should acquire western lands, but instead how to govern them once they were acquired. Franklin suggested the creation of a representative government of the colonies that could establish laws, collect taxes, and raise troops. As LaFeber notes, Franklin envisioned a society free of European corruption and people of "swarthy complexion." In the meantime, the Philadelphian, surrounded by powerful sachems and chiefs at Albany, called first and foremost for the cultivation of Native friendship and trade. Franklin made good relations with the Indigenous peoples a key policy of his proposed colonial government, which he assumed someday would rule Native land.[20]

Franklin's dedication to expansion inspired his virtuoso diplomacy during the American Revolution. LaFeber describes how Franklin initially objected to an alliance with France because he did not want to compromise US freedom of action. To achieve the hoped-for conquest of Canada, the Floridas, and Bermuda, however, the United States would need economic and military aid. As the first accredited US minister to a foreign power, Franklin, by then in his seventies, was a star in Paris, where he deftly cultivated French support while preserving US interests. By playing off Britain and France at the peace negotiations, Franklin, along with John Adams and John Jay, scored a triumphal extension of the US border to the Mississippi River.[21]

After eking out a win in the Revolutionary War, the Americans discovered that "conquering an empire is considerably easier than governing it," writes LaFeber.[22] Britain took advantage of its commercial and naval dominance along the Atlantic coast, around the West Indies, and on the Great Lakes, while Spain closed off the port of New Orleans. Americans, mired in debt and economic depression, were divided over the conflicting agendas of northern, southern, and western states. As LaFeber liked to point out, this era, fortunately for the United States, was distinguished by having a collection of very smart people in charge. Yet even they would struggle with the competing demands of maintaining a republic or building an empire.

James Madison, in particular, studied the successes and failures of past republics. He addressed the formidable conundrum of how to construct a national government strong enough to conduct foreign relations overseas and weak enough to prevent oppression at home. The Virginian believed that individuals as well as nations were motivated by interests and passions, rather than reason. Out of these interests grew factions, the most common source of which was "the unequal distribution of property," as Madison noted in *Federalist No. 10*. The danger, he feared, was that the majority might resort to force over the minority. Rejecting the classical belief that a republic flourished only in a small state, Madison proposed that a republic could be successful "by giving such an extent to its sphere, that no common interest or passion would be likely to unite a majority of the whole number in an unjust pursuit." Factions made up of self-sufficient, property-owning, middle-class citizens, he believed, would check and balance each other, as would a system that divided power at the national level as well as between the state and federal governments.[23]

Madison's solution had its critics. The Antifederalists opposed the new Constitution because they were concerned about the potential dangers of a powerful executive, a large military, unfair taxes, and the diminished authority of individual states. One eloquent critic was Madison's fellow Virginian Patrick Henry, who preferred that power remain in the hands of strong states like his own and brandished what LaFeber refers to as a "swashbuckling attitude" toward foreign nations. Madison responded that the strengthened national government provided in the new Constitution would "render us secure and happy at home," as well as "respectable abroad."[24]

Madison's dream of a people in self-control thanks to an extended sphere complemented the founding vision of continental empire. Thomas Jefferson, in particular, believed that independent, property-owning farmers were the backbone of the republic. Accordingly, those farmers and their progeny needed land. As Jefferson's secretary of state, Madison effectively maneuvered the acquisition of the Louisiana Purchase from Napoleon Bonaparte. As LaFeber observes, however, Madison himself worried that too vast a country could cause republican institutions to crumble. Madison advised that there should be no representative government in the new territories right away because the few settlers out there were not up to the job of ruling themselves. Half the population was Native and Black, while the white people, assumed by Jefferson to be the only people capable of governing the territory, included Creoles, Roman Catholics, and renegades, whom he regarded with suspicion. The vaunted principle of self-determination, it seemed, was meant for some people, but not for others.[25]

In one of his most memorable lectures, LaFeber used the escapades of Aaron Burr to illustrate the fragility of the extended sphere following the purchase of the Louisiana Territory. Soon after Jefferson's vice president fatally shot Alexander Hamilton and fled New Jersey and New York, he conspired with western secessionists and Spanish agents to create a new empire in Mexico. Although Burr's plot failed and he was acquitted of treason, his scheme exposed the weaknesses as well as the strengths of the early republic as it pursued expansion. Jefferson and other national leaders fully intended to extend the nation to the Pacific, but they wanted to do so in a manner that would keep it together.[26]

LaFeber's hero, John Quincy Adams, believed that union and liberty began at home, and that home was a continental empire. In *John Quincy Adams and American Continental Empire* (1965), LaFeber collected speeches, letters, and memoirs that traced the crusade conducted against European colonialism by "the greatest secretary of state in U.S. history."[27] He shows how Adams extended the sphere by way of the annexation of Florida, the negotiation of the Canadian boundary, and the Transcontinental Treaty. He notes that Adams was instrumental in articulating the belief expressed in the Monroe Doctrine that "the Americas were for Americans." Promulgated in 1823 by President James Monroe, the doctrine also celebrated the expansion of the United States along with its growing population, resources, and respectability. "By enlarging the basis of our system and increasing the number of States," the Monroe Doctrine declared "the system itself has been greatly strengthened."[28]

After succeeding Monroe in the White House, Adams envisioned a "civilized" continent tied together by roads, canals, and railroads. "The spirit of improvement is abroad upon the earth," said the sixth president in his first Annual Message (as the State of the Union address was then called). He urged Congress to equip a research expedition for circumnavigating the globe, establish a university, and erect an astronomical observatory. Adams despaired of his failure to establish a national system of internal improvements. He believed that the exceptional United States had a divine mission to set an example for the rest of the world to follow.[29]

A "cruel paradox" confronted John Quincy Adams, LaFeber observes. Expansion might just as easily harm as foster US liberty. Following his service as secretary of state and president, Adams was elected to Congress, where, known as "Old Man Eloquent," he became the foremost opponent of slavery. Adams abhorred any dismantling of the republic, but he believed that "if the Union must be dissolved, slavery is precisely the question upon which it ought to break." He stridently opposed western expansion if it brought more slave states into the nation. He supported the annexation of Oregon, but the admission of Texas, he wrote, was "the heaviest calamity." He objected to the use of force in the war with Mexico. He worried that extending the sphere beyond the continent would create a country too large to govern. He feared that intervention abroad would undermine freedom at home. LaFeber shows the contradictions in a brilliant career of espousing the expansion of a nation whose glory, Adams asserted, "is not *dominion*, but *liberty*."[30]

In *The New Empire*, LaFeber explores how policymakers grappled with this "cruel paradox" following the Civil War. President Harrison wrote to his secretary of state in 1891, "You know I am not much of an annexationist," while stating his interest in obtaining naval bases. Blaine fully agreed, listing "only three places of value enough to be taken"—Hawaii, Cuba, and Puerto Rico.[31] These few lapses were to be regarded as exceptions to US exceptionalism. The United States could still project itself as a beacon of freedom if it did not make a habit of seizing overseas possessions or ruling over people without their consent.

Walter Quentin Gresham, Grover Cleveland's secretary of state, stated his belief that a free government could only acquire territory it intended to include in the United States. His stance did not prevent him from praising the notion of his friend Carl Schurz (a German immigrant who rose to power in the Republican Party and the US Senate) that the United States could enjoy "all sorts of commercial advantages" by negotiating for coaling stations "without taking those countries into our national household on an equal footing" and "without assuming any responsibilities for them." This happy thought, while persuasive, went unrealized. The acquisition of coaling stations, LaFeber points out, would mean "political entanglements and increased military responsibilities."[32]

The New Empire describes how thinkers, policymakers, and business executives assessed the crisis facing the nation at the end of the nineteenth century.

For example, LaFeber cites at length an 1894 *Bankers Magazine* article that echoed Madison as it evaluated the danger of the irreconcilable factions that had brought the national government to a standstill. The symbol of the times was the destitute tramp, it said, and the ethic of the times was founded on "self-aggrandizement, power, and wealth at the expense of everybody else." One alternative to sectionalization, the article proposed, was to centralize power to allow the majority to govern without hindrance.[33]

LaFeber argues that the 1890s were the culmination of a half century of foreign policy dedicated to commercial expansion.[34] President McKinley, he claims, was not breaking with tradition by acquiring Cuba, Puerto Rico, and the Philippines as a result of the war with Spain. He instead was using war to continue the building of a commercial empire interrupted by the crisis over slavery and the Civil War, economic depression, the Cuban Revolution, imperial competition over China, and the realignment of the great powers. LaFeber always felt there was more to do on this period. He so often suggested it to his graduate students that some of them would respond, when asked, that their research topics were US foreign relations with colonial Southeast Asia, World War II Britain, or Cold War Latin America . . . and the 1890s.

LaFeber contributed to the revision of McKinley's reputation as the first modern chief executive. McKinley made his priority the revival of the economy and the restoration of confidence. "The maker must find a taker," the Ohioan said as he promoted the growth of jobs by opening markets at home and abroad.[35] His administration's foreign policy was supposed to make this happen through reciprocity treaties, a modern navy, war, annexation of territory, and the Open Door diplomacy promoted by Secretary of State John Hay. An additional feature of the new empire was an expansion of presidential powers that threatened the checks and balances system. The potential jeopardy for republican government, which LaFeber labeled the "Tocqueville Problem," is discussed in chapter 9 of this book.

In making his case, LaFeber focuses on the formal and informal collaboration among powerbrokers in politics and business who pursued commercial expansion. They understood that the United States was competing in an era of government-run colonization fueled by the rapid transformation of industrial technology. They sometimes failed, but they exuded confidence. LaFeber quotes New York businessman Winthrop Astor Chanler dismissing the danger of war to Henry Cabot Lodge in 1898. If Spanish troops invaded New York, predicted Chanler, "they would all be absorbed in the population . . . and selling oranges before they got as far as 14th Street."[36]

In his 1998 preface to the thirty-fifth anniversary edition of *The New Empire*, LaFeber revisits his commitment to understanding policymakers as human beings of their time and place. He had found it difficult to label them, he said, eschewing terms of contemporary scholarship such as "idealists" or "isolationists." He admits that he grew to respect "the intelligence, discipline, and even courage of officials who had to deal with a terrible depression that transformed the nation's economy, society, politics, and foreign policies—and who used that transformation to make the United States one of the world's greatest powers in a very brief period of time."[37]

He continues, "They nevertheless used that transformation as an excuse to counter most important American principles, notably self-determination, and at times to commit atrocities in Hawaii, Cuba, the Philippines, Central America, and China." In *The New Empire*, LaFeber briefly and bluntly declares who paid the price for expansion. In its early decades, he writes, "the United States annexed a continental empire by undermining, economically and ideologically, British, French, Spanish, Mexican, and Indian control and taking final possession with money, bullets, or both."[38]

LaFeber describes Alfred Thayer Mahan as a man who "drank deeply of the 'White Man's Burden' elixir of his day." Articles like "The Anglo-Saxon and the World's Redemption" echoed Mahan, extolling the spread of US interests into Asia and the Americas. Not everyone was persuaded. LaFeber notes that anti-imperialist Mark Twain questioned how the United States could claim to rule benevolently overseas when it had failed to make things better for oppressed minorities at home.[39]

Looking back, LaFeber took himself to task for not including more on race when he was doing his doctoral research in the 1950s and early 1960s. In his later work, he would do so more extensively and directly. In *The American Age: United States Foreign Policy at Home and Abroad since 1750*, for example, LaFeber considers the resistance of Indigenous people to removal from their lands and the doomed efforts of Queen Liliuokalani to preserve Hawaii from US annexation.[40] With his continued interest in the mindset of policymakers, he notes how the belief in white supremacy, as expressed in the concept of Manifest Destiny, was used to justify expansion. Over and over, "extend the sphere" meant the exploitation of people of color.

Roughly thirty years after the publication of *The New Empire* and, by then, several other books, one of LaFeber's friends, historian Warren Cohen, asked him to write the second volume of the *Cambridge History of American Foreign Relations*. Published in 1993 as *The American Search for Opportunity, 1865–1913*, this project provided LaFeber "an opportunity to rethink the 1890s and place the decade in a context running up to 1913."[41] This less well-known study does considerably more than carry the story of *The New Empire* beyond 1898, and its central thesis, about the impact of US expansion, demands more attention than it has received.

Even more broadly than *The New Empire*, *The American Search for Opportunity* plumbs major transformations in the nineteenth-century United States that, in LaFeber's view, created a "springboard" for the US pursuit of an overseas commercial empire. These included the reshaping of the United States into a much more consolidated nation after the Civil War (and, he notes, the development eventually of a much more powerful presidency). Key transformations also included the emergence of revolutionary new technologies of production and forms of corporate organization in the late nineteenth century (together, he labels these a second industrial revolution). *The American Search for Opportunity* also says more about those Americans over whom this new political and economic complex ran roughshod as this "springboard" was being put together following the Civil War. "Root hog or die" was the predicament of many small farmers as well as those working in the mills and factories, a large share of whom were new immigrants.

The influence of racism on US foreign policy, LaFeber, argues in *The American Search for Opportunity*, was deeply rooted, pervasive, and many-sided. He describes how Senator Albert J. Beveridge advocated acquiring the Philippines. The Republican from Indiana raised the historical precedent of the US treatment of the Indigenous people of the United States to justify treating Filipinos in the same way, which meant, as LaFeber points out, "killing or effectively isolating them." Ironically albeit instructively, the Beveridge Prize that LaFeber was awarded sixty years later for *The New Empire* is named for this expansionist, a longtime member of the American Historical Association and winner of the Pulitzer Prize for his biography of Chief Justice John Marshall.[42]

In the 1890s, suffragists sympathized with Filipinos who faced being governed without their consent, while Elihu Root, McKinley's secretary of war, dismissed the question of voting rights for Filipinos. Root pointed to what he considered the failed Reconstruction-era experiment of granting the right to vote to Black American men. Some anti-imperialists condemned such views, especially as segregation was imposed and lynching increased. Others claimed that the United States already had enough racial trouble without taking on the Filipinos. In the end, LaFeber concludes, imperialists "assumed that if the US government had shown it could keep African Americans and Indians (and women) in their place at home without the vote, it could do the same with Filipinos."[43]

The American Search for Opportunity underscores the sheer scale of the ambition welling up in the consciousness of leading Americans by the end of the century. Americans, LaFeber writes, "set out on a quest for opportunities that destroyed order in many of the areas they targeted." The central thesis of the book relates to the impact of US activity on the economic, social, and political fabric of foreign countries. LaFeber notes how political pressure or economic penetration generally helped to generate disorder or resistance, however much US leaders were ignorant of, or in denial about, the connection. (Indeed, given their ideological blinders, they were more likely to perceive pushback as ingratitude.) As a result, people in the Americas and Asia rebelled against the appropriation of their natural resources, the destruction of their culture, the abuse of their political institutions, and the exploitation of their lives and labor. The assumption of US policymakers that they could keep such people "in their place" was to be repeatedly challenged.[44]

To illustrate the point, LaFeber devotes considerable space to analysis of the late nineteenth- and early twentieth-century revolutions that took place in Cuba, Mexico, and China. Not infrequently, LaFeber points out, US officials responded to such upheavals with force. In the Dominican Republic, US capital backed sugar planters who shoved peasants off the land. To protect the friendly government against its own angry, displaced citizens, President Theodore Roosevelt sent warships, invoked what would be known as the Roosevelt Corollary to the Monroe Doctrine, and justified intervention in the interest of peace and justice. The United States desired no "aggrandizement," TR declared. It merely wanted "the other republics on this continent" to be "happy and prosperous." Such policies would restore order, but also inspire more rebellion, which in turn required more military action to protect commerce and pursue "opportunity." The United States emerged as the globe's leading counterrevolutionary power.[45]

Dollar diplomacy contributed to instability. This "highly dangerous" policy pursued in China and the Caribbean, explains LaFeber, was "a partnership among the government, bankers, military, and the wealthy native *comprador* elite that had integrated itself into the American system." LaFeber pointed out that Willard Straight—Cornell graduate, banker, diplomat, and publisher—called dollar diplomacy "the financial expression of John Hay's 'open door' policy." Straight was correct, as long as one remembered that the United States did not shrink from using guns when money failed to work. To protect US interests and keep Washington's chosen leader in power in Nicaragua, President William Howard Taft sent in the Marines. The "search for opportunity," concludes LaFeber, inspired revolution and justified US retaliation. In short, it "ushered in the American Century."[46]

The American Search for Opportunity explored in detail the "many unfortunate consequences" that came with the ascendancy of the United States to the global position of wealth and power described by LaFeber in *The New Empire*.

The aim of extending the sphere in the late nineteenth century was to solve the problems of industrial overproduction and economic depression. Instead, LaFeber argues, expansion served as an alternative to reform.[47] That left the problems unsolved, which justified more expansion, more military interventions, and more consolidation of power in the executive. It was back to the "cruel paradox" of John Quincy Adams. Extending the sphere might be fundamental to the existence of the republic, but it also endangered the republic.

In *The New Empire*, LaFeber dismisses the popular notion that the United States was isolationist. That was a myth, he wrote there and elsewhere. From the beginning of its independence, the United States needed "an active, successful foreign policy." What US policymakers, from Benjamin Franklin on, really wanted was to avoid entanglements. As it expanded across the continent, the United States preferred to move the British or Mexicans or Indigenous people out of the way. Later, policymakers searched for ways to extend US influence abroad through indirect control without commitments and constraints. In this way, the United States joined the competition among the great powers as a new kind of empire.[48]

What if expansion, "deeply rooted in American experience," were to stop? In *The New Empire* LaFeber explores what the closing of the continental frontier meant for late-nineteenth-century policymakers. Economic transformation led to what John Hay, riffing on the famous Gettysburg Address delivered by his former boss, President Lincoln, referred to as "government of the corporation, by the corporation, and for the corporation." The consolidation of wealth inspired distrust of authority, labor unrest, and the rise of populism, for which overseas expansion was seen as the solution. More than a century later, the administration of President Donald Trump promoted the building of a wall as an answer to the nation's problems. In *The End of the Myth: From the Frontier to the Border Wall in the Mind of America* (2019), the historian Greg Grandin pronounced the wall "a monument to disenchantment."[49]

The story of "extend the sphere" is the story of the republic. LaFeber agrees with Madison that there was no daylight between foreign and domestic policy. In his books and lectures, he examines US expansion around the globe. Like another Walt, he contains multitudes.[50] He writes about intellectuals, industrialists, poets, bankers, journalists, screwballs, con men, and do-gooders. He recounts how Secretary of State William Jennings Bryan was flummoxed by the revelation that Black people in Haiti spoke French. He tells how John Quincy Adams, speaker of six languages, had years of diplomatic experience in the Netherlands, Prussia, and Russia, where he became friends with Czar Alexander. With their talents and fallibilities, US policymakers wrestled with how to balance interests and ideals, or, as LaFeber frequently observes, with how to pursue interests while proclaiming ideals.

In *The New Empire*, LaFeber presents a way of analyzing history that is enlightening to any student. He shows us how to examine the world policymakers lived in, in order to find out what they understood about economics, politics, and ideas. He demonstrates how to investigate what they said and what they did. LaFeber encourages skepticism, not cynicism. Years ago, one of the authors of this chapter met a LaFeber enthusiast who seemed a little embarrassed that he had become a lawyer rather than a historian. He wanted his favorite professor to know he was working on environmental protection. "Tell Walt I'm using my power for good," he insisted. LaFeber urges us to question ourselves along with labels, long-held historical interpretations, and the pronouncements of policymakers. In teaching us how to think otherwise, he extended our sphere.

Notes

1. Evoked vividly in Andrew J. Rotter and Frank Costigliola, "Walter LaFeber: Scholar, Teacher, Intellectual," *Diplomatic History* 28 (November 2004): 628–30.

2. LaFeber famously assigned *The Federalist Papers* in his survey course. For the full text of *Federalist No. 10*, see https://guides.loc.gov>federalist-papers>text, 1–10.

3. Walter LaFeber, *The New Empire: An Interpretation of American Expansion 1860–1898* (Ithaca, NY: Cornell University Press, 1963).

4. John Higham, "Changing Paradigms: The Collapse of Consensus History," *Journal of American History* 76 (September 1989):460–66.

5. Retreat at home of Frank Costigliola, September 2021, "An Oral History of Walter LaFeber," https://www.smu.edu/cph/Lafeber. Among Bowers's handful of publications was "Hull, Russian Subversion, and Recognition of the U.S.S.R.," which appeared in the *Journal of American History* in December 1966, a few months before LaFeber published the first edition of *America, Russia, and the Cold War*.

6. The following discussion of LaFeber's years in graduate school draws on the following: the new preface he wrote for the thirty-fifth anniversary edition of *The New Empire* (Walter LaFeber, "Preface, 1998," in *The New Empire: An Interpretation of American Expansion 1860–1898: Thirty-Fifth Anniversary Edition* [Ithaca, NY: Cornell University Press, 1998], xi–xxix); Walter LaFeber, "Fred Harvey Harrington, Teacher and Friend: An Appreciation," in *Behind the Throne: Servants of Power to Imperial Presidents, 1898–1968*, ed. Thomas J. McCormick and Walter LaFeber (Madison: University of Wisconsin Press, 1993); Lloyd C. Gardner and Thomas J. McCormick, "Walter LaFeber: The Making of a Wisconsin School Revisionist," *Diplomatic History* 28 (November 2004): 613–24; and Paul M. Buhle and Edward Rice-Maximin, *William Appleman Williams: The Tragedy of Empire* (New York: Routledge, 1995), 106–7. The first edition of Williams's *Tragedy of American Diplomacy* was published by Dell Publishing in 1959. On the progressive school, see Richard Hofstadter, *The Progressive Historians: Turner, Beard, Parrington*

(New York: Random House, 1968). Williams discussed Beard in his essays "A Note on Charles Austin Beard's Search for a General Theory of Causation," and "Charles Austin Beard: The Intellectual as Tory-Radical," available in his *History as a Way of Learning* (New York: New Viewpoints/Franklin Watts, 1973), 172–99, 228–42.

7. LaFeber, "Fred Harvey Harrington," 3.

8. LaFeber, "Preface, 1998," xiii.

9. Such work continued to proliferate. After LaFeber's *The New Empire* and Thomas J. McCormick's *China Market: America's Quest for Informal Empire, 1893–1901* (Chicago: Quadrangle Books, 1967) (McCormick was another member of the "Wisconsin school"), other themes and topics related to late-nineteenth-century US activity abroad also began to be explored. For a good sense of the literature overall, see the bibliographic essay in Walter LaFeber, *The American Search for Opportunity, 1865–1913*, vol. 2 of *The Cambridge History of American Foreign Relations*, 2nd ed. (New York: Cambridge University Press, 2013), 229–38. This second edition of volume 2 is the edition cited throughout this chapter, with one exception in a later note.

10. *American Historical Review* 70 (October 1964): 191–92. For other reviews, see Harold Whitman Bradley, *Journal of American History* 51 (June 1964): 94–95; Julius W. Pratt, *Pacific Historical Review* 33 (August 1964): 360–62; J. Blicksilver, *Business History Review* 38 (Autumn 1964): 398–400.

11. LaFeber, "Preface, 1998," xi–xii.

12. James A. Field Jr., "AHR Forum: American Imperialism: The Worst Chapter in Almost Any Book," *American Historical Review* 83 (June 1978): 644–68.

13. Walter LaFeber and Robert L. Beisner, "American Imperialism: The Worst Chapter in Almost Any Book: Comments," *American Historical Review* 83 (June 1978): 669–72.

14. Richard Hofstadter, *The Paranoid Style in American Politics* (New York: Vintage, 1967), 145–87.

15. Henry F. Pringle, *Theodore Roosevelt: A Biography* (New York: Harcourt, Brace and World, 1931; rev. ed., 1956), 121.

16. Ernest R. May, *Imperial Democracy: The Emergence of America as a Great Power* (New York: Harper and Row, 1961), 269–70.

17. The aberration thesis is discussed in Edward P. Crapol, "Coming to Terms with Empire: The Historiography of Late-Nineteenth-Century American Foreign Relations," *Diplomatic History* 16 (Fall 1992): 586–90.

18. Sir John Robert Seeley (1839–95) used the phrase, "fit of absent-mindedness," to characterize Britain's expansion in the nineteenth century. The phrase was applied to US expansion by Robert Osgood in one of the most influential volumes on US foreign relations written in the previous decade, *Ideals and Self-Interest in America's Foreign Relations: The Great Transformation of the Twentieth Century* (Chicago: University of Chicago Press, 1953), 42.

19. LaFeber, *The New Empire*, 361.

20. Walter LaFeber, "Foreign Policies of a New Nation: Franklin, Madison, and the 'Dream of a New Land to Fulfill with People in Self-Control,' 1750–1804," in *From Colony to Empire: Essays in the History of American Foreign Relations*, ed. William Appleman Williams (New York: John Wiley, 1972), 13–14.

21. LaFeber, "Foreign Policies of a New Nation," 18–21.

22. LaFeber, "Foreign Policies of a New Nation," 10.

23. LaFeber, "Foreign Policies of a New Nation," 25–29.

24. LaFeber, "Foreign Policies of a New Nation," 28.

25. LaFeber, "Foreign Policies of a New Nation," 27, 35; Walter LaFeber, "An Expansionist's Dilemma," *Constitution* 5 (Fall 1993): 4–12.

26. Walter LaFeber, "Great Losers—Burr," History 313 Lecture Notes, September 28, 1976, courtesy of Douglas Little; Lloyd C. Gardner and Walter F. LaFeber, *Creation of the American Empire: U.S. Diplomatic History* (New York: Rand McNally, 1973), 72–73.

27. Walter LaFeber, ed., *John Quincy Adams and American Continental Empire: Letters, Speeches and Papers* (Chicago: Quadrangle Books, 1965), 24.

28. Walter LaFeber, *The American Age: United States Foreign Policy at Home Abroad since 1750* (New York: W. W. Norton, 1989), 81; LaFeber, *John Quincy Adams*, 114.

29. LaFeber, *John Quincy Adams*, 14–15, 144.

30. LaFeber, *John Quincy Adams*, 23–26, 46, 143, 148.

31. LaFeber, *The New Empire*, 110.

32. LaFeber, *The New Empire*, 201, 408, 412.

33. LaFeber, *The New Empire*, 184.

34. LaFeber, *The New Empire*, 285.

35. LaFeber, *The New Empire*, 331.

36. LaFeber's focus on power broker collaboration anticipated the emergence of corporatism as a framework for understanding US foreign policy. On corporatism, see Thomas J. McCormick, "Drift or Mastery? A Corporatist Synthesis for American Diplomatic History," *Reviews in American History* 10 (December 1982): 318–30; LaFeber, *The New Empire*, 406.

37. LaFeber, *The New Empire*, xvi, xxxiii.

38. LaFeber, *The New Empire*, xvi, 2.

39. LaFeber, *The New Empire*, 16, 86, 305.

40. LaFeber, *The American Age*, 95–97, 169.

41. LaFeber, "Preface, 1998," xxv.

42. LaFeber, *American Search for Opportunity*, 153, 277.

43. LaFeber, *American Search for Opportunity*, 154–55.

44. As discussed in Chapter 6, LaFeber investigated the consequences of US intervention in *Inevitable Revolutions: The United States in Central America* (New York: W. W. Norton, 1983). Walter LaFeber, "Preface," in *American Search for Opportunity* (1997 reprint), xiii–xiv.

45. LaFeber, *The New Empire*, xxiv; LaFeber, *American Search for Opportunity*, 189.

46. LaFeber used the term *comprador* to refer to local merchants and other businesspeople in the underdeveloped world whose activities largely were aligned with the interests of foreigners. LaFeber, *American Search for Opportunity*, 206–10, 216, 223.

47. LaFeber, *The New Empire*, xxv, xxxiii.

48. LaFeber, *The New Empire*, 2; LaFeber, "Foreign Policies of a New Nation," 19; LaFeber, *The American Age*, 18, 27.

49. LaFeber, *The New Empire*, 17; Greg Grandin, *The End of the Myth: From the Frontier to the Border Wall in the Mind of America* (New York: Metropolitan Books, 2019), 272.

50. LaFeber quotes poet Walt Whitman at length in *The American Age*, including lines from Whitman's 1860 poem "The New Empire": "I chant the new empire, grander than any before." LaFeber, *The American Age*, 88, 93, 129–30.

CHAPTER 5

Reconstructing the Backstory
America, Russia, and the Cold War

FRANK COSTIGLIOLA AND JEFFREY A. ENGEL

Walter LaFeber's imagination and ambition were fired by a brief comment George F. Kennan made in the early 1960s, deploring the lack of a "comprehensive work addressed to the entire span of Russia's relations . . . with the West." Jumping from lower case to all-caps as he typed notes on Kennan's book, LaFeber declared: "WHAT I HOPE TO DO IS THIS, BUT ESPECIALLY TO VIEW IT FROM THE AMERICAN SIDE."[1] The necessities of teaching also played a motivating part. Unable to find good books for a planned seminar on the Cold War, he resolved to write one himself. His wife, Sandy LaFeber, later recalled: "So he delayed the seminar for a year while he began the research for a book on America, Russia and the Cold War. He would write the book he felt necessary for students' understanding of this most important subject."[2] The result was *America, Russia, and the Cold War*, a masterpiece that has provided generations of readers with a deeper understanding of the decades of hostile economic, ideological, and geopolitical rivalry between the United States and the Soviet Union and their respective allies. Appearing in ten editions from 1967 until 2008, the volume reveals not only the trajectory of the conflict, but also the intellectual evolution of the author.

The book merits a wide-angled examination. First, it ranks as a stunningly successful commercial and classroom venture, influencing thousands of readers across multiple decades. Chapter titles, some persisting through all ten editions, encapsulated LaFeber's master narratives of the Cold War. "Two

Halves of the Same Walnut" explained the link between the Marshall Plan and the Truman Doctrine. "Korea: The War for Both Asia and Europe" laid out the stakes of the conflict. John F. Kennedy's "New Frontiers" could not escape "Old Dilemmas."

Second, the four decades between the first and the final editions span most of LaFeber's career, making the book a running commentary on his evolution as a historian and as a witness to a changing world. Third, reflecting the global and frequently all-consuming nature of the Cold War for international and US politics alike, *America, Russia and the Cold War* shines also as a concise history of US foreign relations in the six decades after 1945. The volume's "revisionist" interpretation stresses, especially in its first chapters, the clash between the communist and capitalist systems at the root of the Soviet-US competition and how that clash shaped US foreign policy.

A final aspect is the intellectual context of the book. Undergirding LaFeber's brilliance as a scholar and as a teacher was his wide-ranging engagement with other thinkers. LaFeber's personal library included books filled with marginalia recording his reactions to such luminaries as Carl L. Becker and Reinhold Niebuhr. In nurturing the intellectual development of his students, even after they left Cornell, LaFeber fostered another venue for discussing matters of the mind. He managed to find the time, often after midnight, to exchange ideas and information with these and other friends. Some of what he learned enriched *America, Russia, and the Cold War*. The book thus reflects and refracts, sometimes in surprising ways, LaFeber's mentoring, and the ways he was mentored.

We will begin by examining aspects of the book in the context of the ideas and feelings of five scholars who influenced LaFeber's thinking. First was his graduate school mentor at the University of Wisconsin, Fred Harvey Harrington. The Wisconsin history department, a powerhouse in US history during LaFeber's years there in 1956–59, also boasted William Appleman Williams, a second major influence. A former student of Harrington's, Williams proved an iconoclastic democratic socialist, the soon-to-be-famous guru of the New Left "revisionist" view of US foreign relations history. Though the "Wisconsin interpretation" appealed to LaFeber, he also maintained his independence from it, as he did from most movements. He had not gone to Madison intending to become a radical. He also retained some distance from another hallowed influence, Carl L. Becker, a star of the Cornell history department from 1917 to 1941 and Harrington's own undergraduate mentor.

Kennan was a fourth influence. Though he and LaFeber differed in age, temperament, and attitudes toward power, both were lanky sons of the Midwest who mused about writing a great American novel. With both, a fascination with foreign policy trumped the ambition to follow their literary inspiration, F. Scott Fitzgerald. Kennan and LaFeber had each hoped to use fiction to illuminate the problems of US society. They ended up channeling their ambitions into exploring the troubled past of US diplomacy. With regard to *America, Russia and the Cold War*, therefore, Kennan figures as the book's inspiration, as an instigator and then as a critic of the Cold War, and, finally, as a challenger of revisionist Cold War history.

Last but by no means least in this pantheon of influencers was Reinhold Niebuhr, the theologian whose exploration of the irony in American history, and in the human condition, profoundly appealed to LaFeber. Niebuhr's secular warnings about original sin and about the consequent perils of hubris and overweening power permeate *America, Russia and the Cold War* from the first edition to the last.

LaFeber leavened this potpourri of ideas with his own distinctive view of history—and of much else—internalizing Becker's famous premise that a professor is someone who thinks otherwise.[3] In most aspects of his professional and personal life, LaFeber sustained a degree of autonomy and distance. Despite his warm, affable, and outgoing personality, he shielded his inner persona, which some casual acquaintances mistakenly interpreted as aloofness. Because he was sincerely generous with his time and his attention, it was difficult to perceive that he was also smoothly setting the parameters of such interactions. If one ventured too far into LaFeber's domain by suggesting what he might do, or even by asking what he was doing or how he was feeling, the intruder might well encounter a polite but definite drawing of the curtain as he adroitly shifted attention back to his inquisitor. Most interlocutors, flattered by the attention, failed to notice the move. LaFeber was, in this sense, the observer-participant who remained the observer. Perhaps owing to his being an only child, he felt most comfortable acting independently and retaining his options.

Fred Harvey Harrington

LaFeber's inherent reserve militated against unrestrained feelings for anyone outside his family, but he made a near exception for his graduate school adviser. Fred Harvey Harrington employed a firm hand in directing his graduate seminars at Wisconsin, and decades later LaFeber was still struck by the force of his mentor's personality and intellect. He stressed Harrington's "dominant voice" in the national university community, his "arresting presence," and his "energy-charged style."[4] A Harrington visit late in his life to Cornell, which included an appearance in LaFeber's senior seminar, revealed something his often-intimidated undergraduates could not imagine on their esteemed professor's face: the concern of a student still eager, after so many years, to impress his teacher anew.

Harrington inspired LaFeber's scholarship, including aspects of *America, Russia and the Cold War*. Disdaining labels, Harrington nevertheless pressed his graduate students to become revisionists, believing that rethinking was a necessary step in a scholar's development. He insisted they "break intellectual molds, to think the unconventional, to question the accepted, and, perhaps above all, to deal with the roots, transformations, and effects [of US dominance in world affairs]." In describing what Harrington insisted his graduate students do, LaFeber also summed up his own approach to *America, Russia, and the Cold War* as well as to his other books.[5] "Through it all," LaFeber stressed, "one consistent theme reappeared apart from the manner. That theme was the influence of [Charles A.] Beard, and the understanding and sensitivity with which Harrington and other Wisconsin faculty used Beard's work."[6] Beard, the preeminent progressive historian in the years leading up to World War II, challenged the unequal distribution of wealth and power in the United States while emphasizing democracy's ever-present need for reinvigoration. He famously stressed the importance of economic self-interest for the architects of the US Constitution in the 1780s, for example, and the continued self-interest of wielders of national power since.

Harrington challenged graduate students with a Beardian critique: "Where's the economics in your story?"[7] There certainly was economics aplenty in LaFeber's histories. Moreover, every edition of *America, Russia, and the Cold War* retained two paragraphs that, seemingly more attuned to historiographical loyalty than to Cold War history, defended Beard against such apologists for empire as the Harvard historian Samuel Eliot Morison.[8] Reluctant to embrace radical new ideological constructs either as a student or later as a professor himself, LaFeber nonetheless ensured that more-radical authors, like Beard and then Williams, received the respectful forum their ideas deserved.

William Appleman Williams—and George F. Kennan

Williams also stressed economic motivations in his histories of US foreign policy since 1890, arguing that Washington, D.C.'s primary aim was to expand and sustain an Open Door empire that enabled the United States to export industrial and agricultural surpluses that could not be consumed at home. Harrington thoroughly approved and "handpicked" his former PhD student to return to Wisconsin when a new slot on its faculty opened.[9] Williams's reputation preceded him. LaFeber had already read the iconoclast's 1952 book

American-Russian Relations, 1781–1947, and informed his classmates Lloyd Gardner and Thomas McCormick that their new teacher's text was highly critical of US policy, with a last chapter on containment aimed at Kennan. As teaching assistants for Williams, who was then writing his influential *The Tragedy of American Diplomacy*, the three graduate students grew fascinated with his challenge to conventional notions about the Cold War. Sandy LaFeber later recalled "evenings in Madison with Williams holding forth [on Russia] at his home, once at our apartment with Lloyd and Tom McCormick."[10] A witness to Williams's undergraduate lectures from the room's last row, McCormick would later tell one of the authors of this chapter that his logic was so well-reasoned and inescapable that to study with him meant accepting a fundamental premise: for all their talk of a special mission in history, US leaders had mouths to feed and coffers to fill, just like every nation and empire before.

Despite the allure of Williams and the ingrained appeal of his radicalism (radical for the 1950s, that is), LaFeber was always quick to clarify that he, like McCormick, retained Harrington as his primary adviser. Gardner chose Williams. The division remained long past their dissertations. Sticking with Harrington brought practical benefits as well. As he moved into administration during those years, he encouraged his students to finish quickly. Moreover, Harrington's University of Wisconsin "Big Red Machine" had an especially enviable track record for placing freshly minted PhDs. Those advantages loomed large for the LaFebers, who already had a child.

Although LaFeber learned from Williams and Harrington, he was not their acolyte. Invariably polite and habitually discreet, he often glossed over differences with those whom he respected. Nevertheless, he emphasized that "Harrington's personal ideology" was "framed much more by Beardian categories than by any New Left."[11] That distinction also applied to LaFeber himself, who maintained a respectful distance from Williams's broadest conclusions. This seems to have stemmed from a mix of personality and politics. LaFeber's personal copy of *The Tragedy of American Diplomacy* bore this inscription from Williams: "Don't frown so, Walt, this doesn't mean we *have* to have socialism."[12] Many years later Gardner would recall a strain in some conversations with their mentor long after the trio graduated. "[Sometimes] if we were all together with Bill, and a discussion took place, Walt and Tom clammed up and I was left to debate Bill. I guess they felt it wasn't worth it, or that I was the one who had worked with him, so it was my job to mount the challenges?"[13]

Some of those challenges centered on the history of US relations with Russia. One way to contextualize *America, Russia, and the Cold War* is to bring one of LaFeber's key assumptions—the Cold War's near inevitability—into conversation with conclusions reached by Harrington, Williams, and Kennan. Whether serious conflict between the United States and Russia was avoidable remains the overriding question in the relations between these two giants since 1890. Could alternative paths chosen at critical historical junctures have circumvented most Cold War tensions? Was it possible for US leaders to work out a deal with Bolshevik Russia at the time of the Russian Revolution? Was there a significant chance, as Franklin D. Roosevelt had hoped, for postwar collaboration with Moscow after their wartime alliance of necessity? Did Josef Stalin's death, to borrow the title of Dwight D. Eisenhower's speech at the time, provide "a chance for peace"? Was Russia's experiment with democracy in the 1990s a missed chance for closer ties? In the final analysis, is the history of US-Russian relations more a tale of natural enemies or of botched opportunities?

Ultimately unanswerable, these questions nonetheless offer a framework for comparing the underlying ideas, assumptions, and wishes of these four historians. The conversation requires juxtaposing two challenges: first, the possibility that representatives of the United States might have struck a deal with the new Bolshevik regime in 1918, and second, the possibility of a mutual accord in 1945. While imperfect, the analogy between these moments is revealing. At each critical juncture the Communists in Russia desired US resources to rebuild their war-shattered country, and signaled a willingness to moderate their aims if such aid were forthcoming. While some key Americans favored pursuing possible deals, each potential accord ultimately fell prey to long-standing resentments.

In this context, *America, Russia and the Cold War*, especially in its earlier editions, is itself contained by the Cold War. Despite its revisionist stance, the book remained bounded by the assumptions prevailing in the United States during the conflict. Was conflict with Russia inevitable? LaFeber answers with a firm yes. The first sentence of the first edition reads: "It was October 1945 and war had never ended." The book goes on: "The new issue of Russia's leading doctrinal journal, *Bol'shevik*, warned that . . . the 'imperialist struggle,' which ignited World War II, continued to rage." Meanwhile, in Washington, "President Harry S. Truman delivered a speech larded with references to America's monopoly of atomic power." Even before the reader can turn to page 2, the book concludes: "The triumphant wartime alliance had already split on ideological, economic, and political issues."[14]

Subsequent editions retained the same key conclusion: that the ideological incompatibility between Moscow's demand for a closed sphere of influence in Eastern Europe and Washington's aspiration for an open-door world made struggle between them, a cold war, unavoidable. The introduction to the tenth edition, reviewing US-Russian tensions since the late nineteenth century, concludes that the two nations "finally became partners because of a shotgun marriage forced upon them by World War II." Yet, as the opening line of the ensuing chapter makes plain: "A honeymoon never occurred."[15]

The message changed little over the course of forty years, nor did the implied weight of responsibility for the Cold War that ensued: The United States had given the Soviet Union $11 billion worth of materiel during the war and expected a return on its investment in the form of greater cooperation and an open door to Moscow's empire in Eastern Europe. Wary of repeated invasions from the West, the Soviets desired instead a buffer between themselves and the US-led capitalist world, and believed they had already paid their wartime debt in full. It cost 25 million Soviet lives to defeat the Nazis. American dead totaled 420,000.

Although Roosevelt dominated US foreign policy during the war, LaFeber painted a broader canvas of US designs by focusing on the efforts of lower-level officials to set up an open world order friendly to US exports. He does not mention the 1943 Tehran summit at which Roosevelt and Stalin hammered out differences and outlined postwar settlements, for instance. Missing also is Roosevelt's alerting Averell Harriman (the US ambassador in Moscow) of his conclusion that postwar Soviet domination of Eastern Europe was inevitable no matter how deft his personal diplomacy, at least during a postwar transition. LaFeber thought otherwise, however, remaining skeptical that Rooseveltian magic could somehow bridge the chasm separating capitalists from communists.

Both sides may have feared the other too much for such accord. Quoting Louis Halle, the ranking member of the State Department's policy planning staff, LaFeber told readers that "the West lived under the terror of 'the Muscovite tyranny that was spreading from the East.'" Literature painted the best picture in this instance. "For those who wished to understand such fears, Halle recommended reading J. R. R. Tolkien's trilogy, *The Lord of the Rings*, which Halle believed 'enshrines the mood and emotion of those long years.'"[16]

LaFeber's skepticism about the potential for deals with Russia is especially revealing when juxtaposed with the writings of his influences, whose own work addressed the analogous question of a US-Russian accord in 1918. In *American-Russian Relations*, Williams details how close Raymond Robins, head of the American Red Cross's mission to Russia in World War I, came in 1918 to reaching an agreement with the leaders of Soviet Russia. In Williams's telling, economic imperatives remained crucial, but they figured not as a barrier but as a potential bridge in terms of potential trade and safeguarded US investments in Russia. Though he was not a US government official, Robins enjoyed support from some people close to Woodrow Wilson, and he quickly gained the confidence of Soviet leader Vladimir Lenin. "In his long talks with

Lenin they worked out a comprehensive plan for fostering and expanding Soviet-American economic relations," Williams writes.[17] Such a deal envisioned trading financial support from Washington in exchange for the Bolsheviks' keeping Russia in the war against Germany, and thus implicitly keeping it within the international system as well. Details remained to be hammered out, but such a scenario might have altered the long-term course of US-Russian relations.

The question at hand is not whether the Robins-Lenin deal could have worked, but whether that game-changing prospect captured the imagination of those writing about it. Williams was clearly impressed by what Robins had tried to do. In 1949 he launched the research for his US-Russia book by spending two weeks with Robins, who was then living in Florida and confined to a wheelchair. Flattered by the attention, the elderly man entrusted his voluminous papers to the graduate student. That infuriated Kennan, who soon thereafter launched his own book project on US-Russian relations during the Bolshevik Revolution. With limited access to Robins's papers, Kennan gave Robins only limited attention in his 1956 book.[18]

Harrington, however, singled out Robins for fulsome praise in his review of Kennan's book—written while LaFeber was his student in Madison—critiquing its author in the process. As Harrington saw it, "Robins is the central figure of this volume, but not the hero." The Wisconsin historian criticized Kennan for faulting Robins's amateur efforts, finding him too harsh in judging "this unofficial agent . . . wrong in judgment, tactics, and recollection of events," Harrington wrote, and wrong, most of all, "in believing it possible to work with Lenin and Trotsky." Granted, Harrington conceded, Robins overenthusiastically "engaged on a hopeless or near-hopeless mission. But was it wrong to try?"[19]

Robins appears neither in the pages of *America, Russia, and the Cold War* that discuss the Bolshevik Revolution nor in LaFeber's later textbook, *The American Age*. LaFeber had not totally forgotten, however. Where an account of Robins in 1918 does pop up, is at the end of LaFeber's career, his farewell lecture at the Beacon Theatre in 2006. Here LaFeber devoted three sentences to detailing Robins's criticism of Woodrow Wilson but still failed to mention the aborted deal with Lenin that had so captured the imaginations of Harrington and Williams.

When first published in 1967, *America, Russia and the Cold War* quickly captured a chunk of the rapidly growing market for a fresh take on the Cold War. Reviews in the *American Historical Review* by Barton J. Bernstein and in the *Journal of American History* by George C. Herring Jr. emphasized that this was a well-researched, pioneering "revisionist" account, indeed "a serious challenge to American historians" that packed "contemporary relevance and scholarly importance." Bernstein, himself a rising revisionist star, gently faulted LaFeber for not recognizing how much Truman had repudiated Roosevelt's efforts to get along with Stalin. Moreover, while emphasizing the importance of the US quest for an open-door world at the onset of the Cold War, LaFeber had, Bernstein argued, largely dropped this emphasis in subsequent chapters of the book.[20] This was a keen distinction that persisted through all ten editions. The emphasis on economic causation in the first part of the book did indeed fade in later chapters. A side note of possible significance is that when Bernstein's self-consciously "New Left" field-shaping book of "revisionist" essays, *Towards a New Past*, appeared in 1968, it included a chapter by Lloyd Gardner but not one by LaFeber. Perhaps his absence should not surprise.[21] LaFeber always resisted being pigeonholed, even with friends and colleagues whose viewpoints he largely shared.

America, Russia, and the Cold War appealed to readers not only for its revisionist thesis and plethora of facts, but also for its readability. LaFeber emphasized the "direct and sharp" sentences he had learned to write from Harrington with the kind of pungent quotations and memorable metaphors that enabled Thomas A. Bailey, his master's degree adviser at Stanford, to write such popular textbooks.[22] LaFeber paid special attention to the lead sentence of each paragraph. With few distracting adjectives and adverbs, these sentences of mostly nouns and verbs got readers quickly to where the author wanted to bring them. Two random examples: "Dulles, nevertheless, was not content."[23] And "The President went further."[24] Each sentence succinctly grabbed the reader's attention with the promise of further intrigue. Concluding sentences did the same. "Somehow, with the end of the Cold War, foreign policy was becoming more complex—and dangerous," was followed in turn by a blunt first sentence of its own: "Such dangers grew as the world shrank."[25]

LaFeber also infused his writing, like his lectures, with a sense that there was something important at stake, that this was a story that mattered. Employing irony and tragedy to lend dramatic flair, he also offered many a revealing quip. "And, as Henry Kissinger remarked about Russia," LaFeber wrote of the initial post–Cold War years, "of course history does not always repeat itself. But expansion extending over four centuries does reflect a certain proclivity."[26] Studiously low-key was also his review of a later US leader: "Not even Rambo and Reagan's rhetoric could mask the failures of the President's original policies."[27]

LaFeber also praised, albeit often subtly. Having criticized President George H. W. Bush directly for his handling of the 1991 coup against Soviet leader Mikhail Gorbachev, he rehabilitated the president through comparison to one of his heroes. "The world was changing at a dizzying pace," he wrote of the late 1980s, though historian Henry Adams, who had written of his own dizzying era a century before, "would have felt at home." Why? Because "Adams was one of the few prominent Americans who, terrified by the possible catastrophes that could result from a disintegration of Russia, wanted to cooperate with the Russians and help them adjust peacefully to a new world. Most officials in the new George Bush administration agreed with Adams."[28]

LaFeber narrated with a pronounced certainty, especially in earlier editions of the book. Though intellectually committed to the revisionist project championed by Harrington and Williams, he forcefully got across the message that this was *the* story. The narrative might change in the future to reflect new questions and newly available sources, but for now he was telling it like it was, according to the evidence and his own bedrock beliefs. Primary among these beliefs was that facts were facts. Particularly in the early years of his career, when he first conceptualized *America, Russia and the Cold War*, LaFeber reflected the high modernist moment in US society. Amid the turbulence of the post–World War II period and the tensions of the Cold War, verities endured. Within the profession this conclusion was not as obvious as one might think.

Carl L. Becker

LaFeber's firm belief in the fundamental difference between fact and fiction is reflected in a revealing challenge he posed to his hallowed predecessor at Cornell, Becker, another University of Wisconsin PhD and student of famed historian Frederick Jackson Turner. LaFeber revered Becker for resolutely "thinking otherwise," for his association with Beard and other progressive historians, and for a devotion to Cornell that matched his own. That Harrington had worked with Becker at Cornell no doubt had heightened LaFeber's satisfaction in 1959 at snaring a plum position where Becker had strode the Arts Quad.

LaFeber underscored his connection to this predecessor in his copy of Becker's collection of essays, *Everyman His Own Historian*.[29] In this volume, as in most of his personal books, LaFeber penned his signature on the first page, typically with a single line scrawled under his name. His copy of Becker's essays, however, seemed to emphasize the owner's possession with four strokes of the pen. This was his book, and he probably wanted to think of himself as an inheritor of Becker's tradition.

All the more significant, then, that LaFeber differed so sharply with Becker's 1931 presidential address to the American Historical Association, "Everyman His Own Historian." As a progressive historian, Becker expressed his deeply democratic sensibility about the wisdom of ordinary people. He also displayed a presciently postmodernist ethos that questioned the durability of "facts" and the supposed distinction between fact and fancy. "A myth," Becker explained, "is a once valid but now discarded version of the human story, as our now valid versions will in due course be relegated to the category of discarded myths." To which LaFeber queried on the margin "Myth is History?"[30] Reading through this famous essay, probably preparing a lecture for a Cornell audience, LaFeber signaled further linkage to Becker by inking an addition to the title. It now read, "Everyman His Own & Our Own Historian."[31]

Affinity for Becker did not obviate LaFeber's alarm. Progressing further into Becker's essay, his question marks grew in size, and he pressed the fountain pen harder to the page. He scrawled the largest question mark to the right of a passage that he also underlined and set off with a vertical line. Sparking this concern was Becker's assertion, "The facts do not speak: left to themselves they do not exist, not really, since for all practical purposes there is no fact until someone affirms it."[32]

LaFeber's longest penned comment responded to Becker's eerily prescient postmodern populism. LaFeber underscored the words of Becker printed here in italics. "Berate him as we will for not reading our books, Mr. Everyman is stronger than we are, and sooner or later we must *adapt* our knowledge to his *necessities*. Otherwise he will leave us to . . . cultivate a species of dry professional arrogance growing out of the thin soil of antiquarian research." In Becker's view the stories Americans tell about themselves must prove useful, regardless of where the facts might lead, or they would be discarded by the bulk of the population not just as myths, but as lies.

LaFeber would have none of this. He squeezed into the book's margin a concern that speaks to the challenges faced by scholars in the third decade of the twentieth-first century: "This is close to saying that history must be written according to the Will of the Majority or the strongest interest groups. If the latter, Becker's Liberalism is open to question. If the former or latter, his History is so opened." Four additional strokes of the fountain pen underscored his critique.[33]

LaFeber later explained how Becker's "relativism" rendered him unable to "come to terms with the significance of either Hitler or the isolationist US foreign policy of the 1930s." He quoted Becker's insistence in the late 1930s that "abolishing oppression by suppressing oppressors" would not work. "At a turning point in history," LaFeber noted sadly, "Becker did not turn." The alternative to such paralysis, LaFeber continued, was Reinhold Niebuhr, who understood that "absolute evil could exist and could only be destroyed by counterforce."[34] Niebuhr also emphasized, with particular appeal for LaFeber, that even the destruction of evil demanded limits.

Reinhold Niebuhr

Aside from Harrington and Williams, no one matched Niebuhr's influence on LaFeber's thinking, through numerous works but especially his *The Irony of American History*.[35] Finding the concept of irony both personally and intellectually appealing, LaFeber frequently assigned the text to his students, and he used it in scaffolding *America, Russia and the Cold War*. Niebuhr explained that whereas pathos amounts to bad fortune that just happens, and tragedy entails a conscious choice of evil for the sake of good, irony "consists of apparently fortuitous incongruities" that turn out to be not so fortuitous but instead result from pressing assumed virtue too far. For instance, the unsurpassed power of the United States could lead to excessive confidence, then engagement in unwinnable conflicts, and ultimately weakness arising, paradoxically, from an initial sense of strength. The quest for absolute security could impel risk-taking, such as preventive war, and thus similarly undermine safety. The incongruity of strength engendering weakness is akin to comedy, Niebuhr notes, and indeed "the element of comedy is never completely eliminated from irony."[36]

All this made sense to LaFeber, who infused his writings and lectures with Niebuhr's teachings. The historian saw the theologian as a twentieth-century revisiting of two of his favorite thinkers from the eighteenth century, Jonathan Edwards and James Madison. He also appreciated Niebuhr's emphasis on the dangers of overweening power and the consequent importance of countervailing forces. This is what James Madison had laid out in *Federalist No. 10*. Sensitive to the importance of balance, Niebuhr, like Madison, stressed both the need for political limitations on the marketplace and the limits of such regulation. Appraising the index of Richard Wightman Fox's biography of Niebuhr, LaFeber noted: "No Madison."[37] It was not a compliment.

With commentary penned in the margins and with torn-up slips of Cornell stationery to mark pages, LaFeber's annotated copies of the Fox book and of *The Irony of American History* revealed much of his own philosophy. He coded his degrees of enthusiasm. Two vertical lines and an asterisk in the margin celebrated a critique of blind militarism: "The realists are inclined to argue that a good cause will hallow any weapon. They are convinced that the evils of communism are so great that we are justified in using any weapons against them. Thereby they approach the communist ruthlessness."[38] LaFeber seconded

Niebuhr's endorsement of Kennan's warning of "the evils which arise from the pursuit of unlimited rather than limited ends."³⁹ A slip of paper, double lines, and an asterisk signaled accord with "Man is an ironic creature because he forgets that he is not simply a creator but also a creature."⁴⁰

LaFeber applauded Niebuhr for never having "doubted that political authority should exercise dominance over the economic sphere in the interests of justice."⁴¹ The imperative of restraining the marketplace remained an article of faith for LaFeber, while the notion that economic power itself could be both liberating and limiting can be seen in his ongoing reassessment of the relative strengths and weaknesses of the US and Soviet economies. In later editions of *America, Russia, and the Cold War*, he emphasized, for example, what historian Paul Kennedy dubbed "imperial overstretch."⁴² Both the United States and the Soviet Union suffered a growing inability to solve their own internal and external problems, brought on in part by the cost of expansion, empire, and hubris. By 1991 the Soviet Union had succumbed to the malady. Though ostensibly triumphant, the United States, LaFeber asserted, faced more than ever the same challenges that Madison had signaled at the nation's birth.

Faith in Madison's continuing importance sparked LaFeber's longest marginal comment in Fox's biography of Niebuhr. Responding to the theologian's observation that both the United States and Russia exhibited expansionist tendencies, LaFeber reflected that "globalization is the later playing out of Federalist 10 & expanding the sphere—only without a central Govt Madison deemed essential—or using the market as a farcical substitute."⁴³ By the 2006 edition, appearing fifteen years after the Soviet Union had unexpectedly imploded, LaFeber employed Madison to make a new point, one almost unfathomable in the late 1960s when the Cold War appeared to be a permanent fixture of contemporary international affairs: that the story could be told as one of winners and losers. "I cannot but think . . . that the future growth of Russia . . . [is] not a little overrated," LaFeber quotes Madison as reflecting in 1821.⁴⁴

While surprised (like most analysts) by the sudden demise of the Soviet Union and how quickly the Cold War ended in Europe, LaFeber, like Niebuhr and Kennan, had long nurtured a skepticism about human nature that rendered him leery of social engineering, whether by communists, capitalists, or Christians. LaFeber pulled out all the stops—two lines, four asterisks, and a shred of Cornell stationery—to applaud Niebuhr's dismissing "with utter derision the deepest hope that animated thousands of radical and liberal Christians . . . the inauguration of a community of love."⁴⁵ Not effervescent love but hard-earned justice appealed to LaFeber as well as to Niebuhr.

That value was reflected in LaFeber's reaction to the deepest crisis at Cornell during his nearly half century there: the armed occupation of Willard Straight

Hall in April 1969. As recounted in the chapter 1 of this book, he opposed the armed occupation once violence threatened, and when governance of Cornell seemed up for grabs, looked askance at those pushing for a "community of love" on the Arts Quad and in the mass meeting in Barton Hall. Upon hearing that an emerging unicameral senate composed of students, faculty, and administrators was, like the anti-Beardian intellectuals of the early 1960s, talking "consensus," LaFeber acidly remarked that they would likely "soon arrive at their own Vietnam."[46] In this instance as in others, some who adored LaFeber imputed in him a radicalism that was simply not there. Endorsing Niebuhr's disapproval of his rival, Paul Tillich, for his focus on the senses, emotions, and individual pursuit of the good life, LaFeber caustically penned "the 1960s."[47]

As LaFeber' stance in 1969 illustrated, when it came to governance, whether of the university or of the nation, he preferred cool reason to emotion or force. And yet throughout his life he also loved the exaggerated drama of operas and the ginned-up emotionalism of baseball rivalries. His famous lectures sustained attention because they engaged both the mind and the feelings of listeners. It came naturally to LaFeber to balance reason and emotion with grace.

Detailing the impact of Niebuhr on LaFeber is important not only in terms of understanding the latter but also in explaining why the theologian occupied so much scarce real estate in *America, Russia, and the Cold War*. In the preface to the first edition, LaFeber emphasized the difficulty of fitting his analysis of 1945–66 into the page limit allowed by the publisher. Time only tightened the squeeze for later editions. The first edition's 259 pages allotted twelve pages per year. By the tenth edition, the book had grown to 450 pages, yet had to cover sixty-one years, permitting only seven pages per year. Later editions packed more words onto each page, and even the paper grew thinner. Yet even with space at such a premium, LaFeber retained the sections on Niebuhr. Indeed, they grew, and the repeated summoning of Niebuhr in the conclusions of all the editions of the volume testify to this deepest of influences.

Niebuhr also helps explain the book's appeal to readers. What LaFeber launched in 1967 as a study of US-Russian relations in their larger context expanded into a textbook on US relations with the rest of the world. LaFeber managed to include numerous important global developments while maintaining his readable narrative. The bumper-sticker story line of *America, Russia, and the Cold War* comes straight out of Niebuhr: Emerging from World War II as the most powerful nation in history, the United States spent decades dissipating its power in unwise foreign adventures while neglecting mounting problems at home.

"Not since Jonathan Edwards' day of the 1740s, had an American theologian so affected his society," wrote LaFeber about the onset of the Cold War.

Like Edwards, "Niebuhr emphasized the role of sin and sinful power in that society." Humans' birthright of sin burdened them with avarice, selfishness, and an inability to realize the limits of their own power. These weaknesses led to anxieties and an inability to use freedom constructively. Such emotional reactions engendered a will to power and, inevitably, conflict. Given these dangerous aspects of human nature, reason and even science were easily corrupted and blind to their limits. Underscoring the importance of a liberal arts education, LaFeber, echoing Niebuhr, warned that science "often refused to use the religious and historical insights required to solve secular problems."[48]

All this, Niebuhr argued, made communism especially dangerous. That ideology's true believers failed to perceive that while humankind enjoyed only a limited capacity for good, it suffered an almost limitless inclination to perpetrate evil in the name of good. Hence, the United States had to contain Soviet Russia, as Kennan had urged in 1946–47. Niebuhr, LaFeber explained, "provided a historical basis and rationale for the tone, the outlook, the unsaid, and often unconscious assumptions of this period."[49] In laying out Niebuhr's foreign policy recommendations in 1946–47—Cold War policies that included opposing the Soviet Union, rebuilding Germany and Western Europe, and integrating an economic, political, and military Atlantic community led by Washington—LaFeber's language signaled little space between the theologian's ideas and his own. Left unquestioned by either Niebuhr or LaFeber was whether a lasting breach with the Soviet Union was the necessary and safest course.

In his discussion of the domestically divisive Korean War, LaFeber cited Niebuhr's warning that only a half decade into the Cold War, Americans were already losing their sense of limits. They were also trusting too much in economic growth and scientific advances to solve basic moral and political problems. LaFeber approvingly cited Niebuhr's quoting of John Adams: "'Power always thinks it has a great soul and vast views beyond the comprehension of the weak; and that it is doing God's service when it is violating all his Laws.'"[50] LaFeber also drew on Niebuhr's criticism of the United States' disastrous use of overweening force in the Vietnam War.

The dilemmas of hubris and power infused the final editions of *America, Russia, and the Cold War* with a sense of uncertainty that had been largely absent in earlier versions. The world was moving fast and changing radically. The United States had prevailed in the Cold War—or more accurately, its principal adversary had collapsed. Yet it remained unclear how the United States should deploy its enormous power to better either the nation or the world. Pursuit of the Open Door throughout the twentieth century contributed to conflict. Such was the case, again, after 1991. To be fair, LaFeber's caution when composing the later editions might reflect the heightened prudence of a mature historian faced with a paucity of archival records. Still, the final editions of *America, Russia, and the Cold War* offer almost as many questions as answers, inserting hints of ambivalence even in moments of apparent US triumph. "[George H. W.] Bush's inability to take advantage of the Soviet opportunities" as the Cold War waned "was not because of America's public opinion," he wrote of the transition period between Gorbachev's inadvertent dissolution of the Soviet Union and Boris Yeltsin's bold creation of its Russian successor.[51]

More than a decade after the events he described, LaFeber wrote, "Perhaps the President's great caution was caused by the inability of himself and his top advisers, all of whom had grown up in the Cold War, to imagine a world without the Soviets or a Cold War." The tone differed sharply from the bold assertiveness of earlier editions. "Perhaps it was because Bush, Cheney, Baker, and Scowcroft had all been involved with Gerald Ford in 1976 when détente turned sour and Ford went down to defeat in the presidential election," he surmised. "Perhaps it was due to the administration's fear that if Yeltsin won, the Soviet Union could become so chaotic as to present new dangers."[52]

"Perhaps" indeed. The word signifies caution, an antidote to the hubris that both Niebuhr and LaFeber feared. As the final editions of the book detailed, Presidents George H. W. Bush, Bill Clinton, and George W. Bush each tried to impose order on Russian-US relations after the Soviet Union's collapse. In part because of external factors, but also in part due to their own overappreciation of their own power, none developed a lasting solution. Clinton, for instance, ranked as "the first US President in more than a half century to serve his entire tenure in a world without the Cold War," LaFeber wrote. Yet "even without a Cold War, Clinton raised his military budgets from $260 billion to over $300 billion. Meanwhile, he and Bush sent US troops into more conflicts during the 1990–2000 era than had been sent during any other post-1950 decade."[53] Both presidents proved willing to deploy force, yet neither produced a defining vision for US foreign policy, with bold initiatives such as the Marshall Plan and NATO, that strategists in Truman's age had so effectively developed.

By the mid-1990s LaFeber was gaining a new appreciation for that early Cold War period, especially in comparison with what he saw as the overreach and sloppiness of Clinton's foreign policy. Privately, he appraised National Security Adviser Tony Lake as "more screwed up than even I thought or imagined," and resolved, half-seriously, to get "away from all this and back to the good old days when Men were Men, Women were Women, and Presidents were Harry Truman." He was, literally, returning to the Truman Library to look anew at material on the Truman Doctrine, "which I think raises fundamental questions about whether the United States can ever create a foreign policy if the public has its way."[54] LaFeber seemed understandably uncertain what was worse: democratic paralysis or imperial overreach.

Unable to tap extensive archival sources for more recent years, LaFeber proved adept at logging into the digital age, while information also flowed in from an impressive network of contacts. After decades of teaching courses packed with Cornell students already fascinated by world affairs, or drawn in by the force of his teaching, LaFeber operated at the nexus of his own web of experts at the top ranks of academia, business, finance, law, and, not least, government. In January 2003 during the lead-up to the US invasion of Iraq, for example, LaFeber corresponded with Daniel Fried, a career diplomat then on the staff of the National Security Council. He concluded from this conversation that "oil is of course front and center in the whole thing, although one would never know it from the *NY Times*, *Washington Post*, or the Bush administration."[55]

More than memories of Bailey Hall lectures sustained such valued relationships. A dedicated correspondent, LaFeber wrote long, single-spaced letters, and later emails, to a wide variety of acquaintances and friends. Former undergraduate David Maisel (class of 1968) regularly sent brief notices of this or that story in a newspaper or magazine. LaFeber composed detailed replies. Here was the dedicated professor giving substance to the often-hollow chestnut that teaching complemented scholarship.

LaFeber's success in inspiring students to rise to the highest levels of the US government fostered its own dilemmas. In the years immediately preceding the publication of the tenth edition in 2008, LaFeber could boast (had he been so inclined) of a dazzling array of former students making or carrying out US foreign policy. These stars included not only career diplomats like Fried but also national security advisers, vice presidential aides, and ambassadors. LaFeber took pride in their accomplishments, yet like any citizen or mentor, invariably expressed skepticism and even alarm whenever he thought their policies contravened lessons he'd tried to impart in class.

True to form, he did this quietly. In March 1999, for example, with Bill Clinton's air war against the Serbs in Kosovo seemingly open-ended, LaFeber worried that "the Clinton rhetoric . . . almost exactly repeats that of LBJ and Nixon in Vietnam—'stay the course,' the domino theory underlying it all." He worried that "some people," including Clinton's NSC advisor Sandy Berger (class of 1967), "did not pay adequate attention in their History classes in the 1960s."[56] Skepticism over his former student's role in forging national policy, however, soon morphed into pride. By the time of the 2002 edition of *America, Russia, and the Cold War*, Kosovars were free from Serbian domination, and LaFeber in turn praised Berger for having spurred Clinton's pledge not to deploy ground troops to bolster the air war.[57] Ever cautious about the use of force in foreign relations, LaFeber was relieved that his student had, after all, imbibed the virtue of restraint. "Stories circulated that Clinton, who had an explosive temper, had privately berated Berger for his advice," LaFeber wrote. "The President should have thanked him."[58]

Clinton's international problems paled in comparison to the world his successor confronted after the terrorist attack of September 11, 2001. George W. Bush launched a global war on terror in response, which ultimately included an invasion and occupation of Iraq in 2003, something policymakers a decade before had assiduously avoided during their own conflict in the volatile Persian Gulf. This new generation of leaders believed that their nation's exceptional power could overcome historic ethnic and religious divisions within the conquered country, and furthermore believed it would be possible in the Cold War's wake to export US-style democracy at gunpoint. LaFeber wasn't surprised. Niebuhr had warned of the hubris that stems from power, especially when multiplied by fear and uncertainty. "As world affairs became less predictable after 1989–1991," LaFeber concluded, "Americans continued to rely on their military superiority to deal with much of the unpredictability."[59]

Washington's post-9/11 policies eventually buckled under their own contradictions, dissipating US power and international prestige in the process, leaving LaFeber distressed, albeit largely in private. After President Bush on March 19, 2003, announced the forceful overthrow of Iraq's Saddam Hussein, veteran newsman Jim Lehrer invited LaFeber to discuss the war on PBS Newshour, yet he refused this and other such requests. "I do not want publicly to say how I really feel about current policy," he confided to a friend on March 23, "[but] the more I see of what is going on the angrier I'm becoming. Something has gone really wrong."[60] His tenth and final edition of *America, Russia, and the Cold War* carried the story through 2006, albeit with a tie back to a significant moment in US internationalism. "[Woodrow] Wilson had failed to 'make the world safe for democracy' (as he famously phrased it)" and "had died broken and embittered." Bush was no less a Wilsonian, equally convinced principles could repair a broken world while building a better one in its place. Bush also "emphasized an American mission to create new democracies," LaFeber ultimately concluded, and in doing so "appeared to be a reincarnation of the Woodrow Wilson from nearly a century earlier."[61]

Although LaFeber never grew nostalgic for the Cold War, he ultimately came to appreciate aspects of its certainty. He mused, "It well might be [that] the only way the US can exercise its power in complicated global situations is by telling Americans they have to join a 'crusade,' as Harry Truman did in the Truman Doctrine and Marshall Plan. . . . Otherwise, Americans are great, as someone recently noted, at both globalizing business and navel-gazing at the same time."⁶² The irony was that crusades easily mutated into disasters, especially if US leaders tried to spread democracy in countries ill-prepared for it, such as Vietnam, Iraq, or Afghanistan. In the final edition of *America, Russia, and the Cold War*, LaFeber added a long chapter titled "The World Turned Upside Down, 2001–2006." His tone was coolly analytical as he laid out all the mistakes made by US leaders after 9/11. Privately, however, he flashed anger. In Iraq, Bush and Rice "don't have a clue as to what is happening"; at the same time "Czar Vlad I in Russia [is] systematically eliminating all opposition while we continue to support him." Meanwhile, "the Democrats carry out their plans to execute Bush by firing while standing in their own circle. What a bunch of losers."⁶³ Foolishness, like tyranny, "is rooted in a human nature that cannot be changed, only contained," LaFeber believed.⁶⁴ Hence the importance of Niebuhr's emphasis on limiting both concentrated power and confidence in such might.

Such limits were missing in the curriculum at some key universities, LaFeber remarked in a mostly serious tone. "There really is an arrogance that Yale instills that condemns its students to intellectual unreality—even much more so than Harvard—and as I've told Harvard students in my office, Harvard's most important gifts to the world have been the Vietnam War and the Unibomber. Yale's are the Iraqi/Afghanistan catastrophes and John Kerry."⁶⁵

An emphasis on the importance of limits infused both LaFeber's decades of teaching at Cornell and his dedication to updating *America, Russia, and the Cold War*. The single most telling fact about LaFeber's forty-year odyssey with that book is that he concluded every edition the same way: with Niebuhr. Moreover, from the second edition to the last, he couched the warning against overweening power and unceasing conflict in terms of a somewhat obscure formulation that evidently appealed to him. Niebuhr had unearthed from Romans 7 the passage "I see another law in my members, warring against the law of my mind, and making me captive to the law of sin being in my members." Both Niebuhr and LaFeber interpreted this dichotomy in terms of the Cold War. They viewed the "sin" of the "law in my members"—that is, the weakness and inclination toward evil of the body—as referring to the militarized rivalry that characterized the Cold War, as well as the hard-line, "realist" policies of Washington and Moscow in waging the struggle. In this polarity, the law of the mind and of God figured as negotiation and compromise.

Although a cold war between the United States and Russia was flaring up again in the early 2000s, LaFeber in the last paragraph of the final edition of *America, Russia, and the Cold War* sought to inject restraint into that rivalry by enlisting the last leader of the Soviet Union as a Niebuhrian. He quoted Mikhail Gorbachev, who in 1992 had spoken in Fulton, Missouri, where forty-six years earlier Winston Churchill had made his Iron Curtain speech, as counseling Americans not to take a "monocentric" view and try to dominate the post–Cold War world. Gorbachev sounded, LaFeber affirmed, "much like Niebuhr." He then invoked "the spirit of James Madison warning about the dangers of fragmenting empires." Finally, cruising to the end of this four-decade journey, LaFeber cautioned that growing disorder could lead people around the world to "resort to what Niebuhr called 'the law in our members.'"[66] Little that has happened since, either in the United States or in Russia, suggests that anyone has learned this lesson.

Notes

1. George F. Kennan, *Russia and the West under Lenin and Stalin* (Boston: Little, Brown, 1961), vii. LaFeber most likely made this comment in 1963 or 1964, following publication of his first monograph, *The New Empire: An Interpretation of American Expansion, 1860–1898* (Ithaca, NY: Cornell University Press, 1963).

2. Sandra LaFeber email to Frank Costigliola, August 1, 2022.

3. Becker's own view on the question of academic engagement with society and contemporary affairs, discussed below, mutated during World War I. Critical of Becker's lackluster opposition to the growing Nazi threat in the 1930s, LaFeber nonetheless found classroom inspiration in the ideal of thinking "otherwise." It was, he argued, the ideal way to learn. "One of the things that should happen here [at Cornell] is that you're opened up to other perspectives, and you should be challenged," he told students in 2010. "It doesn't mean you change. What it should be is that if you are right, your reasoning should be reinforced. . . . That's one of the purposes of Cornell, to throw out these kinds of challenges to people, take positions and argue about them." Jenny Proctor, "One Role of a Professor Is to Think 'Otherwise,' says LaFeber," *Cornell Chronicle*, October 18, 2010.

4. Walter LaFeber, "Fred Harvey Harrington, Teacher and Friend," in *Behind the Throne: Servants of Power to Imperial President, 1898–1968*, ed. Thomas J. McCormick and Walter LaFeber (Madison: University of Wisconsin Press, 1993), 3.

5. LaFeber, "Fred Harvey Harrington," 3.

6. LaFeber, "Fred Harvey Harrington," 16.

7. Lloyd C. Gardner to Frank Costigliola, email, August 11, 2022, in authors' possession.

8. See for example, Walter LaFeber, *America, Russia, and the Cold War, 1945–1966* (New York: John Wiley, 1967), 92; LaFeber, *America, Russia, and the Cold War, 1945–2002* (Boston: McGraw-Hill, 2002); LaFeber, *America, Russia, and the Cold War, 1945–2006* (Boston: McGraw-Hill, 2008), 101. Hereafter the date span in each book's title will distinguish the edition.

9. "Timeline—1950—Wisconsin School #2: A History of the University of Wisconsin Department of History," https://history.wisc.edu/department-information/the-history-of-the-history-department/timeline-1950-wisconsin-school-2/.

10. Sandra LaFeber to Frank Costigliola, email, August 1, 2022, in authors' possession.

11. LaFeber, "Fred Harvey Harrington," 17.

12. LaFeber's copy of Williams, *Tragedy of American Diplomacy*. Thanks to Doug Little for sharing his observation.

13. Gardner to Costigliola, email, August 11, 2022, in authors' possession.

14. LaFeber, *America, Russia, and the Cold War, 1945–1966*, 1.

15. LaFeber, *America, Russia, and the Cold War, 1945–2006*, 7.

16. LaFeber, *America, Russia, and the Cold War, 1945–2006*, 13n7.

17. William Appleman Williams, *American Russian Relations, 1781–1947* (New York: Rinehart, 1952), 142.

18. George F. Kennan, *Russia Leaves the War* (Princeton, NJ: Princeton University Press, 1956), 64, fn44.

19. Fred Harvey Harrington, review of Kennan, *Russia Leaves the War*, *Mississippi Valley Historical Review* 44 (June 1957): 165–66. Kennan also believed that there had been a chance for Robins to strike a deal—that is, if Robins had possessed the knowledge of Russian language and history, the diplomatic expertise, and the familiarity with Marxist ideology that Kennan himself commanded. See Costigliola, foreword to Kennan, *Russia Leaves the War* (Princeton, NJ: Princeton University Press, 2023), xxi.

20. George C. Herring Jr., review, *Journal of American History* 56 (June 1969): 184–65; Barton J. Bernstein, review, *American Historical Review* 74 (October 1968): 113–14.

21. Barton J. Bernstein, *Towards a New Past: Dissenting Essays in American History* (New York: Pantheon, 1968).

22. LaFeber, "Fred Harvey Harrington," 8.

23. LaFeber, *America, Russia, and the Cold War, 1945–1966*, 157.

24. LaFeber, *America, Russia, and the Cold War, 1945–2006*, 257.

25. LaFeber, *America, Russia, and the Cold War, 1945–2006*, 373.

26. LaFeber, *America, Russia, and the Cold War, 1945–2006*, 384.

27. LaFeber, *America, Russia, and the Cold War, 1945–2006*, 330.

28. LaFeber, *America, Russia, and the Cold War, 1945–2006*, 346.

29. *Everyman His Own Historian: Essays on History and Politics*, ed. Carl L. Becker (New York: Appleton-Century-Crofts, 1935).

30. Becker, *Everyman His Own Historian*, 247.

31. Becker, *Everyman His Own Historian*, 233.

32. Becker, *Everyman His Own Historian*, 251.

33. Becker, *Everyman His Own Historian*, 252.

34. LaFeber, "Carl Becker's Histories and the American Present," *Ezra* 4 (Fall 2011): 7, 9.

35. Reinhold Niebuhr, *The Irony of American History* (New York: Scribner's, 1952).

36. Niebuhr, *Irony of American History*, vii–viii.

37. Richard Wightman Fox, *Reinhold Niebuhr: A Biography* (New York: Pantheon Books, 1985).

38. Niebuhr, *Irony of American History*, 40.

39. Niebuhr, *Irony of American History*, 149.

40. Niebuhr, *Irony of American History*, 156.

41. Fox, *Reinhold Niebuhr*, 286.

42. Paul Kennedy, *The Rise and Fall of the Great Powers* (New York: Vintage Books, 1989).
43. Fox, *Reinhold Niebuhr*, 245.
44. LaFeber, *America, Russia, and the Cold War, 1945–2006*, 349.
45. Fox, *Reinhold Niebuhr*, 140.
46. LaFeber, conversation with Frank Costigliola in Olin Library, late April 1969.
47. Fox, *Reinhold Niebuhr*, 258.
48. LaFeber, *America, Russia, and the Cold War, 1945–1966*, 40; LaFeber, *America, Russia, and the Cold War, 1945–2006*, 52.
49. LaFeber, *America, Russia, and the Cold War, 1945–1966*, 40–41.
50. LaFeber, *America, Russia, and the Cold War, 1945–1966*, 132–33; LaFeber, *America, Russia, and the Cold War, 1945–2006*, 140–41.
51. LaFeber, *America, Russia, and the Cold War, 1945–2002*, 357.
52. LaFeber, *America, Russia, and the Cold War, 1945–2006*, 361.
53. LaFeber, *America, Russia, and the Cold War, 1945–2006*, 387.
54. LaFeber email to David Maisel, August 22, 1995, David Maisel papers. The authors thank Mr. Maisel for providing copies of some of his correspondence.
55. LaFeber email to Maisel, January 15, 2003, Maisel papers.
56. LaFeber email to Maisel, March 23, 2003, Maisel papers.
57. LaFeber, *America, Russia, and the Cold War, 1945–2002*, 385; LaFeber, *America, Russia, and the Cold War, 1945–2006*, 387.
58. LaFeber, *America, Russia, and the Cold War, 1945–2006*, 387.
59. LaFeber, *America, Russia, and the Cold War, 1945–1992*, 354.
60. LaFeber email to Maisel, March 23, 2003, Maisel papers.
61. LaFeber, *America, Russia, and the Cold War, 1945–2006*, 429.
62. LaFeber email to Maisel, June 28, 1997, Maisel papers.
63. LaFeber email to Maisel, January 4, 2004, Maisel papers.
64. *Cornell Alumni Magazine*, May/June 2006, 41.
65. LaFeber email to Maisel, January 7, 2008, Maisel papers.
66. LaFeber, *America, Russia, and the Cold War, 1945–2006*, 450.

CHAPTER 6

Thinking about Democracy
Inevitable Revolutions

Lorena Oropeza and James F. Siekmeier

In June 1982 Walter LaFeber wrote a piece for the *Atlantic* titled "Inevitable Revolutions," arguing that US policies in Central America had "encouraged what they are supposed to prevent." The article indicted Ronald Reagan's policies toward Nicaragua, El Salvador, and Guatemala for fomenting revolution. Blighted by an "ignorance of history," Reagan and his closest advisors were clinging to the same premises that had undermined John F. Kennedy's Alliance for Progress twenty years before: first, that free markets automatically led to free and democratic governments; and second, that economic progress and political stability depended upon eliminating leftist dissent. Meant to stymie the appeal of a Castro-like revolution, the Alliance for Progress had offered Latin American countries massive economic and military aid and the promise of a brighter future. Instead, LaFeber argued, the Alliance had raised expectations only to crush them, widening the chasm between the rich and the poor in country after country while training national militaries that tortured and killed their own people. Such circumstances inevitably fueled support for leftist revolution, the opposite of the original intention of the Alliance for Progress. Historically, nowhere was US power more pervasive than in Central America. And nowhere were the ravages of political upheaval and economic chaos triggered by US interference more apparent.[1]

With the *Atlantic* article, LaFeber entered contemporary policy debates by deliberately intervening in the nation's understanding of US–Central American relations. He intervened in three ways. First, he provided much needed and accessible historical context to the current crisis. The "Inevitable Revolutions" article appeared when the Reagan administration was seeking to topple triumphant Sandinista revolutionaries in Nicaragua, quash left-wing guerrillas in El Salvador, and keep arms flowing to generals in Guatemala who were confronting unprecedented indigenous protest. Second, as in his analysis of the gap between the purported aims of the Alliance for Progress and its negative effects, LaFeber carefully exposed an inherent contradiction in US policies toward Central America: the United States actually bred the revolutions it hoped to avert. Third, with the memories of the Vietnam War still raw, the article served as a call to action, encouraging an end to contemporary interventions in Central America by exposing how Reagan and his advisors were repeating the mistakes of their predecessors. "With luck and an understanding of the past," LaFeber concluded, the United States could end its longstanding complicity in regional upheaval and exploitation.[2]

The three interventions found in the 1982 *Atlantic* article permeated LaFeber's work regarding Central America. The article served as the genesis for a book with the same title published the following year. *Inevitable Revolutions: The United States in Central America* expanded the scope of the original article both temporally and geographically. Starting with the late eighteenth century and extending to the moment of publication, the book examined US interactions with Costa Rica and Honduras as well as with Nicaragua, El Salvador, and Guatemala. All these nations, LaFeber contended, were trapped in a system that he called "neodependency," through which the United States exerted tremendous economic, military, and political influence and control while Central Americans suffered.[3] LaFeber's involvement with current policy, moreover, began before *Inevitable Revolutions*. Another work, *The Panama Canal: The Crisis in Historical Perspective*, provided readers with much-needed context for the contemporary debate over whether to return the waterway to the Panamanians. Taking a long view again—the first chapter opened with the Spanish explorer Balboa—LaFeber offered a persuasive case for ratifying the 1978 Panama Canal Treaties to assuage Panamanian nationalism. For good measure, he blasted *anti*-treaty arguments in the book's conclusion.[4]

A sign of their continued relevance, both books merited second editions. A 1989 edition of *The Panama Canal* dissected the rise of Manuel Noriega, the Panamanian dictator who was both a US ally in the war against the Sandinistas and a US foe in the "war against drugs."[5] Likewise containing a decade's worth of new material, the second edition of *Inevitable Revolutions* in 1993 covered the blood-soaked 1980s as the contra war raged in Nicaragua and civil war continued to engulf El Salvador.[6] It confirmed, in fact, what the *Atlantic* article had predicted yet sought to avoid: decades of US policy culminating in yet more chaos, violence, and poverty throughout the Central American isthmus.

These works exemplified LaFeber's role as a scholar aiming to inform political debates and shift policy. Although he no doubt would have rejected the moniker "scholar-activist" as overtly political and too rooted in the present for a historian, the term accurately captures the broader impact of his work. In introducing an unfamiliar history to US readers, he dispelled ignorance. By providing a critical reading of US foreign policy objectives and outcomes, he challenged American citizens—including members of the Reagan administration—to grapple with the power their nation wielded in the world for good and, all too often, for ill. By engaging in ongoing policy debates, he cultivated the hope that an informed, educated citizenry might effect change. Together these scholarly interventions revealed how he defined his role as a historian of US foreign relations.

LaFeber's writings on Central America also captured his own complex views of US-style democracy. On the one hand, the sense of urgency with which he wrote signaled a fundamental belief in the American system of government. On the other hand, he clearly saw democracy as a fragile enterprise at home and abroad. In his books on Central America, as in his other works, LaFeber warned of the erosion of individual liberties, given the tendency of power to concentrate in the hands of the executive, especially when conducting foreign affairs. Privately, he also worried about the erosion of democratic norms in general within the United States. In terms of inter-American relations, the implication was clear. With US democracy still a work in progress at home, what business did the United States have trying to export it abroad? Skeptical of the American habit of demanding free elections in other nations, as if elections by themselves had the power to function as a societal panacea or offered certain proof of a just society, LaFeber maintained that in Central America only "fundamental structural change" could address "gross inequities" and stop those inevitable revolutions.[7]

An Unfamiliar History

In *Inevitable Revolutions*, LaFeber juggled the tumultuous histories of five countries with the jagged contours of US foreign relations since 1776. On the US side, the book traced the multiple motivations underlying US actions against an international backdrop that shifted from British dominance in the nineteenth century to Cold War concerns in the twentieth. LaFeber also drew attention to an array of actors within each Central American country across time, including military officers, oligarchs, students, unionists, campesinos, Indigenous people, religious folks, and armed rebels.[8] At the same time, LaFeber carefully distinguished among the five countries in terms of racial composition, class stratification, geography, and economic resources. He organized all this information not only around a powerful thesis critical of the role of the United States in Central America but also with a clear sense of purpose, to inform as many people as possible about "the impact of US policies on the peoples and institutions of Central America."[9] Potential readers for *Inevitable Revolutions* included policymakers, students and their instructors, activists, and everyday US citizens who might have been vaguely aware that their country was deeply engaged in several countries south of Mexico but had little understanding as to why.

Orienting US readers was a chief concern. The book started with a "capsule view" circa 1980 of each Central American country: a brief paragraph that highlighted turning points and tragedies in each nation's history, accompanied by a handful of data points that underscored the tremendous societal differences between the Colossus of the North and the nations of Central America. The data points included rates of illiteracy (50 percent to 70 percent everywhere but Costa Rica, where it hovered around 10 percent), per capita annual income (ranging from $640 to $1,520), and landmass (these were small nations roughly comparable in size to various US states).[10] Together, these capsule views introduced readers to the heartbreaking violence and poverty that had plagued Central America historically and that continued to the present day. They also suggested the massive role the United States had played in Central American affairs for the past hundred years.

Maps amplified the message about US power while also exposing readers to an unfamiliar geography. "Throughout the twentieth century," LaFeber noted, "the overwhelming number of North Americans could not have identified each of the five Central American nations on a map, let alone ticked off the region's sins that called for an application of US force."[11] Conveying the proximity of Central America to the United States, a map of the Caribbean Basin, spread across two entire pages, greeted readers almost as soon as they opened the book. Each chapter began with a similarly sized map, which served as a visual summary of that chapter's contents by noting the location and date of key events. Individually, the maps conveyed just how *busy* the United States had been in Central America at any given time. Seen successively, they confirmed a disturbing and presumably interlocking pattern of US intervention and regional upheaval stretching across a century.

LaFeber, nevertheless, chose to begin his history further back in time, in 1776. Besides 1776 being a familiar reference point for US readers, this periodization allowed LaFeber to distinguish between two types of revolutions: the American Revolution versus the radical leftist revolutions then occurring in Central America. In 1776, he explained, Americans broke away from Britain in the name of individual liberty. Without an aristocracy, they had launched an unprecedented experiment in democracy. Americans, "especially if they were white and male," he wrote, enjoyed a "rough equality." For those who enjoyed the freedom to move, moreover, a landed frontier rich with possibility beckoned. In contrast, Central America had been an economic backwater throughout the colonial period. A tiny population of wealthy landowners profiting from the work of others made for highly stratified societies. Tellingly, Central Americans finally broke from Spain in 1821, not in the name of individual freedom but as a backlash of economic and political elites to liberal reforms emanating from the mother country.

From these different starting points, the histories of the United States and Central America continued to diverge over the course of the nineteenth century. While the Central American isthmus remained poor and vulnerable, the United States emerged as a continental empire, a leading industrial power, and after 1898, an overseas empire by acquiring Spain's last colonies, the Philippines and Puerto Rico and by exerting, as sanctioned by the Platt Amendment, routine interference in Cuba. In Central America, the United States had the luxury of exerting tremendous power without formal acquisition or any Platt Amendment. Working closely with each nation's elites, US investors starting putting their money into Central American coffee and bananas in the 1890s.[12] To protect those investments and to keep the Caribbean an "American lake," the United States in the decades that followed secured economic concessions, backed politicians who did what Washington wanted, wrangled the Canal, and, when all else failed to protect US interests, sent in the Marines.

Military intervention completed a massive switch in US history, according to LaFeber. A revolution fought in the name of individual liberty had made the United States "the world's leading revolutionary nation" at its birth, he wrote. By the twentieth century, however, the United States had "turned away from revolution toward the defense of oligarchs" in Central America and elsewhere.[13] The partners of US investors, these oligarchs needed defending because the benefits of capitalism were so unequally distributed in their respective countries. In the United States, relative prosperity had enshrined the free market as the economic counterpart to political liberty and credited capitalism with helping create a large and politically stabilizing middle class. In Central America, capitalism reaped the reverse. The rise of export economies ensured that what little wealth remained in each country was concentrated in the hands of a small elite who stayed in power through brutal repression if necessary. Consequently, LaFeber explained, revolution became one way, and at times seemingly the only way, to force political change in Central America. Not surprisingly, given the vast class divisions, contemporary revolutionary movements on the isthmus—far removed in time and place from 1776—also tended to be anticapitalist.

To drive home this analysis, the introduction offered one more crucial learning aid: LaFeber coined the term "neodependency" to describe the relationship between the United States and Central American nations. Here he borrowed from Latin American dependency theorists who in previous decades had argued that development and underdevelopment were "two sides of the same coin"—that is, the same capitalist system that created wealth for some nations generated poverty for others primarily because wealthy, more powerful nations determined the prices paid for export crops, such as the bananas and coffee that Central American nations produced.[14] Yet as LaFeber noted, Central Americans experienced plenty of US military intervention and political pressure too. He employed the term "neodependency" to describe a multifaceted system of US informal control. For LaFeber, an emphasis on economic relations alone did not suffice to capture the many manifestations of US power in Central America.

As an additional boon to readers, the notion of neodependency operating as a system of informal control arranged the book's many moving parts into a neatly structured narrative arc. The system needed to be set up (chapter 1), maintained (chapter 2), and updated (chapter 3) before finally collapsing in the wake of the 1979 Nicaraguan revolution (chapter 4) and leaving the Reagan administration to confront the fallout (chapter 5, "The Remains of the System"). What came next? In the revised and expanded second edition, what came next was a new chapter, chapter 6, titled, somewhat awkwardly, "Rearranging the Remains of the System." As an organizing principle for the book, the idea of "neodependency" enabled LaFeber to expertly guide his readers through the rise and relative decline of US power in the region.

Yet this idea also generated significant criticism.

A Controversial Analysis

LaFeber had first grappled with explaining unequal power relations between the United States and Central America in *The Panama Canal*, published five years earlier. At the time, no other book written in English or Spanish detailed the history of US relations with Panama. Yet a lack of knowledge, or what LaFeber flatly termed "vast ignorance," hardly precluded *norteamericanos* from forming strong feelings about the canal. LaFeber approvingly quoted a US Canal Zone officer in the preface: "We believe that 80 percent of Americans agree with us that we must keep the Canal under our control. Unfortunately, half of those Americans are not sure where the Panama Canal is located." Eager to contribute to the ongoing debate about the fate of the canal, LaFeber rapidly produced what he modestly termed "only a survey," organized around a few key themes, among them that Panama did not owe its existence to Theodore Roosevelt and that, "contrary to Reagan's statements," the United States did not buy the canal in 1903 or ever own it.[15]

Describing the US-Panamanian relationship in the affirmative, however, proved tougher. As LaFeber noted elsewhere, Panama's history set it apart from the other five Central American nations that he later focused on in *Inevitable Revolutions*. In 1903 Panama broke away from Columbia, not Spain. Afterward the new nation was even more tightly integrated into the American empire than its Central American neighbors were. A 1903 treaty permitted the United States to act "as if it were the sovereign" in the ten-mile-wide Canal Zone "in perpetuity" and charged the United States with protecting Panamanian independence (in effect sanctioning a US right of intervention).[16] In short order, the United States also gained military bases, ownership of Panama's communication and transportation networks, and control over the Panamanian economy. In Panama, the US dollar was (and still is) legal tender. Control of the canal also granted the United States access to the country's primary revenue-generating stream. Despite subsequent treaties and memorandums of understanding, moreover, US control of the canal remained nonnegotiable for most US citizens for most of the twentieth century. Among those most resistant to change were US canal workers and their families, who lived happily segregated lives in the Canal Zone, a place where they enjoyed vastly better homes, schools, and pay than most Panamanians.[17]

With some hesitation, LaFeber settled on describing the relationship between the two countries as "informal colonialism." In the text, he cited Rupert Emerson's definition of colonialism as an apt characterization of "Washington's ties with Panama." A scholar of international relations and political science, Emerson defined colonialism as "the establishment and maintenance, for an extended time, of rule over an alien people that is separate from and subordinate to the ruling power." In further noting that colonialism was "white rule" over nonwhites, moreover, Emerson paid attention to racism. So did LaFeber.[18] Still, in the absence of any formal recognition by the United States of Panama as a colony, LaFeber favored the term "informal colonialism." Yet he did not stop there.

Contrary to his own advice to avoid long citations, at this point in the text a footnote nearly a page long appeared. In it, LaFeber took the time to explain why he favored "informal colonialism" over "dependency"; the former, he wrote, *"seems* [italics added] a more accurate description." To explain his reasoning, LaFeber inserted a popular definition of dependency by Theotonio Dos Santos, a Brazilian economist and one of the founders of dependency theory. Dos Santos stressed the interdependence of development and underdevelopment and the subjugation of poorer nations by richer ones.[19] In contrast, not only did LaFeber see US power operating beyond the economic realm, but he also argued that dependency failed to account for the range of interactions between developed and less developed countries.[20] LaFeber's concept of "neodependency," which played such a prominent role in *Inevitable Revolutions*, emerged from this key insight.

The footnote contained another reason why LaFeber rejected "dependency." Simply put, the United States treated Panama in a way it would never dare treat the powerful Southern Cone nations of Argentina, Brazil, or Chile. LaFeber revisited this idea in *Inevitable Revolutions* when he stated that the frequency with which the United States resorted to military intervention in the region distinguished US relations with Central American countries, and with Caribbean ones too, from its relations with the rest of Latin America.[21] Still, an air of uncharacteristic tentativeness accompanied his initial grappling with dependency theory. As a non–Latin Americanist, LaFeber admitted, he was still a learner. He concluded the footnote by thanking his "most helpful" Cornell colleague, Thomas Holloway, for his "continued and often unavailing efforts . . . to initiate me into the mysteries of dependency theory."[22]

That LaFeber felt the need to explain his rejection of dependency theory speaks to the popularity of this set of ideas at the time when he wrote. Dependency theory originated in Latin America as an alternative to 1960s modernization theory. As articulated by Walt Rostow, an economist who worked in the Kennedy and Johnson administrations, modernization theory proposed that capitalist development occurred along a series of stages. While Western countries had reached the highest stage of development, or what Rostow called the era of "high mass consumption," other, poorer, countries, like those in Latin America, had yet to reach "take-off."[23] The built-in biases were hard to ignore. By viewing capitalism as a phenomenon that occurred strictly *within* nations, modernization theory conveniently suggested that some countries—and implicitly some people—were more backward than others. Latin American scholars (some of whom, like Dos Santos, were Marxists) rejected that premise. They countered by coming up with a set of insights, eventually known as "dependency theory," that prioritized the economic relationship *between* countries. To quote LaFeber quoting the theorists, they proposed that "development and underdevelopment were two components 'of one unified system.'"[24] They disagreed as to what came next. More radical *dependentistas* advocated leftist revolution as the only means of escaping capitalist exploitation.[25]

LaFeber did not. Still, the term "neodependency" was close enough to "dependency," according to the critics who attacked him for daring to use an idea so closely associated with a leftist intellectual tradition. In a particularly harsh assessment that appeared in *Reviews in American History*, Robert Freeman Smith accused LaFeber of offering a "totally deterministic interpretation of history by following the neo-Leninist, 'dependency' theory to explain everything about Central American history." Although Smith had been LaFeber's graduate classmate at Wisconsin, his politics had subsequently swerved aggressively to the right. To Smith, *Inevitable Revolutions* offered a simple "story of domination and exploitation" in which the United States was motivated solely by the drive to "advance and protect capitalist interests in the region."[26]

Arthur Schlesinger Jr., in a review that appeared in the *Washington Post*, likewise found fault with LaFeber's work. Schlesinger had been a special assistant to the president on Latin American affairs during the Kennedy administration, the same administration that, in LaFeber's view, was responsible for the massively ineffectual Alliance for Progress.[27] In a defensive ploy, Schlesinger chided LaFeber by posing a rhetorical question. "Does anyone suppose that, if the United States had been a communist state from the start, it would not still have insisted on dominating Central America," he asked, "and have done so even more crudely and brutally?" Ignoring what the *actual* United States had done in Central America, the question strongly suggested that LaFeber was overly critical of US actions. In contrast, Schlesinger described LaFeber's "invocation of dependency theory" as entirely "uncritical."[28] LaFeber's careful distinction between "neodependency" and "dependency" was lost to both reviewers.

Despite their criticism, LaFeber never marched along a determined path dictated by any theory. Certainly LaFeber took pride in elevating economics within the study of US diplomatic history. As he once wrote, adopting that approach at the beginning of his career made him and his like-minded colleagues "heretics in a field that always seems in need of a few more."[29] Comfortable being a "revisionist"—he once said that all good historians were—LaFeber nonetheless tended to shy away from the word "theory" (and any accompanying mysteries).[30] The smallest details matter here. Only once in his work on Central America did he even mention "a theory called 'dependency,'" a turn of phrase that still contained a bit of distancing.[31] Otherwise, he referred to "dependency" alone versus "dependency theory." Equally telling in this context was his choice to define neodependency more vaguely as a "system" versus a "theory." Terminology aside, neither idea provided a "testable hypothesis" with any predictive value. Instead, LaFeber took what James Mahoney and Diana Rodríguez-Franco characterized as a "theory frame" approach to the Latin American scholarship that informed his work. He gained a "series of orienting concepts" and "general questions for analysis," not a rigid set of assumptions.[32] In sum, LaFeber borrowed from Latin American theorists, but he never aspired to join their ranks. As a historian of US foreign relations, he sought to deliver a blistering critique and analysis of US interventions in Central America based upon the demonstrated evidence of their impact. Neodependency was his means to that end.

All hesitation gone, LaFeber's forthright use of the idea of neodependency in *Inevitable Revolutions* allowed him to expand the *Atlantic* thesis backward in time. In the book, the Alliance for Progress still acted as a key pivot point, a last-ditch attempt to save a system about to collapse under the weight of its own contradictions. But LaFeber now introduced another contradiction, or tension, that dated back to the nation's Founders. Thomas Jefferson liked to talk about an "an empire of liberty," but championing self-determination soon fell to the wayside as the United States expanded across a continent and then projected its power overseas.[33] The long view illuminated enduring themes in US foreign relations as they pertained to Central America. John Quincy Adams's doubts about the likelihood that newly independent Latin American nations would ever follow the democratic example of the United States—"arbitrary power, both military and ecclesiastical, was stamped on their education, upon all their habits, and upon their institutions," he once wrote—foreshadowed the reluctance of Washington, D.C., to view Latin Americans as the cultural equals of Anglo-Americans. Similarly, James Polk's aggressive war against Mexico in 1848 portended the unequal power relationship between the United States and Central American nations.[34]

As LaFeber noted, the United States intervened militarily in Central America no fewer than twenty times between 1898 and 1920.[35] In chapter 1, "Setting Up the System," he explained why: Washington came to see political volatility in Central America as a threat to its own regional dominance. Extrahemispheric powers might see regional unrest as an opportunity to expand their influence by, for example, by forcibly taking over the customhouses of a nation that was not paying back its debts. To prevent this scenario, Theodore Roosevelt claimed international police power and sent in the Marines.[36] Critical of such a rough approach, Woodrow Wilson advocated self-determination but eventually sent in even more Marines.[37] For both Progressive Era presidents, LaFeber wrote, the desire for order over chaos translated into favoring order over self-determination. Order was good for US investments, good for US strategic control, and, the thinking went, good for Central Americans, who might at some later date be ready to participate in a US-style democracy.

By the 1920s, US policymakers grew increasingly concerned about their nation's reputation on the world stage. In wielding a big stick, it had appeared to be a big bully. The Good Neighbor Policy of Franklin Roosevelt, LaFeber asserted, resolved in the most cynical way possible the contradiction between championing self-determination and exerting control. New police forces like the National Guard in Nicaragua were now charged with the job of maintaining order. If they killed or tortured their own people, no matter. Under the banner of the "good neighbor," the United States suddenly began championing self-determination once again and proclaiming the virtues of nonintervention.[38]

For LaFeber, the final step in setting up the system of neodependency, and the chief accomplishment of the Good Neighbor policy, was the rise of military dictatorships that stood ready to quiet domestic unrest. By the close of the 1930s, he noted, military men ruled four out of five Central American nations, not coincidentally the same ones where "2% of the population controlled the land and hence the lives of the other 98%." Costa Rica, with a greater tradition of representative government and more equitable land redistribution, was the only exception. But there too, the United States exerted tremendous power. Throughout the isthmus, the US priority was to keep neodependency operating.[39] On the eve of World War II, the future looked bright from the perspective of Washington. As a system of informal economic and military control, LaFeber wrote, neodependency "looked like it could go on forever."[40]

Instead, the second contradiction inherent in the system of neodependency dominated the postwar period. As LaFeber had argued in the *Atlantic*, US foreign policies bred precisely the type of revolution that US policymakers hoped to avert. A close call occurred in Guatemala in 1954. During the 1930s, LaFeber wrote, Guatemala was a "case study" of how neodependency ensured US objectives without the burden of formal colonialism.[41] It was also a military dictatorship. The Guatemalan Revolution of 1944, however, launched an unprecedented era of democracy that lasted for ten years. In 1950 "the freest elections in the country's history" put Jacobo Arbenz, a champion of land reform, in the presidential palace. At the time, roughly half the country's agricultural population eked out a living on about 4 percent of the land. In contrast, the United Fruit Company owned approximately 42 percent. The poorest of Guatemala's poor, overwhelmingly of Indigenous descent and landless, meanwhile endured working conditions that kept them all but enslaved. A 1952 law that Arbenz backed sought to redistribute wealth through land reform. A middle-of-the-road proposition, given the country's vast inequities, the law called for the expropriation only of uncultivated lands and contained provisions to compensate landowners.[42] Such details hardly mattered to US policymakers who were determined to maintain a system of neodependency.

Convinced that Arbenz's agenda smacked of communism, and in a decision as far removed from self-determination as possible, the Eisenhower administration authorized a coup. With the covert help of the Central Intelligence Agency, a Guatemalan general swiftly replaced Arbenz. Afterward John Foster Dulles, Eisenhower's secretary of state, went on national television to "congratulate the Guatemalan people" for thwarting "the evil purpose of the Kremlin to destroy the inter-American system."[43] Yet, contrary to Dulles's post facto spin, the Kremlin did not pose a threat. Nor did a onetime shipment of arms from Czechoslovakia. On this point, LaFeber and Eisenhower's military strategists were in accord.[44] The real threat to US interests, LaFeber argued, were Guatemalan reforms that, in his words, "pecked at" private property ownership.[45]

Five years later, the Cuban revolution directly inspired the Alliance for Progress. Designed to thwart the appeal of communism as a model of change, the Alliance for Progress promised to invest roughly $20 billion of US funding in Latin America to spur peaceful development and socioeconomic reform along capitalist-friendly lines. Unfortunately, it failed to deliver on its promises several times over, LaFeber wrote. First, truly impressive statistics of per capita growth rate during the 1960s in Central American countries masked growing economic inequality, as US aid went overwhelmingly to US firms or familiar oligarchs, ensuring the continued concentration of wealth. Second, the Alliance for Progress spurred the movement of people from the countryside to the city. Some moved expecting the Alliance to produce new industrial jobs (it failed to do so), while others were pushed off the land as export crop production expanded. An impoverished, disappointed population concentrated in urban areas, LaFeber points out, was ripe for radicalization. Third, the Alliance for Progress as a program of economic aid lasted only for the Kennedy administration. Lyndon Johnson, distracted by Vietnam, soon tipped the scales almost exclusively toward military aid. Conveniently, since 1946 the Pentagon's School of the Americas in the Panama Canal Zone had been churning out hundreds of US-trained Latin American army officers, groomed to protect Central American elites and advance US interests.[46] The upshot? A decade after the launch of the Alliance for Progress, Central American societies were still grotesquely stratified, and the populations of each country, again with the sole exception of Costa Rica, were more at the mercy of their own brutal militaries than ever before. In Guatemala by the 1970s, violent uprisings of Indigenous peoples could also be traced to decades of repression conducted by post-coup military governments.

The United States could not find an alternative way forward even as the system veered toward collapse. To the surprise of some reviewers, LaFeber's neodependency thesis prompted him to condemn the policies of Jimmy Carter just as vigorously as those of Ronald Reagan.[47] The problem with Carter's human rights emphasis, LaFeber argued, was that it was mostly talk. In a damning assessment, considering his prior analysis, he wrote that it was "the moral equivalent of Kennedy's Alliance for Progress."[48] Because another quality that LaFeber brought to the task of telling the multifaceted story of US–Central American relations was the clarity of his writing, his comparison of how both Kennedy and Carter futilely sought a nonexistent middle ground in Central America warrants quoting at length:

> Both men talked about revolution when they meant painfully slow evolution. Both men desired more democratic societies in Central America as rapidly as possible but without the radical changes that those desires entailed. Both wanted the military-oligarch elites, long nourished by and dependent on the United States, to share power and distribute the wealth more equitably, but neither wanted to lose US power and influence that had always worked though those elites. Both men wanted change in Central America, but they dreaded revolution. In the end, when they realized that one was not possible without the other, both presidents backed away from the consequences [of their calls for change].[49]

As was the case with Wilson half a century earlier, Kennedy and Carter said one thing but did another, a combination that always earned some of LaFeber's sharpest criticism. Not that Reagan was spared. While Reagan claimed that the Soviet Union "lay behind all the unrest in the world," LaFeber, looking at the evidence, dismissed that proposition as misguided, as much so during the 1980s as it had been during the 1950s. But that was not the only mistake that Reagan seemed doomed to repeat. The reification of the free market and reliance on military power ensured that the United States was still committed to a system of neodependency that made Central American revolutions inevitable.

Ironically, LaFeber's expert analysis of the devastating role the United States historically had played in Central America left him open to a second set of criticisms. Some reviewers charged that LaFeber focused too much on the US side of the story. They noted, for example, the relative absence of Spanish-language sources. In fact, nowadays writing a book on the history of US–Central America relations without accessing Latin American archives would be a tough sell to a publisher. More broadly, however, the criticism mimicked one that was soon directed at dependency theory itself. By emphasizing how economic relations trapped Latin Americans in a system of exploitation, the argument went, the concept failed to leave them much agency.[50] Similarly, other reviewers contended that in demonstrating the overwhelming nature of US power, LaFeber had diminished the role that Latin Americans played in their own history and presented them mainly as victims.[51]

LaFeber's books were more complex than that. On the one hand, he did show Latin Americans vigorously acting to advance their own interests. Tellingly, each chapter in *The Panama Canal* was organized around the intersecting narratives of three men. As a result, Panamanian leaders centered the narrative as much as American presidents did. Elsewhere in Central America, those "military-oligarchy elites" who had long partnered with the United States also provided a constant source of consternation. Determined to protect their own privilege, they threw up roadblocks to halt even the most modest socioeconomic reforms proposed by the United States. Moreover, although the United States designed the Organization of American States to keep hemispheric matters under US control (and beyond United Nations oversight), Latin American member nations were quick to use the forum in ways that ran counter to US priorities, by investigating human rights abuses by Nicaragua's Anastasio Somoza in 1978, for example.[52] By the 1970s, moreover, Mexico and Venezuela had stepped up as two Latin American countries that, by pursuing their own foreign policy objectives, were offering an "alternative" to the US system in Central America.[53] By the 1980s tiny Costa Rica was spearheading a regional peace process, much to the displeasure of the Reagan administration.[54]

On the other hand, LaFeber may not have portrayed Central Americans as passive, but he most assuredly presented many who lived in the regions as victims targeted by the hemisphere's one and only superpower working in cooperation (most of the time) with each country's elites. Here LaFeber's attentiveness to how US-style racism shaped and misshaped the relationship between the United States and Central American nations merits mention. Demonstrating that his concept of neodependency was expansive, he traced how, despite different ideas about race and race-mixing, the power elite in the United States often found common ground with similarly hued economic and political elites in Central America, to the detriment of darker-skinned folks. In Panama, for example, where the local population resented the importation of West Indian workers to the Canal Zone, antiblackness became an occasion for bonding between two presidents.[55] At other times, LaFeber noted, the United States abandoned nuance in favor of assuming the racial inferiority of Latin Americans, elites included. Theodore Roosevelt's 1904 corollary emerged from a conviction that

Latin American governments throughout the Caribbean Basin were "small bandit nests of the wicked and inefficient type" incapable of self-rule.[56] Again assuming blanket inferiority, and augmenting anti-American sentiment, the Canal Zone's two-tiered salary system paid all Panamanians less than "white" workers until the 1950s.[57]

Most tragically, LaFeber linked racism to widespread death and destruction. Put aside debates about agency: dead people have none. All too often, he reminded readers, US priorities, by supporting right-wing repression and fueling left-wing upheaval, cost Central Americans their lives. Repeatedly pointing out instances of torture and death inflicted by US-supported military forces, LaFeber lamented the bloodshed. He called out suffering. And he assigned blame. In the second edition of *Inevitable Revolutions*, a single understated sentence summarized LaFeber's disgust with eight years of the Reagan administration's failed attempts to topple the Sandinistas in Nicaragua and the destabilizing consequences that reverberated elsewhere in Central America as a result. "As North Americans debated and escalated," he wrote, "Central Americans grew poorer and died."[58]

In short, LaFeber paid attention to the historic cheapness of brown lives.

A Scholar-Activist

In a 1984 review of Tom Buckley's *Violent Neighbors: El Salvador, Central America, and the United States* in the *Washington Post*, LaFeber praised the journalist for providing "some of the most powerful writing yet published on the charnel houses of El Salvador and Guatemala that pass as Central American governments." LaFeber counterpoised the Reagan administration's sanitized reference to the "unlawful and arbitrary deprivation of life" to Buckley's graphic description of a "disposal site" in a country where 40,000 people had already lost their lives to right-wing repression. There, Buckley wrote, the countless victims, male and female, young and old, carried on their bodies evidence of rape, torture, and mutilation. "For death squads [in El Salvador]," LaFeber wrote, "death is not enough."[59]

This level of seemingly endless violence, and US complicity in it, inspired LaFeber to write and revise *Inevitable Revolutions*. In a closely related proposition, he sought to end US military interference in the region. LaFeber wrote the bulk of *Inevitable Revolutions* between 1981 and 1983 in direct response to the ratcheting up of tensions that had accompanied Ronald Reagan's election in 1980. Direct US military involvement in Central America suddenly seemed much more possible given Reagan's hard-line anticommunist stance. The question was whether events in Central America proved such a threat to US national security that a military response was required. To LaFeber, the answer was no. Daniel Ortega, the Sandinista leader, to paraphrase a LaFeberian insight, was no Adolf Hitler.[60] LaFeber knew all too well, moreover, that military intervention risked turning into an unjustifiable slog. After William Howard Taft sent US troops to Nicaragua in 1911, they stayed until 1925, only to return the following year and remain until 1933. In 1975, just a few years before LaFeber began writing *Inevitable Revolutions*, a decade of massive US military intervention in Vietnam had finally and ingloriously ended.

Such was the backdrop to LaFeber's activist scholarship. A response to contemporary debates, his work on Central America stood out for its urgency and drive; in these texts LaFeber met a critical need. Just as *The Panama Canal* helped educate the US public about the waterway's history at a time when no other similar book, or book on Panamanian history for that matter, existed, when LaFeber wrote *Inevitable Revolutions*, historical monographs regarding US relations with any Central American nation except Guatemala were scant.[61] One of the few historians who had published on the Caribbean region as a whole, including Central America, was Dana G. Munro, who earlier in his career had worked at the State Department implementing some of the same early twentieth-century policies that he later wrote about. Suffice it to say that his perspective, particularly in eschewing the role of economics, was much less critical than LaFeber's.[62]

To LaFeber, however, recording events in line with Washington's interpretations and priorities, absent any critical analysis, betrayed the responsibility of a professional historian. For that reason, a rush of popular self-congratulatory histories about US foreign policy and policymakers that accompanied the end of the Cold War failed to impress him. "Triumphalism always sells better than negativism," he dismissively commented.[63] Like Fred Harvey Harrington, his mentor at Wisconsin, and like Carl Becker, Harrington's mentor at Cornell, LaFeber was predisposed "to think otherwise" regarding US foreign policy.

Harrington, Becker, and other "progressive historians" insisted that change was possible, particularly if a more educated public could counter the power of economic elites. Yet despite foregrounding class conflict in their work, they did not advocate it. Instead they confined their scholarly activism to improving existing democracy. What logically flowed from these priorities and assumptions was a strong belief that historians ought to write books in the service of democracy, books that addressed critical issues, offered insightful analysis, yet were still accessible to a broad audience. In other words, they ought to write the type of books that LaFeber did, as exemplified by his work on Central America.

The "progressive legacy" was apparent in LaFeber's work in another way. As critical as he could be of US foreign policy, LaFeber had zero interest in chucking the US system of government. He made that clear in a 1985 tribute to Harrington, in which LaFeber wrote approvingly of how fellow historian Jerald Combs had characterized Harrington's students.[64] Borrowing from Combs, and indirectly responding to critics of neodependency theory along the way, LaFeber wrote:

> While some Harrington students have been outspokenly critical of capitalist development, and have used Marxist categories to explain that development, they—unlike leading Western intellectuals who have used the same categories—have not called for change through violence. They instead believe in the system's ability to recognize its problems, debate the alternatives, peacefully construct other and better institutions, and thus rationally carry out much needed reforms.[65]

LaFeber was one of those students. He may have assigned Lenin's "Imperialism, the Highest Stage of Capitalism," to his own students in the second half of his survey of US foreign relations, but LaFeber's political pole star was democratic reform, not leftist revolution.

To critics who implied otherwise, LaFeber typically responded publicly, if he responded at all, with grace and wit. In 1999 he admitted that for the past fifteen years or so he had usually chosen not to respond to, or even read, reviews, because, whether positive or negative, they tended to be a distraction from the current project at hand.[66] An exception occurred in 1989 when the *New Republic* faulted *The American Age* for failing to mention certain themes and concepts that the reviewer argued were essential. Considering the review "so bad I had to answer," LaFeber in his response simply—but devastatingly—tallied how often he mentioned these themes and concepts according to the book's index.[67] In 1985 LaFeber responded with humor after a conservative think tank scholar lazily described him as an "American Marxist historian" in the pages of the *Wall Street Journal*.[68] As LaFeber pointed out, actual Marxist scholars had criticized his Central American and Cold War studies for their failure to concentrate on economic factors alone. "Perhaps I should be flattered. By describing my writings as Marxist, Mr. [Mark] Falcoff does ascribe a consistency and coherence to them that are, unfortunately, not there," LaFeber teased.[69] Privately, LaFeber explained that he had responded in part because he knew that the *Journal* was indexed, thereby ensuring that his was the last word. (Future researchers, using the *Journal*'s index to find reviews of *Inevitable Revolutions*, would discover not only Falcoff's review, but also LaFeber's rebuttal of it.)[70] LaFeber took an even softer approach toward fellow Wisconsin alumnus Robert Freeman Smith. In the tribute that he wrote about Harrington, LaFeber obliquely acknowledged, but did not bother to dismantle, Smith's criticism of *Inevitable Revolutions*. To disabuse the idea that Wisconsin graduate students were a left-leaning monolith, LaFeber wrote, one only had to look at the reviews that Smith recently had started writing about other members of the so-called "Wisconsin School."[71]

Although he never bothered to respond to Arthur Schlesinger's damning assessment of *Inevitable Revolutions*, LaFeber did reveal much about his priorities as a scholar-activist in an exchange about the review with a former student:

> I think Schlesinger probably killed the book in Washington. He really wrote a savage and from my view unfair review. Arthur has always worked over people from Wisconsin whom he suspects of "revisionism"—whatever that is. No doubt he also did not like my fundamental criticism of Kennedy's Alliance for Progress, on which the entire book turns—especially since Arthur was working on the Alliance in the White House. But he never mentions that in the review. Interesting thing is that the Associate Editor of the POST wrote a letter of apology to me for the review—but published it anyway. The book is selling well in New York City, Boston, and other places, but clearly not having much effect on the crazy people in the Reagan Administration.[72]

Clearly blunter in his private correspondence than in his public pronouncements, LaFeber in public held to a standard of polite discourse that encouraged reasonable debate, a position consistent with his high opinion of democracy's capacity for improvement. Therefore, he deeply regretted that Schlesinger's review may have kept his work from reaching its main target: Reagan administration policymakers.

In *Inevitable Revolutions*, he noted with concern the damage this same group was also doing at home. When lecturing, LaFeber often spoke with admiration of "small 'd' democrats"—that is, US citizens who valued democratic government and recognized its fragility. Not many were to be found in the Reagan White House, he feared. Although unlikely to join a protest himself, LaFeber reserved some of his most scathing comments for the damage done by that administration to individual liberties during the late 1980s. He detailed the illegal spying and harassment endured by those who opposed official US policy, such as the members of CISPES, the Committee in Solidarity with the People of El Salvador.[73] His summation of the damage wrought by the Iran-Contra affair, in which US agents sold arms to Iran to fund the contras, was scorching: "The Iran-Contra scandal posed a dangerous threat to the United States. Unelected and unaccountable military officers in the N.S.C. [National

Security Council] worked with key State Department personnel to defy US laws. They did so for the sole reason that they thought their case was right and that all opposition, even from Congress and [Secretary of State George] Schulz, was wrong. They dragged the Constitution, US policies in Central America, [and] Americans' reputation and credibility around the world through the mud." These unelected zealots abandoned the rule of law, LaFeber continued, for a policy that was doomed to fail.[74] As LaFeber showed in the second edition of *Inevitable Revolutions*, US attempts to isolate and undermine the Sandinista government succeeded only in pushing it further to the left. Once again, US policy had reaped the opposite of what it attempted to sow.

As he revisited that point, LaFeber made clear the extent to which historical scholarship was his chosen mode of activism. His career was devoted to unmasking and analyzing the hard "realities of power" as manifested by the United States across the globe.[75] Thus, just as LaFeber considered the transition of the United States from a nation that inspired revolution to one that opposed it as "one of the central questions in US diplomatic history," he viewed the rapid transformation of the United States from a collection of former colonies to a global superpower in less than two centuries as a crucial topic of inquiry, arguably the most crucial, in US history overall.[76] Endlessly pursuing this line of scholarly inquiry, LaFeber maintained a sharp focus on power in all his books.

When combined with his extraordinary writing skills and painstaking research, this unrelenting focus helps explain LaFeber's remarkable ability to pivot from topic to topic in his books. Not by chance did LaFeber's work on Central America showcase themes that appeared in his other works, including the close connection between domestic welfare and foreign policy, the US penchant for unilateralism, the nation's constant hunt for economic opportunity, and, consequently, an inability to blame Cold War tensions solely on Soviet aggression. Another common theme particularly relevant to Central America, and indicative of LaFeber's views on democracy, was his questioning of the on again/off again habit among US policymakers of championing self-determination and democracy in the form of holding elections. Elections simply could not bear the weight of upholding democracy, he wrote, in the absence of "independent and fair judiciary systems, consensus on political and secular norms, responsible governing institutions that can check as well as extend power, and a functioning economy providing the needs of life."[77] Notably, in Central America most of these pieces were missing. But they were missing in other parts of the world, too.

LaFeber's unshakable conviction that the rise of US power across the globe was an essential topic in US history also shaped his measured response to the constant criticism directed at the field over the course of his career. Chief among them was that the field of US diplomatic history, to use an old-fashioned term, was too focused on white men and too US-centric. Consequently, critics labeled US diplomatic history as hopelessly out-of-date, irrelevant, and worst of all, boring.[78] Although he did not buy the criticism, LaFeber saw room for some improvement. As he once pointed out in seminar, US presidents and secretaries of state were, at least until recently, all white men, a circumstance that skewed the field away from easy incorporation of the dominant themes of race, class, and gender that had captivated US historians in the wake of 1960s social movements.[79] Nevertheless, LaFeber showcased racism as a function of US power in his work on Central America, as part of his endeavor to "move beyond the usual diplomatic history—that is, what we said to them, they to us, and we to ourselves."[80]

Recognizing gender as a category of analysis took LaFeber more time. Initially resistant to including women and family history within a US history textbook that he cowrote, LaFeber and his coauthor "finally caved in" on that point, deciding to add a third author to do what they literally considered women's work.[81] In 1998, however, LaFeber contributed a blurb to Kristin L. Hoganson's *Fighting for American Manhood*, a gendered look at 1890s expansionism, in which he praised her "pioneering, imaginative and provocative analysis." The book could not be ignored, he explained, "in part because of the spirited debate about its innovative approach."[82]

Nonetheless, to LaFeber the tragedy of 9/11 settled the debate about what were relevant research priorities and approaches within the field of the history of US foreign relations. In the aftermath of that tragedy, LaFeber detected with satisfaction a renewed interest in what some considered old-fashioned diplomatic history. "All those jazzy cross-cultural, ethnic, gender descriptions seem to have given way to more traditional categories since 9/11," LaFeber noted in 2002. He had a theory as to why: "Those traditional ways of studying the field have rebounded, not least in my view, because the less traditionally trained scholars have done a lousy job of trying to explain what happened on 9/11."[83] Not surprisingly, both before 9/11 and afterward, LaFeber demonstrated little patience with any approach that decentered the United States as a hegemonic power. "A major problem with transnational history or, as many job descriptions now call a variation, international history, is that, in the effort to be inclusive, the realities of power are too often avoided," he insisted in an article in *Diplomatic History* in 2007. Not all players on the international stage were created equal, he insisted. As for cultural studies of "soft power," they might be fun to read but lacked analytical heft. If the history of US foreign relations was a traditional field, at least it was directed at understanding important matters. By default, the fields that LaFeber labeled "minor" were not. "Some day scholars will look back at this era and wonder why so many researchers and teachers were pushing minor (if different) perspectives when the guts of the issue, American foreign policies in key countries, were failing—and too few in the United States either cared or analyzed the problem," he wrote to a friend in 2010, seven years into the Iraq War.[84]

Ironically for a student of power as it operated among nations, LaFeber cultivated a narrow view of it elsewhere. As much attention as he paid to the prevalence of racism in the history of US foreign relations, LaFeber never was captivated by the notion of structural racism, despite its growing popularity among his academic peers. Nor did patriarchy ever truly interest him. To be sure, LaFeber deplored injustice at a personal level. That five of his last six PhD students were women was more than a coincidence. When he himself was a graduate student, he was surprised by the pervasiveness of segregation in Washington, D.C.[85] Yet in a well-visited episode, he strongly condemned the forcible occupation of Willard Straight Hall, Cornell's student union, in April 1969 by African American students outraged by a cross-burning and other incidents on campus. After white fraternity members attempted to evict them, the students smuggled in guns.[86] LaFeber was appalled at the time by the takeover and angered by the Cornell administration's promise of no reprisals for those involved. Long afterward he continued to insist that the armed display of Black power in 1969 was "essentially raping the major principle of the university"—namely, the free and peaceful interchange of ideas.[87]

LaFeber likewise opposed the Latinx gun-free four-day sit-in at Cornell's Day Hall in November 1993. Angry over a vandalized art exhibition on campus, students, who were already frustrated about the lack of progress in hiring "Hispanic" faculty and staff, entered the building and refused to leave.[88] While Professor Tom Holloway, the history department's Latin Americanist, considered the demonstration "a semi-spontaneous act . . . of civil disobedience," in the style of Gandhi, Martin Luther King Jr., and César Chávez, LaFeber's reaction was less sanguine. According to Holloway, LaFeber looked as close to angry as Holloway ever recalled seeing him in twenty-five years of being colleagues: "I think Walt saw the Latino students' actions in 1993 through the lens of 1969 and he didn't like what he saw one bit."[89] Notably, despite his disapproval, LaFeber also modeled the behavior that he preferred by writing directly to the student leader of the Day Hall protest, a history major whom he had taught. The note outlined his disagreement with the protest, according to that leader, "but not in a way that ruptured our relationship."[90]

Ultimately LaFeber's idealized view of the university as a place that shed light, not heat, as a hallowed ground for reasoned debate, directly paralleled his appreciation of democracy as, in its best incarnation, a forum to advance reform. Unfortunately, however, neither optimistic perspective had much to do with the founding of ethnic studies programs across the United States. Again and again, universities have been convinced to found ethnic studies and other similar programs not because of rational arguments but almost always in the wake of student takeovers, hunger strikes, and other forceful demands.[91] A proud Cornellian, LaFeber failed to recognize that power infused the institution that he loved.

Still, we can all be grateful that LaFeber's commitment to understanding, teaching, and writing about the history of US foreign relations was unwavering. He, too, was a small "d" democrat whose endeavors regarding Central America were written to sway the course of US foreign policy in an area of the world that most people in the United States knew little about. Determined to change that, in *Inevitable Revolutions* he advanced the proposition that, for the United States the Central American isthmus was the most important area in the world, based on its geographic proximity, deep historical ties, and Reagan-era fearmongering. Although that claim might be disputed from the perspective of the 2020s versus the 1980s, few could dispute that LaFeber elevated the region's importance to academics, policymakers, and the reading public by weighing in on the topic of US–Central American relations in a time of crisis. Today the term "neodependency" has found more of a home among theorists interested in the fate of poorer people of the Global South than among historians of US foreign relations.[92] Nevertheless, by introducing the idea of neodependency into the lexicon of diplomatic history, LaFeber cleverly positioned himself as both an ardent critic of US actions and—distinct from Marxists of either the academic or the guerrilla variety—a strong opponent of revolutionary violence.[93] Arguably, his careful analysis set the terms of debates for the hundreds of publications on this topic that followed in his wake during the 1990s and beyond.[94]

Moreover, LaFeber set the stage for understanding "blowback" in the Central American case, meaning the unintended consequences of US actions abroad. Coined in the 1950s by the CIA, the term was popularized by Chalmers Johnson, a political scientist who in 2000 published a book with that title and theme.[95] Since 1993, crises in Central America have continued and often have been entangled with US foreign policy. Not by coincidence did immigration from Central America remain paltry until the 1980s, when Central Americans started fleeing massive political violence and economic chaos. Many of these new arrivals moved to urban areas, where, as the new Latinos on the block, some young people joined gangs to survive. Meanwhile the United States made it easier to deport immigrants who were arrested or convicted of crimes, even if they were in the country legally. That tougher policy ensured the exportation of a US-grown criminal element to poor and politically unstable nations. One result was that the gang MS-13 became an international criminal organization. Another was more suffering for the people of El Salvador, who in 2022 were caught between gang-related criminal violence and, under the rubric of a national anti-gang campaign, brutal government-backed human rights violations.[96] In 2021, more Central Americans than Mexicans congregated along the US-Mexico border hoping to cross.[97] What might LaFeber have said about this chain of events? We miss his wisdom.

We also miss his courage and his general demeanor of polite unflappability. As often as he earned extraordinary praise for his career and publications, he was also targeted with sharp, often unfair, criticism for daring to take a hard, analytical look at the course of US foreign policy. One attempt at a "gotcha" moment was particularly telling. A scholar reviewing eight foreign policy courses for bias (the proposition itself was indicative of the writer's own conservative leanings) slammed LaFeber for describing the war in Vietnam as "the most pointless, costly, and bloody war in our nation's history." Casualty rates in the Civil War and both World Wars exceeded the number of dead in Vietnam, the reviewer pointed out. That is true, but only if one looks only at US combat deaths and ignores the estimated three million Vietnamese who died in the war.[98] Not inclined to describe the other wars as "pointless," LaFeber also did not ignore the Vietnamese when writing that sentence. He studied the impact of US foreign relations at home and abroad, upon the people of the United States and upon other peoples. He did so, moreover, by maintaining the highest historical standards. Even that seeker of bias had to admit that he detected, in *Inevitable Revolutions* no less, "a genuine professional scruple . . . on LaFeber's part to respect the facts."[99] Similarly, the scolding Schlesinger conceded that *"Inevitable Revolutions* deserves to be read by everyone concerned with saving the United States from further folly in Central America."[100] By marrying the highest standards of scholarly excellence with an unwavering commitment to make a difference across decades, Walter LaFeber epitomized the best type of scholar-activist—even though he most likely would have objected to the description!

Notes

The authors would like to thank David Langbart, Stephen Streeter, Rachel Jean-Baptiste, Lisa G. Materson, Andrew S. Higgins, and participants in a workshop that took place on the Cornell campus in October 2022 for their contributions to this article.

1. Walter LaFeber, "Inevitable Revolutions: US policies in Central America Have Encouraged What They Were Supposed to Prevent," *The Atlantic*, June 1982, 74–83.

2. LaFeber, "Inevitable Revolutions," 83.
3. Walter LaFeber, *Inevitable Revolutions: The United States in Central America* (New York: W. W. Norton, 1983), 16–18.
4. Walter LaFeber, *The Panama Canal: The Crisis in Historical Perspective* (New York: Oxford University Press, 1978).
5. Walter LaFeber, *The Panama Canal: The Crisis in Historical Perspective*, updated ed. (New York: Oxford University Press, 1989).
6. Walter LaFeber, *Inevitable Revolutions: The United States in Central America*, 2nd ed., rev. and expanded (New York: W. W. Norton, 1993).
7. LaFeber, "Inevitable Revolutions," 83.
8. LaFeber, *Inevitable Revolutions*, 341. Unless indicated otherwise, citations are to the first (1983) edition.
9. LaFeber, *Inevitable Revolutions*, 341.
10. LaFeber, *Inevitable Revolutions*, 8–12.
11. LaFeber, *Inevitable Revolutions*, 13.
12. LaFeber, *Inevitable Revolutions*, 31.
13. LaFeber, *Inevitable Revolutions*, 13.
14. Omar Sánchez, "The Rise and Fall of Dependency Theory: Does It Inform Underdevelopment Today?," *EIAL (Estudios Interdisciplinarios América Latina)* 14 (2003): 13. Probably the most-cited book on dependency theory in Latin America is Fernando H. Cardoso and Enzo Faletto, *Dependency and Development in Latin America* (Berkeley: University of California Press, 1979). For excellent overviews of dependency theory, see Louis A. Pérez, "Dependency," in *Explaining the History of American Foreign Relations*, 2nd ed., ed. Michael J. Hogan and Thomas G. Paterson (New York: Cambridge University Press, 2004) 162–75; and Robert Pakenham's thoughtful *The Dependency Movement: Scholarship and Politics in Development Studies* (Cambridge, MA: Harvard University Press, 1998).
15. LaFeber, *The Panama Canal* (1989), x–xi. Unless indicated otherwise, citations are to the 1989 edition.
16. LaFeber, *The Panama Canal*, 30, 33, 56.
17. LaFeber, *The Panama Canal*, 36, 58, 60–62.
18. LaFeber, *The Panama Canal*, 52–53.
19. For an initial articulation in English, see Theotonio Dos Santos, "The Structure of Dependence," *American Economic Review* 60 (1970): 231–36.
20. LaFeber, *The Panama Canal*, 53.
21. LaFeber, *Inevitable Revolutions*, 18.
22. LaFeber, *The Panama Canal*, 53.
23. W. W. Rostow, *The Stages of Economic Growth: A Non-Communist Manifesto* (Cambridge: Cambridge University Press, 1960).
24. LaFeber, *The Panama Canal*, 53.
25. Sánchez, "The Rise and Fall," 32.
26. Robert Freeman Smith, "The United States and the Caribbean–Central American Region: Empire, System, or Legitimate Sphere of Influence?," *Reviews in American History* 12 (September 1994): 445.
27. Schlesinger's exact job title was found in the guide to his personal papers deposited at the John F. Kennedy Presidential Library and Museum, https://www.jfklibrary.org/asset-viewer/archives/AMSPP, Papers.

28. Arthur Schlesinger Jr., "The US and Central America: A No-Win Game," *Washington Post*, November 6, 1983.

29. Walter LaFeber, "Fred Harvey Harrington," *Diplomatic History* 9 (Fall 1985): 312.

30. Lloyd C. Gardner and Thomas J. McCormick, "The Making of a Wisconsin Revisionist," *Diplomatic History* 28 (November 2004): 612–24, reprinted as chapter 2 of this book. Lorena Oropeza remembered that he made the comment about revisionists in a graduate seminar.

31. LaFeber, *Inevitable Revolutions*, 16.

32. James Mahoney and Diana Rodríguez-Franco, "Dependency Theory," in *The Oxford Handbook of the Politics of Development*, ed. Carol Lancaster and Nicolas van de Walle (New York: Oxford University Press, 2018), 24. Like Sánchez, these authors note that many *dependentistas* likewise reject the labeling of their ideas as a fixed theory.

33. LaFeber, *Inevitable Revolutions*, 22.

34. LaFeber, *Inevitable Revolutions*, 23, 29.

35. LaFeber, *Inevitable Revolutions*, 79.

36. LaFeber, *Inevitable Revolutions*, 37.

37. LaFeber, *Inevitable Revolutions*, 49–54.

38. LaFeber, *Inevitable Revolutions*, 67–74.

39. LaFeber, *Inevitable Revolutions*, 81. LaFeber noted that although US economic interests and State Department interests usually converged, they did not always do so, in which case protecting the system was what mattered. "In nearly every instance, the interests of the State Department and North American business coincided. When they did not, the business interest usually gave way, as indeed it had to if a *system* was to be maintained" (*Inevitable Revolutions* [1993], emphasis in the original).

40. LaFeber, *Inevitable Revolutions* (1993), 95.

41. LaFeber, *Inevitable Revolutions*, 78.

42. LaFeber, *Inevitable Revolutions*, 116–17.

43. LaFeber, *Inevitable Revolutions*, 124.

44. For the shift of US military policy toward Latin America from hemispheric defense to Latin American internal security, see David M. K. Sheinin, *Argentina and the United States: An Alliance Contained* (Athens, GA: University of Georgia Press, 2007), 123.

45. LaFeber, *Inevitable Revolutions*, 124. "Pecked at" in the sense that the land law had modest aims and included compensation for landowners. Any attempt to redistribute wealth, however, threatened not only US influence in Central America but also power relations throughout the hemisphere.

46. LaFeber, *Inevitable Revolutions*, 104, 109. The School of the Americas moved to Fort Benning, Georgia, in 1984 and was closed in 2000.

47. He was not alone in this criticism. See Peter Smith, *Talons of the Eagle: Latin America, the United States, and the World*, 3rd ed. (New York: Oxford University Press, 2008), 146–47.

48. LaFeber's wording also slyly referred to Jimmy Carter's having labeled the 1970s energy crisis "the moral equivalent of war" in a 1977 speech. The phase originally came from the philosopher William James.

49. LaFeber, *Inevitable Revolutions*, 212.

50. Essentially, the critics argued that highlighting the relationship *between* nation-states ignored the range of processes within states. For a summary of this critique,

see Claudio Katz, *Dependency Theory after Fifty Years: The Continuing Relevance of Latin American Thought*, trans. Stanley Manilowitz (Boston: Brill, 2022) 76–77.

51. See William M. LeoGrande, review, *Political Science Quarterly* 101 (Spring 1986): 152–54; Mark L. Kleinman, review, *UCLA Historical Journal* 5 (1984): 133–34. Schlesinger made a similar point in his review. Before the second edition of *Inevitable Revolutions* was published, LaFeber revealed his impatience with this type of criticism. In a letter to Jim Siekmeier, he commented about a book that grouped him among historians who, in analyzing US support for the Somoza dynasty in Nicaragua, had underestimated its "dark political brilliance" and its ability to defy democracy-minded Americans. With a dollop of irony, given how often the label had been applied to him, LaFeber wrote, "Sometimes I can't stand revisionists." The quotation about brilliance can be found in Paul Coe Clark Jr., *The United States and Somoza: A Revisionist Look, 1933–1936* (Westport, CT: Praeger, 1992), xviii.

52. LaFeber, *Inevitable Revolutions*, 232.

53. LaFeber, *Inevitable Revolutions*, 213–18.

54. LaFeber, *Inevitable Revolutions* (1993), 340–44.

55. LaFeber, *The Panama Canal*, 66.

56. LaFeber, *Inevitable Revolutions*, 37.

57. LaFeber, *The Panama Canal*, 52.

58. LaFeber, *Inevitable Revolutions* (1993), 323.

59. Walter LaFeber, "Eyewitness to Terror," *Washington Post*, April 8, 1984, https://www.washingtonpost.com/archive/entertainment/books/1984/04/08/eyewitness-to-terror/43a71bfc-2370-4524-a93c-8d5b9ffdd1a0/; Tom Buckley, *Violent Neighbors: El Salvador, Central America, and the United States* (New York: Times Books, 1984).

60. LaFeber made this point about relative threats in an article for a Cornell campus publication. LaFeber "Carl Becker's Histories and the American Present, *Ezra*, Fall 2011, 8–9, https://ezramagazine.cornell.edu/FALL11/Viewpoint1.html.

61. For Guatemala, see Richard H. Immerman, *The CIA in Guatemala: The Foreign Policy of Intervention* (Austin: University of Texas Press, 1982); Stephen Schlesinger and Stephen Kinzer, *Bitter Fruit: The Untold Story of the American Coup in Guatemala* (Garden City, NY: Doubleday, 1982). Rigoberta Menchu's, *I, Rigoberta Menchú: An Indian Woman in Guatemala*, published in English in 1984 (New York: Verso) had appeared in Spanish the year before. See Menchú with Elizabeth Burgos, *Yo me llamo Rigoberta Menchú y así me nació la consciencia* (Havana, Cuba: Casa de las Américas, 1983).

62. Dana G. Munro, *Intervention and Dollar Diplomacy in the Caribbean, 1900–1921* (Princeton, NJ: Princeton University Press, 1964); Munro, *The United States and the Caribbean Republics, 1921–1933* (Princeton, NJ: Princeton University Press, 1974).

63. Jeff Sharlet, "Why Diplomatic Historians May Be the Victims of American Triumphalism," *Chronicle of Higher Education*, September 24, 1999, A19.

64. Jerald A. Combs, *American Diplomatic History: Two Centuries of Changing Interpretations* (Berkeley: University of California Press, 1983).

65. LaFeber, "Fred Harvey Harrington," 318. For an interesting view of how LaFeber's political position compares to that of Gabriel Kolko, whose politics and scholarship were more overtly leftist, see Nick Witham, "Functions of Revisionist Historiography during the Reagan Era," *Left History* 15 (Fall/Winter 2010–11): 65–86.

66. Walter LaFeber letter to Douglas Little, August 25, 1999. The authors thank Mr. Little for providing a copy of this and several other letters.

67. See David Hendrickson "Trivial Pursuits: The American Age—US Foreign Policy at Home and Abroad, since 1750," *New Republic*, May 1, 1989; Walter LaFeber, "History Lessons," *New Republic*, June 19, 1989. LaFeber explained his decision to respond in a May 15, 1989, letter to David Langbart, a former student who shared some of LaFeber's correspondence with the contributors to this book.

68. Mark Falcoff, "Bookshelf: A Will to Power—The Making of a Sandinista," *Wall Street Journal*, July 22, 1985. Falcoff reviewed Omar Cabezas's *Fire from the Mountain: The Making of a Sandinista* (New York: Crown, 1985), which included an afterword by LaFeber.

69. Walter LaFeber, "Marxist Label Won't Stick," Letters to the Editor, *Wall Street Journal*, August 9, 1985.

70. LaFeber letter to Little, February 28, 1986.

71. LaFeber, "Fred Harvey Harrington," 313.

72. LaFeber letter to Langbart, November 13, 1983.

73. LaFeber, *Inevitable Revolutions* (1993), 295–96.

74. LaFeber, *Inevitable Revolutions* (1993), 338, 334.

75. Walter LaFeber, "Some Perspectives in US Foreign Relations," *Diplomatic History* 31 (June 2007): 424.

76. LaFeber, *Inevitable Revolutions*, 115.

77. LaFeber, "Some Perspectives," 426. LaFeber credited Fareed Zakaria's concept of "illiberal democracy" for informing his thinking on this point. See Walter LaFeber, "The Tension between Democracy and Capitalism during the American Century," *Diplomatic History* 23 (Spring 1999): 263.

78. Walter LaFeber, "Response to Charles S. Maier, 'Marking Time: The Historiography of International Relations,'" *Diplomatic History* 5 (Fall 1981): 362–64.

79. Among his students, Brenda Gayle Plummer has brilliantly captured the explanatory power of race and racism in her books, including *Rising Wind: Black Americans and US Foreign Affairs, 1935–1960* (Chapel Hill: University of North Carolina Press, 2009) and *In Search of Power: African Americans in the Era of Decolonization, 1956–1974* (Cambridge: Cambridge University Press, 2012).

80. LaFeber, *Inevitable Revolutions*, 341.

81. LaFeber letter to Langbart, April 14, 1986. The textbook, initially coauthored with Richard Polenberg, was called *The American Century* (Hoboken, NJ: John Wiley, 1975). Later editions featured Nancy Woloch as a coauthor. Jim Siekmeier remembered looking through LaFeber's books in the late 1980s in McGraw Hall Room 425, his office for many years, and finding a book by Mary Beth Norton, a Cornell colleague, who taught women's history at Cornell. The inscription read: "Walt—More Consciousness-raising—Best, Mary Beth."

82. Kristin L. Hoganson, *Fighting for American Manhood* (New Haven, CT: Yale University Press, 1998). The blurb is from the back cover.

83. LaFeber letter to Langbart, November 2, 2002.

84. LaFeber email to Langbart, July 21, 2010.

85. LaFeber email to Langbart, September 13, 2015.

86. Donald Alexander Downs, *Cornell '69: Liberalism and the Crisis of the American University* (Ithaca, NY: Cornell University Press, 1999), 178–79, 181.

87. Downs, *Cornell '69*, 18. From the perspective of 2024, LaFeber's use of gendered language also stands out.

88. For details about the art exhibition vandalism, see Sascha Hernández, "Recalling the '93 Day Hall Takeover by Latino Students," *Cornell Chronicle*, October 30, 2014, https://news.cornell.edu/stories/2014/10/recalling-93-day-hall-takeover-latino-students. Also see Glenn C. Altschuler and Isaac Kramnick, *Cornell: A History, 1940–2015* (Ithaca, NY: Cornell University Press, 2014), 308–15.

89. Email from Thomas H. Holloway to the authors, January 23, 2023. In another email exchange, Professor Tim Borstelmann, another member of the Cornell History Department at the time, also remembered that Walt LaFeber "was upset." Email from Tim Borstelmann to Lorena Oropeza, February 4, 2023.

90. Email from Eduardo Peñalver to Lorena Oropeza, February 5, 2023, authors' possession. Peñalver returned to Cornell as a law professor in 2006 and became dean of the law school in 2014. In 2023 he was the president of Seattle University.

91. In California in the late 1960s, for example, Third World student strikes at San Francisco State and the University of California, Berkeley, launched ethnic studies. See Andrew S. Higgins, *Higher Education for All: Racial Inequality, Cold War Liberalism, and the California Master Plan* (Chapel Hill: University of North Carolina Press, 2023). LaFeber had a point about the consequences: Higgins traced Reagan's ride to the California governorship to his opposition to these strikes.

92. A recent example: Adrián Sotelo Valencia, "Neo-Imperialism and Neo-Dependency: Two Sides of the Same Historical-Political Process," *Sub-Imperialism Revisited: Dependency Theory in the Thought of Ruy Mauro Marini*, ed. Sotelo Valencia (Leiden: Brill, 2017).

93. His ability to thread that particular needle may have prompted LaFeber's being included in in a 1985 CIA-generated list of potential speakers who would offer agents-in-training an "alternative or revisionist view" regarding the administration's policies toward Central America. Memo, Director of Training and Education to Chief, Intelligence Training, January 16, 1985, CIA-RDP90-00998R000100010019, CIA FOIA Online Reading Room, www.cia.gov/reading room. There is no indication that an invitation was ever issued or accepted.

94. LaFeber, *Inevitable Revolutions* (1993), 413.

95. Chalmers Johnson, *Blowback: The Cost and Consequences of American Empire* (New York: Metropolitan Books, 2000). Coined by the CIA, the term itself dates to the 1950s.

96. Jonathan Blitzer, "The Rise of Nayib Bukele, El Salvador's Authoritarian President," *New Yorker*, September 5, 2022, https://www.newyorker.com/magazine/2022/09/12/the-rise-of-nayib-bukele-el-salvadors-authoritarian-president.

97. John Gramlich and Alissa Scheller, "What Is happening along the US-Mexico Border in Seven Charts," November, 9, 2021, https://www.pewresearch.org/fact-tank/2021/11/09/whats-happening-at-the-u-s-mexico-border-in-7-charts/. Arguably another "blowback" phenomenon is climate change, which is also triggering migration. See Maria Christina García, *State of Disaster: The Failure of US Immigration Policy in an Age of Climate Change* (Chapel Hill: University of North Carolina Press, 2022).

98. André Ryerson, "The Question of Bias: How Eight College Courses Teach American Foreign Policy," *Academic Questions* 1 (1988): 14.

99. Ryerson, "The Question of Bias," 7–8.

100. Schlesinger, "The US and Central America," 5.

Chapter 7

Turning to Asia
The Clash

ANNE L. FOSTER AND ANDREW ROTTER

                    Walkerton, Indiana, was named for James H. Walker, a banker who in the middle of the nineteenth century helped build the Cincinnati, Peru, and Chicago Railroad. The CP&C ran through Walkerton. The town was planned by surveyors for the railroad; its track went straight north and south, and as in hundreds of midwestern towns, the streets were laid out in a strict grid, every turn a right angle. Walter LaFeber was raised in Walkerton. Its population, three years before he was born, in 1933, was 1,137. His father ran a grocery and dry-goods store. Walt worked in the store from a very young age, stocking shelves and eventually managing the cash register. His close friend and colleague Thomas McCormick once said: "If you want to understand Walter LaFeber, you have to visit Walkerton, Indiana"; McCormick told one of the authors of this chapter (Rotter) he himself had once done this.

    LaFeber was not the only prominent US diplomatic historian to come from a small town. Lloyd Gardner grew up in Delaware, Ohio. William Appleman Williams, who helped train LaFeber, McCormick, and Gardner at the University of Wisconsin, hailed from Atlantic, Iowa—an aspirational place name if there ever was one. Wayne Cole, another Wisconsin PhD from the same period, came from Manning, Iowa, a town of 1,800 people during his youth. And it was not only foreign relations revisionists who hailed from small towns. Thomas A. Bailey, LaFeber's MA supervisor at Stanford, was born on a prune orchard near San Jose, California. John Lewis Gaddis was born in 1941 in Cotulla, Texas, which in 1940 had a population of 3,600.

It may seem counterintuitive that historians interested in the place of the United States in the world would grow up in towns like Walkerton, Delaware, and Atlantic. Yet there are several possible reasons this might not be a coincidence. To begin with, it might be because, as Gardner has suggested, "there were not enough problems in small towns, so historians-to-be sought out the wider world—if even in historical imagination."[1] Bright, curious youngsters might chafe against the limitations of small towns. They read and dream of far-off lands, creating for themselves a vicarious cosmopolitanism that offered intellectual and emotional release from their perceived isolation. This is a common enough theme in fiction and memoir—Jay Gatsby? Ronald Reagan?— and one that makes sense to Gardner from his own experience. Its lessons may apply most fully to historians with international interests, and perhaps with particular strength to those whose feet remain planted in the United States, unwilling or unable to detach from the home place entirely, but eager to look outward from it in the search for encounter, interaction, or comparison.

It is also worth noting that LaFeber, Williams, Gardner, and McCormick all grew up in the Midwest. David S. Brown has argued that historians "beyond the frontier" developed a uniquely regional perspective on US history and the nation's place in the world. Starting with Frederick Jackson Turner and continuing through Charles Beard, then to the Wisconsin historians John Hicks, Merle Curti, William Hesseltine, Fred Harvey Harrington (LaFeber's graduate mentor, who was raised in upstate New York but moved to Wisconsin, and stayed), and Williams, these thoughtful midwesterners developed a worldview that embraced popular dissent in the service of grassroots democracy, a populism generally shorn of its sour impulses for racism and antisemitism, and a faith in community that far more closely resembled Portage, Wisconsin (where Turner grew up), or Papillion, Nebraska (Curti's birthplace), than it did Manhattan, New Haven, or Cambridge. To paraphrase John Quincy Adams, they went not abroad in search of monsters to destroy. There were monsters enough at home, in the form of unbounded laissez-faire capitalism, East Coast elitist hubris (usually found in liberal internationalists), and politicians whose commitment to democracy was no better than skin deep. The Indiana-born Beard and his midwestern successors at Wisconsin crafted a critique of US foreign policy that, as Brown has written, "appealed to both a neo-isolationist right and an anti-imperialist left." Their populism did not diminish their curiosity about the wider world.[2]

Yet the isolation of small towns and the cosmopolitan dreams they might have inspired can be overstated. The Walkertons of the world were not nearly as distant from international networks or knowledge as the mythology of the frontier would predict. Having moved from the East Coast to the midwestern college town of Urbana-Champaign, Illinois, in 1999, the historian Kristin Hoganson set out to examine her new, smallish city, in search of the heart of the heartland. Seeking the local, she found instead the global, "the histories of foreign relations" and "a mesh of global entanglements stemming from searches for security and power." She learned that it had long been thus; even in the nineteenth century, Urbana-Champaign and its surrounding county had been closely connected to world markets and affairs that appeared to be far distant but in truth were as present each day as the prairie wind.[3] The twin-cities of Urbana-Champaign was considerably more populous than Walkerton in 1930, but Champaign County was a good deal smaller than St. Joseph's County, Indiana, which held not only tiny Walkerton but vigorous South Bend, a short drive away.

Common to both counties and towns was the railroad. In the late nineteenth century the Illinois Central, underwritten by British capital, carried pork in its refrigerated cars from West Urbana (now Champaign) to Chicago and ports beyond, then ships conveyed it to markets in Europe, where prices for meat were fully a midwestern concern.[4] In Walkerton, during the same era, C. W. N. Stephens' General Store stood near the CP&C station. At its height, it employed twenty-two men, sold general merchandise, livestock, and grain, and occupied two stories of a storefront measuring forty-four feet by one hundred feet. Streets of the town were named "Michigan," "Virginia," and "Georgia." They were flanked by large grain elevators—the Midwest's version of skyscrapers. By the 1890s, telephones were in use in most businesses and in some residences, and at least several could be used for calling long distance.[5] Walter LaFeber & Son, Grocery and Dry Goods, was not as big as Stephens's store. But it sold a wide variety of products from many places, and it served as a gathering spot for the Walkerton community, a place where people met to shop and gossip.

The CP&C ran to Chicago, and it carried not just goods but passengers. Walter LaFeber often took the train to the Windy City to go to Chicago Cubs baseball games at Wrigley Field. His father had served in the Navy in France during the First World War, and he had evidently brought home with him a sense of the wider world, as most soldiers and sailors did. His family recalls that Walt visited New York when he was in high school, and that in his sophomore year at Indiana's Hanover College he spent a semester in the United Kingdom, which according to family members left a lasting impression. Hanover offered a wide-ranging liberal arts education delivered by dynamic classroom teachers like LaFeber's mentor, Robert E. Bowers, who urged him to pursue graduate work in history, first at Stanford and then at the University of Wisconsin. Whatever the mythology of the midwestern small-town boy, it is clear that Walt LaFeber had a curiosity about the world "built in," as his son puts it.[6] He was no provincial. Like his father, he knew about the wider world.

LaFeber & Son may not have carried any Japanese items during the 1930s. The Smoot-Hawley Tariff of 1930, as intended, put financial roadblocks in the path of US imports of many products from around the world, among them the silk that made up almost two-thirds in the value of Japanese products that earned US dollars. Still, the Midwest was attached to Japan in other ways. Hundreds of graduates of midwestern colleges and universities traveled to Japan as missionaries. University of Illinois agronomist O. H. Peabody learned Japanese farming methods during a three-year stint in Japan, then returned to teach them to Champaign County farmers.[7] St. Joseph's County had a visitation of a different sort: the arrival from Japan in 1830 of the invasive plant species autumn olive, which overwhelmed some native varieties by blocking the sunlight they needed to thrive.[8]

It is unlikely, of course, that young Walter LaFeber was aware of these many connections between Japan and his native Midwest. Asia as a whole played a limited role in LaFeber's teaching and scholarly interests, at least prior to 1975. The exception to this was China, about which the "Wisconsin School" showed a great deal of curiosity, and about which McCormick wrote his dissertation and first book, *China Market*.[9] LaFeber himself brushed against East Asia in his first book, *The New Empire*, which considered the run-up to war with Spain and the burst of overseas imperialism that accompanied it, including the annexation of the Philippines in 1898.[10]

Readers of that book, or of chapter 4 in this book, will know that its focus is on domestic economics and politics in the United States, and that its secondary concerns are the European imperial powers and Spain and Cuba, not the Philippines itself. LaFeber's subsequent publications included edited books on the diplomacy of John Quincy Adams and the Cold War—each of which includes some material on US relations with Asia—and monographs on the Cold War (largely in Europe), the US response to revolutions in Central America, and the Panama Canal.[11] In a series of short articles published during 1968–70, three in *Current History* and one in *The Nation*, LaFeber considered the US exercise of power in Asia, with a focus on the triangular relationship among the United States, Japan, and China. In 1975 LaFeber published "Roosevelt, Churchill, and Indochina: 1942–1945" in the *American Historical Review*. The article's title suggests its emphasis, which was on high policymaking in the United States and Britain, not so much on Indochina—a portmanteau place-name conferred by imperial France. Excellent and much-cited, the piece nevertheless appeared to be a one-off, for after its publication LaFeber turned his attention to Central and South America.[12]

As was often the case, part of what spurred LaFeber to turn to Asia was current events. There was, of course, the war in Vietnam. And then, starting in the late 1970s and reaching fever pitch in the 1980s, much of the US public feared that Japan, the United States' erstwhile protégé after World War II, was bent on overtaking the United States and poised to do so, at least economically. Harvard professor Ezra F. Vogel's *Japan as Number One: Lessons for America*, was one of the most provocatively titled and carefully argued (and therefore probably least read) of a series of articles and books trumpeting Japan's rise.[13] More popular was Michael Crichton's novel *Rising Sun*.[14] The *Kirkus Review* caught the essence of the book and of the moment in US-Japan relations: "The Yellow Menace returns in Crichton's shocking, didactic, enormously clever new mystery-thriller—only now he wears a three-piece suit and aims to dominate America through force of finance, not arms. 'The Japanese can be tough,' says one character here. 'They say "business is war," and they mean it.'"[15] Sayuri Guthrie-Shimizu, who worked on *The Clash* with LaFeber while she was finishing her PhD at Cornell, recalled that the publisher approached LaFeber about the possibility of providing more robust historical context to the US-Japan relationship than journalists and other political commentators were writing.[16]

There are some hints that LaFeber's interest in Japan was growing even before that ask. In 1993 he published *The American Search for Opportunity, 1865–1913*, the second volume in the four-volume *Cambridge History of American Foreign Relations*.[17] The book required a broad ambit, given its function in the series and its chronological scope. Its index cites Japan on thirty-seven different pages. That compares with eight citations for France and twenty-one for Germany. It may be that these years—involving the advent of the Meiji Emperor, Japan's economic growth, and its military victories over China and Russia, the latter mediated by Theodore Roosevelt—simply demanded this emphasis. Or maybe the chance (or the need) to learn more about Japanese policy during these years piqued LaFeber's interest in the longer-term US relationship with Japan, the patterns that shaped the years covered in his book, and those that emerged from it. In any case, *The Clash* would become his next book.

The book has twelve chapters along with a preface and conclusion. LaFeber begins the story in 1850 and concludes it in the 1990s. He explains in his preface that the title refers to the fact that although the US-Japan relationship over the nearly 150 years covered in the book seemed mostly cooperative, with the obvious exception of 1931–45, in truth the relationship was full of "sometimes highly dangerous clashes," since the two nations had "two different forms of capitalism."[18] The two nations clashed most frequently in or over China. Chapters 1–7 cover the years 1850–1941, and chapters 8–9 treat World War II and the Occupation. LaFeber dispatches the years from 1951 into the 1990s in just three chapters, chapters 10–12. This simple observation reveals much about one of the main arguments of the book: since their formal inception in the middle of the nineteenth century, US-Japanese relations have been characterized more by continuity than by change. LaFeber makes the continuity of clash clear in the preface, but other continuities reveal themselves in the narrative.

Chapters 1–2, covering the years 1850 to 1900, introduce the theme of cultural misunderstanding. This theme characterizes the relationship throughout the book, although the nature of misunderstanding changes, and it is complicated by the fact that some people from each country wish to learn about the other. US citizens and the Japanese, although the former more forcefully and with more harmful consequences, have racial views shaping their interactions with each other and with other Asians. Chapter 1 tells the "opening of Japan" story a bit differently from what high school history typically teaches, demonstrating that by the mid-nineteenth century, Japanese officials were seeking the most sensible way to engage with the rest of the world. US actions did force their hand, but the Japanese also saw the US effort as their best opportunity to structure their broader engagement on their own terms. In chapter 2, LaFeber argues that the relatively low level of actual contacts during 1868–1900, as each nation worked more on internal matters than on expanding their power in Asia, resulted in "never better" relations.[19] LaFeber has written about these late nineteenth-century years many times from the US perspective. His interpretation of US actions does not change much from that in *The New Empire* or *The American Search for Opportunity*. Japan and the United States are presented in these chapters as having a competitive affinity.

Already in chapter 3, covering 1900–1912, and then even more in chapter 4 (1912–20), the affinity is fading in the face of the competition. Both nations expanded their territorial holdings in Asia during these years. The United States claimed to be expanding to support its Open Door policy, serving its ever-increasing demand for markets for its goods. Japan more frequently closed doors where it expanded, wanting to ensure its access to both raw materials and markets in the hard-won colonized spaces. During these years competition was particularly fierce over investment in Manchuria, a region rich in resources that Japan needed, and a location of significant development. Expansion in Manchuria was likely to prompt competition in any case, but the overt racism of US immigration policy, and in the ways Japanese immigrants to the United

States were treated, caused friction. After California attempted to require segregated "Oriental" schools for Japanese, Chinese, and Korean immigrants in 1906, President Theodore Roosevelt negotiated a compromise to prevent that, but the Gentlemen's Agreement required Japan to limit further immigration to the United States. Japanese officials agreed, but they understood what the agreement signaled. Relations became so contentious that both countries drafted war plans aimed at the other.[20]

Officials in both Japan and the United States worked on ways to demonstrate both power and peaceful intentions, and through World War I, managed peacefully. Potential problems arose again in the aftermath of that war, when Japanese officials sought what they believed was their due as an Allied power and a great nation: land and rights in China, Germany's former possessions in Asia, and a racial equality clause. President Woodrow Wilson, constrained by both his racism and his concern for traditional US policies toward China, tried to thwart Japanese ambition. He only halfway prevailed, but that was sufficient to alert Japanese officials that the United States was more a stumbling block than an equal.

In chapter 5 (1921–31), chapter 6 (1931–37), and chapter 7 (1937–41), the conflicts grow. During the 1920s the United States had the upper hand and used its power to continue to restrict Japanese ambitions. LaFeber allotted twelve pages, one of the longest subsections in the book, to discussing the Washington Conference of 1921. This conference represents well the US vision for world order after World War I. The United States got nearly everything it wanted out of the conference. The Anglo-Japanese alliance ended. Japan agreed to build fewer battleships and heavy cruisers than Britain or the United States, in return for access to US capital markets. All participating nations agreed to respect the Open Door in China. So long as US capital flowed, each nation prioritized financial development over political or military power—and both Britain and Japan subordinated their interests to what the United States found acceptable—peace reigned.

The US vision for the world would not prevail for long. It abruptly collapsed with the onset of the Depression. During the early 1930s, US capital ceased to flow. The Japanese responded by prioritizing their political and military ambitions, although whether they did so in service of or instead of financial ambitions depends on one's point of view. Much of chapter 6 reveals the inadequacy of US policy tools for confronting a nation, in this case Japan, which had stopped subscribing to the US view of the world order. Expansion into China and a closed economy initially seemed to help Japan, which had lower unemployment and faster growth than the United States. But as LaFeber writes, the Japanese decision to join Germany and Italy in the Anti-Comintern Pact of

1936 "began a five-year era in which Japan moved from weakness to weakness and the United States moved from weakness to strength."[21]

Japan's direct clashes with US interests in China revealed that Japan was more dependent on the United States, its market, its capital, and its technology, than it had recognized. In 1937 the United States was not yet prepared to capitalize on this Japanese weakness. President Franklin D. Roosevelt's disastrous attempt to balance the federal budget caused more economic distress, the depression deepened, and dissension erupted among policymakers and politicians about the exercise of US power. Chapter 7, covering only 1937–41, reads like that section of a tragedy when all the actors know they are walking toward their doom, yet they cannot take steps in any other direction. LaFeber takes the reader through the painstaking transformation that both policymakers and the public went through in these years as they came to grips with the realization that FDR's preferred method for ordering the world—US economic power backed up by exhortation and diplomacy—had completely failed.

The other critical part of this story is Japan's dependence on imported raw materials, and what Japanese policymakers believed they needed to do to preserve their access to these. As LaFeber notes, in Japan the militarists' solution, "to cordon off large parts of Asia to obtain economic self-sufficiency," increasingly won out during the late 1930s. In the United States, disputes between officials with more experience in China and those with more experience in Japan meant that the United States continued to pursue both negotiations with Japan and military support for China after 1937. Negotiations revolved, as always, around China. Japanese officials insisted that their troops must stay in China. US officials insisted that they must leave. At stake: Who would get to trade with and invest freely in China? It turned out that only war could settle that question.

The war years 1941–45, covered in chapter 8, are a familiar story well told. LaFeber emphasizes the disparity in resources—how scarcity drove Japan, and abundance enabled the United States, to pursue military strategies and choose diplomatic policies leading to defeat for one and victory for the other. Even while emphasizing that the United States fought to destroy closed economic blocs and to promote "free markets globalized," LaFeber also highlights the pernicious effects of race on the war in Asia, noting that many US officials believed that unless Japan was "destroyed to the point of unconditional surrender," it would rise again to lead the rest of Asia to oppose all white people. The anti-Japanese sentiment prompting the US government to send Japanese Americans, but not German Americans or Italian Americans, to concentration camps the US government called relocation camps, is also part of the war story in *The Clash*.

The bulk of this long chapter focuses on the interplay between military strategy, which after mid-1942 was shaped by the knowledge that the United States was in position to win the war even if it might take some time, and by plans for the postwar world, which still looked to be a contentious one. China, Britain, and the United States had different visions for world order in postwar Asia, and US officials even quarreled among themselves. All the US officials agreed, however, that this time the US vision would be backed by more than diplomacy and economic power. As the war in Europe wound down in the spring of 1945, and Josef Stalin began to make plans to honor the Soviet pledge to enter the war against Japan, hints of the full scale of postwar conflict began to emerge. The new US president, Harry Truman, scrambling to make sure that the war ended on US terms and with the United States prepared to be the sole occupier of Japan, authorized the dropping of atomic bombs on Hiroshima and Nagasaki.

The US effort to transform Japan into the shepherd of the US order in Asia during the postwar Occupation is the story of chapter 9, which covers just 1945–51. LaFeber evokes the seesaw emotions of 1945, with jubilation at victory and elation at the massive amounts of US economic, military, and political power vying with fear about Soviet intentions and the levels of poverty and destruction in Japan, China, and Europe needing to be addressed immediately, as well as latent worry about a resurging depression. In Japan, US officials moved to completely remake politics and the economy during the immediate postwar years; but continued economic turmoil, concerns about disorder worldwide, and growing Soviet power prompted a more conservative turn after 1947. As LaFeber argued, Japan was "less an end in itself than the means ... for achieving the larger regional and global purposes of US foreign policy."[22] Japanese views and voices are muted in this chapter compared to others, although reading carefully reveals that Japanese officials were biding their time and influencing what they could. The outbreak of war on the Korean peninsula made Japan's task easier, so much so that LaFeber quotes Japanese prime minister Yoshida Shigeru as calling the conflict "a gift from the gods."[23] The United States needed a stable, prosperous Japan more than it needed a democratic Japan; it also needed lots of supplies for the US effort in Korea. Both US needs helped Japan's economy recover and its politicians reassert their authority.

Chapters 10–12, the last quarter of the book, cover the years 1951 through the mid-1990s. Another historian tasked as LaFeber was with providing context and correctives to anti-Japanese commentary in the 1980s might well have written primarily about World War II and the years after. LaFeber devoted only a small portion of his book to these years, demonstrating in the first nine chapters that the misunderstandings had a much longer history. But chapters 10–12 are as lively as the rest of the book. LaFeber calls the 1950s "the pivotal decade."[24] Japanese officials carefully maneuvered to run especially their economy but also their foreign relations to suit Japanese rather than US interests. Having learned the lessons of the 1920s very well, they made sure that domestic companies could get sufficient Japanese capital and would not have to rely on foreigners. Japan also began as early as 1952 to pursue trade relations with the People's Republic of China, a move the United States did not relish. US policymakers still held many cards, including the fact that the United States provided military protection, raw materials, and a market for Japan.

In many ways, chapter 10 (on the 1950s) and chapter 11 (covering 1960–73) recall the economic contention between the two countries in the early twentieth century, as each had a different vision for how to interact with and develop China. The stage was bigger now, since Japan and the United States now also had important interests in Southeast Asia. Neither country sought political control over places supplying raw materials or markets, but both sought to promote their own ways of doing business in order to profit both their companies and their nations. In some ways it was a return to the competitive affinity of the very early twentieth century, tipping again into pure competition after the mid-1960s when Japan began consistently to run a positive trade balance against the United States. Chapter 12, the final chapter, covering the years 1973 until the time the book went to press, explores those years when Japan's economic successes coincided with US weakness in the aftermath of the war in Vietnam, resulting in US fears that Japan would surpass the United States in global power. Japan's factories were producing high-quality, desirable consumer products, from televisions to video recorders to cars, at a good price, but Japan was facing its own growing pains from corruption at home to conflict abroad over the best way to deal with a resurgent China or protests in Southeast Asia. LaFeber uses the mutually beloved sport of baseball to explore cultural affinities and conflicts in the mature US-Japan relationship of the 1980s and 1990s. The United States and Japan no longer competed to see who could control China, and instead traded ideas about how best to handle the rise of Chinese economic power in the early 1990s, a fitting end to this particular story.

The Clash was one of three winners of the Bancroft Prize in 1998. Reviewers praised the book for its range and comprehensiveness. Writing a "Featured Review" in *Diplomatic History*, Charles E. Neu lauded *The Clash* as "the fullest account of American-Japanese relations ever written" and called it a "thoughtful, richly detailed analysis."[25] Nicholas Kristof, who (like several others) reviewed *The Clash* alongside Michael Schaller's *Altered States*, told readers of *Foreign Affairs* that LaFeber had brought "a fresh eye and a wonderful historical sweep to his work," while Mark Beeson called the book "a masterly survey of the historical interaction between Japan and the United States."[26] That LaFeber was a US foreign relations historian, rather than a Japan expert, offered the advantage (according to Carol Gluck, herself a Japan expert) "of distance from the afflictive claustrophobia of many Japan specialists," presumably such as herself.[27]

Yet the reviews were hardly uncritical. The reviewer for the *New York Times* found the book, at over 400 pages of text, heavy going.[28] Edward Drea pointed to weaknesses in LaFeber's treatment of military history—vital, he said, to an understanding of the US-Japan relationship over time.[29] Gluck and other reviewers recognized that LaFeber was not a Japan expert, and while that was not in their view altogether a drawback, it did lead, according to E. Bruce Reynolds, to some errors in LaFeber's account of pre-Meiji Japan. Neu pointed out that *The Clash* neglected "important themes, such as the role of American missionaries in Japan, the interaction of popular culture, the images held by elite groups, or the misconceptions and misunderstandings bred by the great chasms between the two cultures." Kristof detected a category error that led to an excessive focus on politics and diplomacy to the detriment of sociological and anthropological perspectives; in a backhanded compliment, he praised LaFeber for writing "so knowledgeably without the benefit of the Japanese language that I wondered why any of us ever bothered to slave away over it."[30] China, which in LaFeber's telling was the main object of the clash between the United States and Japan, was treated as a passive country, what Gluck called "a more or less inert object of competing imperial attentions," an especially serious shortcoming in light of events at the end of the twentieth century and a poor predictor of diplomacy in the new millennium.[31] Eileen Scully's long review in *Reviews in American History* picked a variety of bones with *The Clash*, most significantly with its title (and thesis), which flirted with "teleology" in its insistence that "every interaction between the two [nations]—even if ostensibly cooperative—embodies, portends, and accelerates their inevitable collision."[32] The *American Historical Review* and the *Journal of American History* evidently did not commission reviews of *The Clash*, probably because it was published by a trade press.

LaFeber surely anticipated some of these criticisms. He knew that his lack of Japanese language limited his understanding of half the relationship. He thus relied entirely on Sayuri Guthrie-Shimizu to choose Japanese documents appropriate to the study and to translate them. Guthrie-Shimizu remembers, fondly, that LaFeber trusted her to do this work, but adds that he called her frequently to press her on the nuances of her translations. It was, she recalls, an impressively rigorous process.[33] LaFeber conceded that his perspective was, as William Appleman Williams had once admitted (and celebrated) about his own, "a view from the provinces." For that he would not apologize. As always, he was unwilling to depart from the conviction that the analysis of power in the twentieth century must begin with the United States.

Nevertheless, LaFeber was at pains to avoid provincialism, to channel not just Walkerton but South Bend, Chicago, New York, and London. He also knew the book was dauntingly long. While it was still in draft form, he wrote to one of the contributors to this book: "Few people will read the book. It is now about 600 pages (instead of the original 800), so I doubt if I'll want to read it again myself," LaFeber quipped. "Too bad—there is a good story and some instructive morals buried in the relationship, and I might have gotten them out in the open if I had not lost control of the thing. Never had this kind of problem with a book before."[34]

LaFeber's interest in getting the translations right, in telling the story fully from the Japanese side, followed his process from his previous work. He sought expert help from friends, colleagues, and students, immersed himself in the literature, spoke with experts, and visited Japan several times. *Inevitable Revolutions*, first published in 1983 but with a greatly expanded edition in 1993, also dove deeply into Central American history, resulting from the same kinds of reading, consultations, and visits. In that book LaFeber's goal was to understand "the impact of U.S. policies on the peoples and institutions of Central America."[35] In *The Clash* the story is more reciprocal, showing impact in both directions. In this sense it demonstrates the promise of international history. It might be a cautionary tale for international historians that the book took LaFeber took twice as long to write as he had expected.[36]

The contrasting biographies of US and Japanese leaders featured in several chapters of *The Clash* reflect both the still-traditional approach in this book, focused as they are on the individual leaders and their potential to effect change, and the effort to explain historical developments from both sides. Chapter 4, covering the pivotal years 1912–20, opens with vivid descriptions of Japanese leader Yamagata Aritomo and US president Woodrow Wilson. Both men had been shaped by political upheaval taking place in their youth, which both saw in part as stemming from racial contention, although they perceived that contention in different ways, naturally. For each, ensuring political stability at home depended in part on exerting sufficient power overseas.[37]

Between 1912 and 1920, Japan and the United States clashed in significant ways—over immigration, the racial equality clause Japan championed at the Paris Peace Conference, and in their different visions for China. The backgrounds of Yamagata and Wilson helped shape the nature of those disputes and their resolutions. Rarely did history see a pair of leaders so instructively matched in background and outlook. In later chapters, too, compelling biographies help illuminate the history, as in the chapter 10 discussion of Kishi Nobusuke, the Japanese prime minister, and his efforts to help navigate a particularly tense time in US-Japanese relations in the mid-1950s.[38] LaFeber drew attention to Kishi's ardent nationalism, his love of aspects of US culture, and his shrewd ability to maneuver through a variety of difficult situations throughout his career.

LaFeber's efforts to understand both sides stretch beyond biography. Given that at least part of the impetus for writing the book was US pundits' crude criticisms of Japan in the 1980s, it is not surprising that the chapters on 1960 through 1973 (when Japan first began consistently to run a positive trade balance with the United States after 1966) and 1973 into the 1990s (when the US public began to believe Japan had potential to overtake the United States economically) pay particular attention to the Japanese rationale for following economic as well as political and strategic policies that ended up benefiting Japan significantly more than the United States.

In the midst of the US war in Vietnam, for instance, Japan carefully began looking for ways to distance itself from the United States. It joined ASEAN, the Association of Southeast Asian Nations, even providing one-fifth of the initial funding. As LaFeber wrote, US officials, "absorbed in Vietnam," completely "missed the importance" of ASEAN.[39] Conflict only grew from that point. Japanese officials were "confused" by statements from President Richard M. Nixon and Secretary of State Henry Kissinger that seemed to suggest that Japan should perhaps acquire nuclear weapons.[40] *The Clash* still has as its primary purpose explaining how and why the United States acted as it did in relationship with Japan, but more than his other works, it also represents the views and goals of Japanese officials for that relationship.

Because *The Clash* concerns US-Japan relations, it is in one sense as traditional a study as they come in the foreign relations subfield—the revisionist branch, of course, in which subtitles tended to offer some small variation on "The United States and [Your Choice of Other Country Here]." It is, in many respects, vintage LaFeber. Despite having the breadth and feel of a textbook, its sources include, as most of his books do, archival documents, in this case from Washington, New York, Princeton, Cambridge (Massachusetts), and New Haven, and every presidential library from West Branch, Iowa (Hoover), to Austin, Texas (Johnson). Its emphases are economics and diplomacy. Make no mistake: *The Clash* follows the revisionist playbook, in which problems are mostly caused by the United States' material overreach and a Japanese reply in kind, call and response, and strategic crises follow especially from the US-Japan rivalry in China, where both nations pursued their own visions of an Open Door for trade. The entries in the book's index are mainly names, places, and periods. The images it contains are mostly cartographic, or photographic reproductions of Great Men, Americans and Japanese: "maps and chaps." The prose style of *The Clash* is, in the judgment of the authors of this chapter, some of the best LaFeber ever wrote. It is direct, conversational without being loose or chatty, evocative, clear, and witty. There are notes of Thomas Bailey in LaFeber's storytelling, though not in his analysis. One can assume accuracy in rendering source materials; no one needs to fact-check Walter LaFeber.

But look closer. The book also demonstrates the ways in which LaFeber was grappling with changes in the profession, particularly the effects of the end of the Cold War, the development of what was then called international history, and the nascent cultural turn. In some ways, though, the most unusual quality of *The Clash* is that it is his only book focusing solely on the full chronological sweep of a bilateral relationship.[41] This particular canvas, geographically focused and chronologically broad, allowed LaFeber to paint the full scene as he envisioned it. Economic motives provided the broad brushstrokes, but culture, race, and strategy filled in the colors. LaFeber was skeptical of the newer developments, the purported end of the Cold War, international history, and the cultural turn, but as always, curious about them. He argued in 1992 that thinking of the Cold War only in terms of a post-1945 US-Soviet struggle was too limited, and he drew attention to continuities in US foreign relations since the 1890s.[42]

We can perhaps infer his sentiments about international history, as it was then called, from the many probing questions he asked one coauthor of this chapter in the early 1990s, as she pursued an international history approach in her dissertation. His obvious skepticism seems to have stemmed from two suspicions. First, he represented the best of a traditional kind of scholar, someone who returned again and again to similar themes and topics, investigating them ever more deeply and from a variety of angles, to try to answer puzzling questions about a place. That place, for him, was chiefly the United States. How did the United States, with all its many contradictions, become what it is, and particularly how did it come to exercise power in the world as it did, and with what consequences for the polity? He seemed to think that an international history focus might lead easily to divorcing the study of foreign relations from deep investigation of the societies creating those relations. He was prescient, in some ways. Many scholars today deploy technology and reasonably good funding to conduct research in more archives and countries and languages than they can possibly deeply study.

His second suspicion centered on the ways that international history developed in the 1980s and 1990s, focused more on politics and strategy than economics. International history, as more recent scholarship demonstrates, is eminently compatible with a focus on economic motives, but that was not the trend in the 1990s. What is perhaps most impressive, though, is that LaFeber was grappling with these developments at all. He had no real need to, as an eminent senior scholar. But his own curiosity and his relationships with a wide range of scholars prompted his openness to at least considering new approaches.

In his acknowledgments, LaFeber thanks many scholars—he was always generous—including a number of Japanese, and we know that he and his wife, Sandy, went to Japan several times. His son, Scott, recalls LaFeber conversing about Japan with the eminent foreign relations historian and US-Japan specialist Akira Iriye.[43] The book begins by contrasting US and Japanese cultures— the people, not their nations. Americans were, as Alexis de Tocqueville saw them: restless, striving, acquisitive, noisily democratic, and bent on maritime trade. The Japanese valued "consensus and harmony."[44] LaFeber makes numerous references to culture, broadly defined, in the text. He discusses films—*Patria, Thirty Seconds over Tokyo, Godzilla,* and Akira Kurosawa's peculiar *Rhapsody in August*—and cites Walt Whitman and Lafcadio Hearn.[45] He quotes at some length Townsend Harris, the first US consul to Japan, who described what he considered the peculiarities of Japanese life, including the bats, rats, and spiders with whom he cohabited, and the pervasive, and to him distressing, nudity of the people at toilet.[46] When a Japanese delegation first came to the United States in 1873, its leader, Iwakura Tomoni, made sure to avoid the cultural faux pas of bringing along his preferred clothing and condiments, and the Japanese noted with dismay the "boldness and coquetry of American women." LaFeber mentions baseball, the excited reception in Tokyo of Theodore Roosevelt's Great White Fleet, and the summer Olympics in 1964. The US public believed the Japanese were conformist and often inscrutable. The Japanese deplored what they saw as the casualness of US violence.[47]

The index of *The Clash* contains fifty discrete page references to race, a category of analysis not generally associated with revisionism during most of LaFeber's career. He clearly takes seriously the racial aspects of US-Japan relations. He describes US and Japanese struggles to place each other along the ladder of civilization, a racialized concept that both societies believed in deeply. There were moments in the relationship particularly susceptible to mutual misperceptions based on racism. During the first visit by a Japanese delegation to the United States, in 1860, the Japanese were subject to racist taunts, as when one Philadelphian asked a US naval officer accompanying a Japanese delegate, "Is that your monkey you have got with you?"[48] The racialized misperceptions were pervasive and could be subtler than references to monkeys. Japanese observers often commented on the lewdness and lack of discipline among Americans, while Americans expressed surprise when Japanese demonstrated knowledge and initiative.

The heart of the dilemma was Japan's ambition to join the ranks of great powers as an equal, which included an ambition to be an Asian imperial power. As they steadily achieved that ambition, they attracted both grudging admiration and racialized scorn. LaFeber reported the words of Finley Peter Dunne's character Mr. Dooley: "A subjick race is on'y funny whin it's raaly subjick. About three years ago [1904] I stopped laughin' at Japanese jokes."[49] Mr. Dooley evoked Japan's growing power in the Pacific, but in the United States, Japanese faced school segregation in California, a Gentlemen's Agreement to end that segregation leading to de facto exclusion of Japanese immigration, with that exclusion codified in the 1924 Exclusion Act, as well as anti-Asian riots. Race was deployed to restrict Japanese global ambitions. Woodrow Wilson feared threats to the "white race" as he considered committing the United States to war in 1917, and at the Paris Peace Conference, he took extraordinary steps to defeat Japan's proposed racial equality principle for the Covenant of the League of Nations.[50]

Such measures demonstrated to Japan that the great power club would never be open to them. They set about achieving their ambitions on their own, an effort ending in World War II, a struggle shaped by race and racism. Japan claimed that the purity of the Japanese race meant Japanese were uniquely qualified to rule Asia, and regarded Americans as dirty. Americans were equally racist. LaFeber quotes the famous war correspondent Ernie Pyle as saying, "The Japanese were looked upon as something subhuman or repulsive." This sentiment was reinforced by President Roosevelt's executive order creating the so-called relocation camps for Japanese and Japanese Americans on the West Coast.[51] Even after the US victory in the war, racism persisted. LaFeber notes that as late as 1989 in Rhode Island, an effort to end the celebration of Victory Day (colloquially called Victory over Japan Day) drew people wearing "American Legion and Veterans of Foreign Wars paraphernalia" and using racist epithets.[52] The pervasiveness of racism and racial imagery shaped relations between Japanese and Americans, although in *The Clash*, anecdotes and examples tend to speak for themselves. LaFeber does not explore their meaning and effect at length; race is perhaps not quite a discrete category of analysis for him.

The Clash was published just as an influential group of historians were turning to culture—again, broadly conceived—as a way of explaining US foreign relations. Cultural history itself was having an extended moment. Borrowing from anthropology, most notably the Weberian cultural anthropologist Clifford Geertz, who defined culture (both productively and confoundingly) as "webs of significance," historians increasingly told stories about common folks, finding meaning in their everyday practices, religious rituals, language, and gestures.[53]

Foreign relations historians found ways to apply cultural history to their own practices. They were open to using sources then alien to those in the field, among them fiction, visual images, notes in the margins of texts, and accounts concerning diplomatic etiquette or the expression of emotion. To some this meant investigating nonstate actors and their organizations. Others saw culture inscribed in the actions of the state itself. Michael Hunt's influential book *Ideology and U.S. Foreign Policy*, published a decade before *The Clash*, borrowed from Williams the analytical category "ideology," which Hunt couched in cultural terms, praising Geertz but shying away from substituting "culture" for "ideology," evidently because the former lacked sufficient parsimony or rigor.[54] Others proved less hesitant. Some argued that categories of analysis such as race, gender, and religion were part of the larger construct of culture, being ways of weaving webs of significance or creating "structures of meaning," another Geertzian definition.[55] The interdisciplinary field of cultural studies had a role here too, insisting on interrogating the United States as an empire, not unlike other empires—an argument congenial to the revisionists, though the ponderous use of theory and often abstruse language of cultural studies scholars limited their influence on foreign relations historians.[56]

Walter LaFeber was not a foreign relations culturalist. His references to culture were broad, subject to binary descriptions that an unfriendly critic might today scorn as "essentialist." Again and again, *The Clash* advanced revisionist arguments, such that there was no mistaking the centrality of economic factors in its analysis. Convinced that power mattered most and that it inhered only in the state, aware of the cultural turn in the field, and doubtless aware that some of his students and former students were at minimum curious about it, LaFeber seems to acknowledge it without endorsing it. At one point, discussing the early John F. Kennedy administration's policy toward Japan, he writes: "The two cultures might have appeared to be converging, but foreign policies do not always follow culture."[57] Summing things up at the end of the book, he adds: "That much of the conflict is due to centuries-old cultural differences is apparent. Other causes, however, are too often lost. There is little culturally based about US free trade, 'one-world' policies after 1945."[58] The final sentence of *The Clash* declares that "the primary cause" of conflict between the two nations—"the centuries-old rivalry to decide which system was to lead in developing Asian and especially Chinese markets"—would remain the chief influence on US-Japan relations.[59] It could hardly be clearer: economics mattered most.

For LaFeber, culture was a feature of US-Japan relations, but it did not determine them, nor did it shape them significantly. Race, independent in his view of a larger cultural framework, helped to explain mutual misperceptions and likely affected behavior, as was the case after US immigration restriction and in battle during the Pacific War. It is tempting to ascribe to LaFeber's analysis a belief in the culture of capitalism, the view that faith in private property and free enterprise and the relentless pursuit of foreign markets brought with it a way of thinking about the world. Or perhaps it was the other way around—that is, that capitalism, US-style, was predicated on an uncommon geography, certain habits of thought about democracy and individualism, and a particular sort of history that made for a peculiarly, if not uniquely, US culture.

As readers of chapter 9 in *Thinking Otherwise* will discover, LaFeber's fascination with Tocqueville suggests something deeper than a belief in the crass desire for profit as the root of all foreign policy decisions.[60] Revisionism was never solely about economics. Students, in their own ways, of Beard, Harrington, Williams, and LaFeber were interested in how US domestic policy shaped the nation's foreign relations. Much of this had to do with economics. But not all. The revisionists took ideas seriously, placing economics within the more spacious category of ideology—*Weltanschauung*, as Williams called it. Harrington was interested in religion—his book was titled *God, Mammon, and the Japanese*—and Williams, too, understood the importance of religious thinking among US policymakers, writing that the first forty years of the twentieth century saw "the rise of a new crusading spirit in American diplomacy," which emphasized "the virtues (and necessities) of Protestant Christianity."[61] For his part, LaFeber would place the theologian Reinhold Niebuhr front and center in *American, Russia, and the Cold War*.

Walter LaFeber was a revisionist to the end—emphatically a small "r" revisionist, given his insistence on challenging accepted wisdom, whatever that might be. These traits are likely familiar to many small-town midwesterners. LaFeber never abandoned his conviction that US foreign relations had their basis in material factors, that the pursuit of an economic Open Door abroad was the predicate for a US empire that put aside the pursuits of liberty and modesty, as empires do, and that tragically eclipsed the quest for justice at home. But his mind, and his sensibility, were capacious enough to entertain more than one big idea at once. It has been remarked that, in his brilliant classroom lectures, Walter LaFeber dispensed a powerful radicalism while wearing a suit or coat and tie, an ideological wolf in the traditional sheep's clothing of the male academic.[62] Culture, and especially race, appeared in a similar way in *The Clash*: another way of thinking about foreign relations, another way of thinking otherwise, another part of what made Walter LaFeber so astonishingly appealing and influential.

Notes

1. Lloyd Gardner email to Andrew Rotter, June 21, 2021, in authors' possession.
2. David S. Brown, *Beyond the Frontier: The Midwestern Voice in American Historical Writing* (Chicago: University of Chicago Press, 2009), quotation at 129.
3. Kristin L. Hoganson, *The Heartland: An American History* (New York: Penguin, 2019), xxvi.
4. Hoganson, *The Heartland*, 106–7.
5. History of Walkerton, http://www.walkerton.org/wordpress1/history/#:~:text=Walkerton%20was%20named%20for%20James,store%20from%20nearby%20West%20York.
6. Conversation with Scott LaFeber, Anne Foster, and Andrew Rotter, August 29, 2022, notes in authors' possession.
7. Hoganson, *The Heartland*, 166.
8. St. Joseph County Soil and Water Conservation District, "Invasive Species," https://www.stjosephswcd.org/invasive-species.
9. Thomas J. McCormick, *China Market: America's Quest for Informal Empire, 1893–1902* (Chicago: Quadrangle Books, 1967). Note that Fred Harvey Harrington's most famous book concerned US relations with Korea (and Japan). See Fred Harvey Harrington, *God, Mammon, and the Japanese: Dr. Horace N. Allen and Korean-American Relations, 1884–1905* (Madison: University of Wisconsin Press, 1944).
10. Walter F. LaFeber, *The New Empire: An Interpretation of American Expansion, 1860–1898* (Ithaca, NY: Cornell University Press, 1963).
11. Walter F. LaFeber, ed., *John Quincy Adams and American Continental Empire* (Chicago: Quadrangle Books, 1965); LaFeber, ed., *The Origins of the Cold War* (New York: John Wiley, 1971); LaFeber, *America, Russia, and the Cold War, 1945–1966* (New York: John Wiley, 1967, with nine subsequent editions); LaFeber, *The Panama Canal: The Crisis in Historical Perspective* (New York: Oxford University Press, 1978); LaFeber, *Inevitable Revolutions: The United States in Central America* (New York: W. W. Norton, 1983).
12. See, for instance, the following articles by Walter F. LaFeber: "Our Illusory Affair with Japan," *The Nation*, March 11, 1968, 330–38; "China and Japan: A Matter of Options," *Current History*, September 1968, 153–58, 179–80; "Before Pearl Harbor," *Current History*, August 1969, 65–70, 114; "China and Japan: Different Beds, Different Dreams," *Current History*, September 1970, 142–46, 179–80; "Roosevelt, Churchill, and Indochina: 1942–1945," *American Historical Review* 80 (December 1975): 1277–95.
13. Ezra F. Vogel, *Japan as Number One: Lessons for America* (Cambridge, MA: Harvard University Press, 1979).
14. Michael Crichton, *Rising Sun* (New York: Knopf, 1992).
15. *Kirkus Review*, March 10, 1992.
16. Sayuri Guthrie-Shimizu, comment, LaFeber Tribute Workshop, Ithaca, NY, October 29–30, 2022, tape recording available at www.smu.edu/cph/LaFeber.
17. Walter LaFeber, *The American Search for Opportunity, 1865–1913* (Cambridge: Cambridge University Press, 1993).
18. Walter LaFeber, *The Clash: U.S. Relations with Japan throughout History* (New York: W. W. Norton, 1997), xviii.
19. LaFeber, *The Clash*, 32.

20. LaFeber, *The Clash*, 89–91.
21. LaFeber, *The Clash*, 182.
22. LaFeber, *The Clash*, 271.
23. LaFeber, *The Clash*, 287. We follow here LaFeber's ordering of Japanese names, with surname listed first.
24. LaFeber, *The Clash*, 296. This is the title of chapter 10.
25. Charles E. Neu, "Feature Review: American and Japan in the World Arena," *Diplomatic History* 23 (Summer 1999): 571.
26. Michael Schaller, *Altered States: The United States and Japan since the Occupation* (New York: Oxford University Press, 1997); Nicholas D. Kristof, "Japan's Full Story: Inside and Outside of the Cabinet," *Foreign Affairs*, November/December 1997, 141; Mark Beeson, review Article, *Journal of Contemporary Asia* 32 (2002): 267.
27. Carol Gluck, "A Not So Special Relationship," *Times Literary Supplement*, June 26, 1998, 31.
28. Sebastian Mallaby, "Uneasy Partners," *New York Times*, September 21, 1997.
29. Edward Drea, review of *The Clash*, *Journal of Military History* 62 (October 1998): 924–25.
30. E. Bruce Reynolds, review in *History* 26, no. 4 (Summer 1998): 208; Neu, "Feature Review," 573; Kristof, "Japan's Full Story," 141, 144. Sayuri Guthrie-Shimizu recalls that Japanese area studies experts largely "shunned" *The Clash*. Sayuri Guthrie-Shimizu, comment, LaFeber Tribute Workshop.
31. Gluck, "A Not So Special Relationship." See also Robert G. Kane's review in *Orbis* 42 (Summer 1998): 480.
32. Eileen P. Scully, "Men, Maps, and Markets: First Causes and Last Resorts in US-Japan Relations," *Reviews in American History* 26 (1998): 762.
33. Guthrie-Shimizu, comment, LaFeber Tribute Workshop.
34. LaFeber letter to David Langbart, July 10, 1996, in Langbart's possession.
35. LaFeber, *Inevitable Revolutions*, 361 in 1984 ed., 421 in 1993 ed.
36. LaFeber, *The Clash*, 481.
37. LaFeber, *The Clash*, 101–4.
38. LaFeber, *The Clash*, 314–21.
39. LaFeber, *The Clash*, 345.
40. LaFeber, *The Clash*, 349–50.
41. It could be said that the book is actually about that triangular relationship LaFeber wrote about in the late 1960s, but in *The Clash*, while China receives sustained attention, it is acted upon rather than actor.
42. Walter LaFeber, "An End to Which Cold War?," *Diplomatic History* 16 (January 1992): 61–65.
43. Conversation with Scott LaFeber, Foster, and Rotter.
44. LaFeber, *The Clash*, 6–7.
45. LaFeber, *The Clash*, 24, 52–53.
46. LaFeber, *The Clash*, 19.
47. LaFeber, *The Clash*, 38–39, 63, 356, 90–91, 338, 348, 400.
48. LaFeber, *The Clash*, 24.
49. LaFeber, *The Clash*, 88.
50. LaFeber, *The Clash*, 113, 123–34.

51. LaFeber, *The Clash*, 218–19.
52. LaFeber, *The Clash*, 381.
53. Clifford Geertz, *The Interpretation of Cultures* (New York: Basic Books, 1973), 5.
54. Michael H. Hunt, *Ideology and US Foreign Policy* (New Haven, CT: Yale University Press, 1987).
55. For example, see Emily S. Rosenberg, *Financial Missionaries to the World: The Politics and Culture of Dollar Diplomacy, 1900–1930* (Durham, NC: Duke University Press, 1999); Andrew J. Rotter, *Comrades at Odds: The United States and India, 1947–1964* (Ithaca, NY: Cornell University Press, 2000).
56. An influential work that made this argument in the mid-1990s is Amy Kaplan and Donald E. Pease, eds., *Cultures of United States Imperialism* (Durham, NC: Duke University Press, 1994). This scholarship influenced Foster's dissertation and later book: Anne L. Foster, *Projections of Power: The United States and Europe in Colonial Southeast Asia, 1919–1941* (Durham, NC: Duke University Press, 2010).
57. LaFeber, *The Clash*, 333.
58. LaFeber, *The Clash*, 399.
59. LaFeber, *The Clash*, 405.
60. LaFeber, *The Clash*, 30–31.
61. Harrington, *God, Mammon, and the Japanese*; William Appleman Williams, *The Tragedy of American Diplomacy*, rev. ed. (New York: Dell, 1962), 53.
62. Andrew J. Rotter and Frank Costigliola, "Walter LaFeber: Scholar, Teacher, Intellectual," *Diplomatic History* 28 (November 2004): 628.

CHAPTER 8

Demystifying Globalization and US Power
Michael Jordan and the New Global Capitalism

SAYURI GUTHRIE-SHIMIZU AND JESSICA WANG

Walter LaFeber loved sports. He played varsity basketball in high school and was on the freshman team at Hanover College, but he ultimately decided it took too much time away from his studies. When recruited to the Cornell faculty, he made the mistake of thinking that Cornell's football team being the best in the Ivy League meant that the team actually played well. The poor quality of Cornell football did not prevent him from crowing over the team's victories, however, as his long-time friend Lloyd Gardner can attest.

He reveled in baseball most of all, especially his beloved Chicago Cubs. Walt's wife, Sandy LaFeber, recalls that on the first morning of her first visit to Walkerton, Indiana, LaFeber's hometown, Walt roused her out of bed early. He had tickets to an afternoon Cubs game and they needed to catch the train to Chicago. Gardner and Richard Immerman also recall an infamous outing to a Cubs–Reds game during a meeting of the Organization of American Historians in the early 1980s. Cold, rainy weather at a time when the two teams were absolutely abysmal did not deter LaFeber, which speaks volumes about his diehard loyalty to the Cubs, not to mention his preference to avoid academic conferences. His daughter Suzanne fondly recalls a father-daughter trip to a playoff game at Wrigley Field in 2015, where after the game her father came away with a baseball signed by Billy Williams, a favorite former player from the 1960s and 1970s who later joined the coaching staff, and whom

LaFeber admired for his basic decency, humility, and devotion to the Cubs. A year later, LaFeber finally enjoyed the ultimate reward for decades of beleaguered fandom, when his cherished team finally won the World Series.[1]

LaFeber preferred college basketball and football to their professional counterparts, however, so his 1999 book, *Michael Jordan and the New Global Capitalism*, was not an exercise in self-indulgent fandom. Instead, Jordan's iconic global stature, combined with Nike's ability to sell sneakers and sports imagery all over the world, grabbed his scholarly attention.[2] In the same year that the Michael Jordan book came out, LaFeber also delivered his presidential address to the Society for the History of American Foreign Relations (SHAFR) on "Technology and American Foreign Relations." Together the two works provided occasions to grapple with the evolution of global capitalism, the mobilization of knowledge, culture, mediated imaginaries, and their implications for US power.

Of course, such issues had always featured prominently in LaFeber's work. Already in *The New Empire*, for example, culture and ideational spheres provided a driving force of US foreign relations with the "intellectual formation" of economic and racial anxieties that gave rise to the new US empire of the late nineteenth century. But by the 1990s, Emily Rosenberg's pathbreaking work on business, popular culture, and US global relations, combined with histories of science and technology increasingly attentive to the social, political, and institutional dimensions of knowledge production and dissemination, provided more robust foundations for LaFeber's ever-fertile historical imagination.[3] In an immediate post–Cold War era that seemed to guarantee US hegemony for the foreseeable future, LaFeber focused more intently on how soft power, in the form of mass consumerism, mass communications, scientific knowledge, and technological systems, constituted the key means for the United States to amass and deploy global political capital. In his 1999 SHAFR address, secretaries of state William H. Seward, Elihu Root, and George P. Shultz emerged as movers, shakers, and visionaries who understood and exploited modern technology as means of power, whereas in the Michael Jordan book, "His Airness" provided a vehicle for interrogating the blend of corporate power, mass media, mass consumerism, and the cult of celebrity that undergirded US cultural hegemony in the 1990s. In both accounts, knowledge and culture, by being embedded within and mobilized by well-organized and powerful corporate and political institutions, defined and perpetuated US power well beyond what the more limited accouterments of formal diplomacy and military dominance could offer.

These works on global capitalism, culture, and corporate power strongly reflected their early post–Cold War moment, in which LaFeber described the

LaFeber loved baseball and was an avid fan of the Chicago Cubs, but he actually played college basketball for the Hanover Panthers. Courtesy of Sandra LaFeber.

historical past as a gradual unfolding of accumulated US power that ultimately consolidated US hegemony. By contrast, the present-day era of a hollowed-out middle class, an increasingly unstable and polarized US political system, a complex multipolar global order, and the almost apocalyptic upheaval of warfare, climate change, and a global pandemic allows no such confidence about the durability of US power, or even US nationhood itself. Where does LaFeber's analysis of technological change, corporate power, mass media, and the globalization of sports fit within a radically changed present-day context? In this chapter we offer an appreciation of LaFeber's late 1990s writings about capitalism, while also suggesting the ways in which the so-called cultural and international turns in historical scholarship, as well as the dramatically reduced circumstances of the United States itself two decades later, challenge LaFeber's findings. In particular, global and transnational approaches now emphasize the need for a more dramatic decentering of US power and recognition of a more fluid set of processes and diffuse centers of gravity at work, defined by the co-creation of US and global orders through the reciprocal give-and-take of exchange.

LaFeber himself had reservations about the international turn in the history of US foreign relations and rightly objected to a historiographical leveling that downplayed vast asymmetries of power between different countries and societies. Yet the revisionists' own emphasis on the limitations of US power invited interpretations that emphasized the agency of parties beyond US borders and the exercise of power from below. Although the United States enjoyed and capitalized upon massive advantages within the international system, thanks to the endowment of a settler colonial empire and its wealth of natural resources, the parochialism of US history and its particular strain of US exceptionalism ultimately overestimated US hegemony.[4] From that standpoint, the globalization of US history does not obscure or whitewash the role of the United States within the international system so much as it explains the intricacies of power within a world of uneven, yet interdependent, development. At the end of the day, however, LaFeber was not trying to write global history. Throughout much of his career, he sought to understand the United States and explain how its foreign policy exposed and exacerbated the particular vulnerabilities of the US political system. He sought nothing less than to warn his readers about the ever-contradictory and often tenuous state of US democracy and its aspirations, and on those terms, he eminently succeeded.

LaFeber, the Wisconsin School, and the History of Capitalism

Capitalism as an object of historical study has experienced a remarkable resurgence over the past decade. The 2008 financial crisis gave new urgency to discussions of capitalism's ability to unleash chaos, ruin, and widespread human miseries. Meanwhile, the ever more apparent and alarming effects of global climate change and environmental degradation have raised profound questions about capitalism as a way of life and the impossibility of continuing to ignore as exogenous the massive physical mobilization and cycling of energy and materials that the present-day global economy requires.[5]

In the midst of these developments, Sven Beckert's *Empire of Cotton: A Global History* (2014) and a self-proclaimed movement for a "new history of American capitalism" revived interest in the history of US economic life and made the history of capitalism a flourishing area of research. Exponents of the new history of US capitalism acknowledged that their research program rested upon ample precedents. Beckert and Christine Desan observed in a 2018 essay that "disciplinary trends in history, economics, political science, and law"—particularly earlier scholarship in economic history, the revelations of the new social history of the 1960s and 1970s, the movement launched in the late 1970s to bring the state back into historical analysis, and more-recent investigations of political economy—had all paved the way for a reinvigorated history of capitalism. Surprisingly, however, despite an emphasis on the global as one of the hallmarks of the new literature, Beckert and Desan omitted US foreign relations from their overview.[6] Seth Rockman, in an earlier overview, also identified multiple historiographic lineages as candidates for the field's progenitors. In a long list that included New Left labor history, the scholarship on US political development in the 1980s and 1990s, and William Cronon's stunning meld of economic and environmental history in *Nature's Metropolis*, the Wisconsin School once again went without mention.[7]

Such lacunae did not pass unnoticed. In a lively roundtable in the *Journal of American History*, Peter James Hudson identified internationalism as critical analytical terrain and took historians of US capitalism to task for their blinkered and truncated vision. "Despite the recent turns to diaspora, empire, and transnationalism," he observed, "U.S. history remains provincial."[8] Writing in another forum, Paul A. Kramer similarly welcomed the promise of the field's breadth and ambition, although he expressed skepticism about "the hype" in which "the 'new history of capitalism' label proved an effective brand." In an incisive, rigorous, and theoretically informed analysis, Kramer went on to highlight the legacy of the Wisconsin School and underscore the need to continue to move historical investigations of capitalism beyond the national frame.[9]

The Wisconsin School itself, Kramer pointed out, emerged from a powerful pre–World War II tradition that had aimed an unsparing critique at US financial imperialism in the Caribbean and at a collusion between corporate interests and government that it held responsible for a disastrous US entry into World War I. In a Cold War era that rendered critiques of capitalism unwelcome and even politically risky, William Appleman Williams and the Wisconsin School unapologetically placed capitalism at the center of historical analysis.[10] For observers in a late nineteenth-century era of sensational economic swings between boom and bust, foreign markets promised the magical solution to surplus production at home and all of its attendant social ills, particularly the economic immiseration and labor unrest that threatened the basic stability of an increasingly urban and industrial society. To those who charged him with indulging leftist ideological dogma, Williams had a ready retort that the desperate allure of markets abroad sprang not from any wild imaginings on his part but from the preoccupations of tradesmen, businessmen, journalists, labor leaders, politicians, religious leaders, and other writers in the pages of trade journals, popular magazines, personal correspondence, and policy documents throughout the 1890s. One simply could not read basic sources from the time period without being hit over the head by repeated calls for US goods to resolve domestic political problems by finding foreign markets.[11]

At the same time, Williams did not merely follow and report upon his sources. In an era dominated by narrative approaches to US political history, his writings displayed an unusual command of political economy, social theory, and comparative analysis. Critics who accused Williams of economic determinism and Marxist assumptions about the inherent instabilities of capitalism and its inevitable crisis missed the centrality of ideology as the driving force in his conception of US foreign relations. Williams, along with other like-minded historians, sought to challenge a neoclassical overconfidence that naturalized liberal economics as the unfolding of its own internal, inexorable logic.[12] As a corrective, Williams appealed not to a rigid Marxian framework but to the power of ideology and its imaginaries to show how political and cultural orders constructed and maintained economic systems and their folkways. At the root of the American dilemma, Williams argued, lay a nineteenth-century liberalism that believed that a harmony of interests could emerge from the individual pursuit of economic self-interest.[13] From the *Weltanschauung* of liberal economics came the Open Door as the imagined and hoped-for solution to US problems that would simultaneously enrich the world. Tragedy then ensued from the US refusal to accept others' qualms about the liberal economic order, particularly Americans' inability to countenance the legitimacy of the alternative ideas and grievances that led to revolutions.[14]

Williams's historiographical roadmap paved the way for a generation of scholarship at the University of Wisconsin. As discussed elsewhere in this book, LaFeber's writings throughout his career bore the imprint of Williams's influence. Williams's strident invocation of the Open Door ultimately proved too blunt an instrument for LaFeber's more subtle and fluid analytical leanings, especially when it came to the Cold War, in which a Manichean ideology of geopolitical struggle decoupled itself from late nineteenth-century economic anxieties and gained a life of its own. But other topics—the economic developmental aspirations of the United States from the American Revolution onward, the economic, strategic, and ideological formulations of US leaders and intellectuals in the late nineteenth century, American overconfidence in the virtues of liberal order, and the counterproductive nature of American antipathy toward other countries' revolutionary political movements in the twentieth century—built upon Williams's ideas to become classic themes in LaFeber's own writings throughout his career. LaFeber also reached beyond political economy to incorporate questions of culture, race, gender, and knowledge-making into his understanding of US foreign policy. All of these themes came together in his efforts in the late 1990s to reckon with what capitalism had become and how it had gotten there.

In late June 1999, days before the official release date of *Michael Jordan and the New Global Capitalism*, LaFeber delivered his SHAFR presidential address, "Technology and American Foreign Relations." At a time when the vast majority of studies in the history of US foreign relations focused on the post-1945 period, the SHAFR lecture epitomized LaFeber's ability to take the long view on both capitalism and US power. As he pointed out in his opening words, dramatically accelerated economic growth distinguished capitalism post-1750 from the previous thousand years of economic activity in Europe. Although LaFeber boldly declared that "technological evolution drove capitalism," he was no technological determinist. In his telling, "technological change" was shorthand for the combined force of innovation, novel forms of social organization, and the human ambitions behind the political and cultural currents that made nineteenth- and twentieth-century capitalism possible. Visions of US prowess and the world-historical destiny of the American nation to serve as the model for all humanity in the age of republicanism also drove US nation-building from the beginning. The early leaders of the United States—men such as George Washington, Alexander Hamilton, and James Madison, and in the next generation, LaFeber's beloved John Quincy Adams—firmly believed in a glorious future for their country, even as the realities of US weakness relative to European powers required a more modest and tenuous strategy of attempting to navigate a predatory geopolitical order as a neutral trading state. In the 1840s when William H. Seward, then senator and a future secretary of state, maneuvered to create a legal and political environment that could maximize the capacities of steam power and rapid communications by wire to support US imperial prospects, he tapped into this already well-established exceptionalist tradition at the heart of American nationhood.[15]

Seward, Root, and Shultz, as embodiments of technologically savvy foresight and nationalist ambition, provided LaFeber with a framing device to analyze what he defined as three distinct periods of economic and political development in the United States: the first and second industrial revolutions, followed by the information revolution of the late twentieth century. Seward recognized early on the transformative possibilities opened by steam power and telegraphy. As he moved in his career from the governorship of New York to the US Senate, he mobilized law and political capital to support railways, telegraphy, and other new technologies as drivers of US commercial expansion and enhanced global political status. Like many of his contemporaries, when he contemplated steam-powered ships, he foresaw an ever-burgeoning trade across the Pacific. As secretary of state, Seward also aggressively pursued US dominance in telegraphy, albeit with mixed success. Although Seward did not live to see the age of US technological dominance and economic preeminence, he grasped what LaFeber eloquently described as the "nationalizing, centralizing, and imperialistic" potential of the first industrial revolution. It took a civil war to reconstitute the political edifice required for those nationalizing possibilities, but with the transition from the first to the second industrial revolution came a new era of US power.[16]

For LaFeber, Elihu Root personified the late nineteenth- and early twentieth-century world of the second industrial revolution, in which the age of electricity and the combustion engine amplified to dizzying new heights the scope and scale of globalized commerce and labor migration. According to LaFeber's rendering, Root—who held many notable positions, including serving as both secretary of war and secretary of state for Theodore Roosevelt—understood that ever more powerful technologies of communications, industrial production, and warfare, made possible by increasingly purposive efforts to tie scientific research to direct commercial and industrial applications, required the vigorous deployment of governmental authority. Only the federal government could assemble the organizational might to advance national agendas through control of strategic waterways, communications, and access to global markets for US trade and finance. Root and his contemporaries felt keenly the vertiginous pace of the twentieth century's global entanglements, which embedded the United States in an intricate web of connections that signaled both opportunity and danger. A technological age of modern capitalism promised progress and unprecedented prosperity. Dangers also loomed, though, owing to failures of political imagination, the self-immolating tendencies of imperial power, and the revolutions spawned by the intense instability of modern economic, political, and social life. For Root, the United States had no choice but to live in an ever-changing present in which, as LaFeber put it, "the train of the second industrial revolution was already successfully roaring down the tracks." The ongoing professionalization and bureaucratization of governmental institutions, as in the early twentieth-century reorganization of the US military and consular service, along with the strengthening of the Republican Party's alliance with corporate America, were key means by which Root sought to meet the challenges of a globalizing era.[17]

LaFeber then nimbly jumped ahead to George P. Shultz and the postindustrial information revolution of the late twentieth century, in which the challenge of political revolutions abroad that had already confounded Root's generation continued to defy US pretensions of order. For Shultz in the 1980s—and for LaFeber at the end of the 1990s—the full implications of digital technology and its informational possibilities were not yet apparent, and indeed, they remain elusive even today. Shultz had pursued a successful academic career for two decades as an economist before joining the Nixon administration in 1969 as secretary of labor. He subsequently served as director of the Office of Management and the Budget and then secretary of the treasury, before returning to private life as executive vice president of the Bechtel Group, a prominent engineering and project management company. Shultz would eventually head the Bechtel Group as its director and president.[18]

Already in the 1950s Shultz had begun to sense the revolutionary possibilities of computing for US business enterprises. As secretary of state under Reagan, he continued to track developments in computing, satellite communications, and scientific and technological advancement more generally, and he hailed information technology as the basis of states' economic and political power. States would either learn to exploit new technological capabilities, like the rising Asian "tigers" did, or they could sink into obsolescence and decay, a trend that the Soviet Union was hard put to reverse in the 1980s. Information technologies, Shultz quickly perceived, also portended new foreign policy challenges through their decentralizing potential, which would empower and embolden nonstate actors ranging from corporations to terrorists.[19] Shultz sometimes overreached, as revealed by his irrational exuberance in the 2010s for a young entrepreneur named Elizabeth Holmes and what would ultimately turn out to be her fraudulent claims to unprecedented advancements in blood-testing technology by her company, Theranos.[20] Long before disruption became a twenty-first-century watchword in the heady, hyped-up world of Silicon Valley startups, however, Shultz and other apostles of digital technology in the 1980s believed a new age in capitalism and global affairs had already arrived.

In his SHAFR address LaFeber had discussed traditional political elites as a way to explore the coevolution of technology, capitalism, and US power. In *Michael Jordan and the New Global Capitalism* he turned to basketball stardom, the Nike Corporation, and satellite television to foreground culture and US soft power within a novel stage of corporate capitalism's relentless evolution. Americans in the 1990s, LaFeber argued, found themselves living in a new era, not because of the end of the Cold War, but because of "the information revolution, the new power of US capital and transnational corporations to drive that revolution, and the reaction—sometimes violent—in the United States and abroad to that revolution."[21] At the center of these tectonic shifts stood the GOAT (Greatest of All Time), the already legendary Michael Jordan.

The transformation of the National Basketball Association (NBA) from fading US sports league into global supercommodity in the 1980s and 1990s epitomized what LaFeber called "the new global capitalism." Although basketball, a quintessential US invention, globalized early and began to travel with Christian missionaries from the United States to Asia and other parts of the world in the 1890s, the NBA throughout most of its early history was an anemic business enterprise that, by the early 1980s, looked destined for bankruptcy. The NBA turned itself around through shrewd business acumen, which tied professional basketball's fortunes to the expanding horizons of the multinational corporation and the new arena of satellite communications. Nike, as an exemplar of multinationals' increasingly agile organizational structures, blended technological innovation, marketing, and nimble, spatially defused modes of cross-border operation, particularly the exploitation of cheap and well-regimented labor available in Asian factories. As globalization reshaped the geography of manufacturing, it also created new markets and consumerist fantasies. With satellite television, US media corporations developed global audiences and made the NBA into the stuff of excitement, desire, and sociability worldwide.[22] In this dizzying, technologically driven opening of economic possibility, Jordan's image of show-stopping athleticism and on-court commanding presence provided the currency and cultural capital that generated ever-ballooning profits for Nike and transformed US sports into a global commercial enterprise.

As NBA basketball drew in new viewers and the Swoosh garnered more and more consumer dollars, Jordan himself carefully, albeit not without missteps, tended to his public image and cultivated a strictly apolitical persona. Promoting his brand and maximizing his wealth appeared to be MJ's priorities. As LaFeber observed, Jordan remained conspicuously silent when it came to labor conditions in Chinese factories, a relative dearth of opportunities for African Americans within Nike's corporate structure and the NBA's managerial echelons, and stark episodes in which the consumerist allure of Air Jordan sneakers fomented inner-city violence among covetous teens. Jordan also carefully avoided comment on election campaigns that challenged entrenched racism, such as Harvey Gantt's attempt to unseat Jesse Helms in North Carolina's US Senate race in 1990. Although critics might have wished for Jordan to emulate Jackie Robinson, Muhammad Ali, Arthur Ashe, or other African American athletes who transcended the entertainment value of sport with their political commitments, perhaps it could be said that Jordan perfectly embodied the economic values of an evolving neoliberal era. LaFeber grimly noted that in a United States where a third of African American children lived in poverty, Nike's and Jordan's signature advertising slogan, "Just Do It," rang of empty promise for young people who had to make their way in a postindustrial US economy. Meanwhile, as Nike navigated the era of Title IX by creating sneaker lines for US women, female workers on production lines in Asia suffered from low wages, gendered labor exploitation, and worse.[23]

LaFeber was not the first writer to cover these intertwined developments, but as a historian of US foreign relations, he tied the dynamics of late twentieth-century capitalism, new technologies, and sports-based consumerism to US globalism in the form of soft power and US cultural hegemony. As commodities, NBA basketball, Nike sneakers, and Jordan's image of transcendent athletic prowess added up not merely to a multibillion-dollar industry. Combined they captivated foreign consumers across global ideological fault lines with US popular culture's universalist messages of energy, innovation, and abundance. Jazz and Hollywood films in the 1920s and the "Coca-colonization" of the Cold War had already long served US interests, but "the power of that popular culture," LaFeber contended, "multiplied with the technological marvels" that appeared in the 1960s and 1970s. The globalized power of media, combined with ever more sophisticated marketing and advertising techniques, shaped "the language, eating habits, clothes and television watching of peoples around the earth."[24] But even as critics in the 1980s and 1990s, like their predecessors earlier in the twentieth century, indulged in endless handwringing about US cultural imperialism, LaFeber also identified the ease with which new communications technologies would defy centralized control and US dominance. In his postscript to the book's post-9/11 edition, he pointed to the expanded reach of global terrorism as evidence of the limits of US consumer culture to win allegiances abroad. In addition, he highlighted the deft ability of Osama bin Laden's al-Qaeda network to exploit satellite phones, the internet, traditional Islamic financial systems that were largely invisible to big corporate banks and to governments, and a global media environment more diverse and less penetrable by US capital than most Americans acknowledged.[25] The promise of US soft power ultimately gave way to the more open-ended, multivalent proclivities of global capitalism itself.

Culture, Knowledge, and the Decentering of US power

LaFeber's approach to technology and foreign relations focused on a United States always ready to capitalize upon innovation as a means of building and maintaining hegemony, while his account of global sport assumed that economic and cultural power radiated inexorably outward from an American core. In both cases he wrote within a US-centered tradition of historical writing, in which the global constituted an ecosystem in which US leaders strategized and US power flowed. Other societies either accepted or resisted the US juggernaut, but the extent to which these societies—or states—actively shaped the form and direction of technological systems, knowledge production, popular culture, or global capitalism remained largely unexamined territory.

More recent scholarship on US foreign relations has challenged such US-centric narratives and analytical framings. Historians have increasingly sought to decenter the United States in favor of globalized conceptions of power that emphasize local agency and the complex dynamics by which ideas, goods, economic conditions, and political relationships evolve through reciprocal interchanges instead of top-down, unidirectional impositions or diffusion from metropolitan centers. The new social history of the 1960s and 1970s, with its concern for the rich texture of everyday lived experience and agency from below, did more than simply expand the range of historical actors who attracted scholarly attention—it upended assumptions about the hegemonic nature of power. For example, where historians of chattel slavery had once taken for granted the helplessness and powerlessness of persons subjected to involuntary servitude and systematic violence, Eugene Genovese's pathbreaking study, *Roll, Jordan, Roll*, lavishly described a social world of the enslaved that was rife with deliberate obfuscation and other forms of resistance. The enslaved subverted authority at every turn, whether by maintaining spiritual traditions, celebrating the virtues of the trickster, denying remunerative labor to slaveholders, attempting escape, or otherwise contesting the totalizing aspirations of a brutal institution.[26] A decade later, James C. Scott's influential *Weapons of the Weak* similarly emphasized peasants' challenges to the self-proclaimed logics of markets and modern state power, not just through formal political organization, but through everyday acts of resistance.[27] Such writings made it increasingly difficult to insist on either the top-down power of the state or the overweening influence of a global superpower within the international system, when resistance, creative adaptation, and the resilience of local folkways shaped the nexus between state, society, and international relations even amid massive asymmetries of power.

By the 1990s, right around the time that LaFeber was tackling Michael Jordan and global capitalism, other scholars increasingly appealed to cultural encounter and cross-pollination as analytical alternatives to cultural imperialism, in which symbiotic processes of give-and-take made foreign and local parties both actors and acted upon. For example, one important intervention in the field, the edited volume *Close Encounters of Empire: Writing the Cultural History of U.S.-Latin American Relations* (1998), stressed the blurred boundaries, messy exchanges, and local remaking of meanings that defined the US cultural presence in Latin America, even as the United States undeniably possessed and mobilized unmatched economic, political, and military resources. The challenge, as the volume's editors put it, required recognizing "the unequal nature of Latin America's encounter with the United States" while simultaneously offering "a history that is culturally sensitive, multivocal, and interactive."[28] Rumors in the Dominican Republic about worm-infested "gringo chicken," for example, suggested that US-style production methods had become dominant in the Dominican poultry industry but also that Dominicans were resisting agri-business and its globalizing, homogenizing threat to the locally raised patio chickens that betokened home, family, and Dominican identity.[29]

By the late 1990s, anthropological studies of big-name US brands and their reception abroad also focused on how locals made their own meanings out of novel cultural experiences. The contributors to James L. Watson's edited volume *Golden Arches East: McDonald's in East Asia* (1997) uncovered a broad range of responses to fast-food burger consumption that had little to do with corporate executives' imagined marketplace or the ability of US corporate capitalism to Americanize foreign consumers. In a 1990s Beijing still adjusting to the corrosive novelty of global capitalism, McDonald's encompassed diverse meanings: a worldly dining experience that created a fictive and vicarious sense of travel to foreign capitals, an encounter with Western-style modernity for parents anxious to acquaint their children with a new economic future, or a clean, well-lit, and wholesome site for long dates by young people. Even local appetites responded differently to the same number of calories. The *xianbing*-like burger, with a bun rather than rice, was a mere snack that left one hungry for a full meal afterward.[30] Such localized findings suggested that for people in East Asia, whatever it might mean for them to eat a McDonald's hamburger, they are not simply falling victim to a homogenizing Coca-colonization. From this perspective, a cultural study of Nike sneakers, basketball, and NBA superstardom might look very different in a close ethnographic study of consumption, adaptation, and localization than it did in LaFeber's account of US-driven market penetration and the unidirectional emanation of US cultural power. A soft power so malleable that it is endlessly transmutable and transmissible might, in the end, not be power at all.

Global histories and their decentering ethos have remade historical understandings of knowledge production as well. In his SHAFR address, LaFeber presciently accorded knowledge production a central role in his account of technology and US power, and he did so at a time when historians of science had only just begun to go beyond traditional intellectual history approaches to incorporate society, politics, and global power relations into their analyses.

History of science originally imagined the field as studying the unfolding of an analytical architecture of scientific ideas according to their own internal logic of discovery, and with a premium placed on understanding the emergence of key concepts, such as Newtonian mechanics, Darwinian evolution, or Einsteinian relativity theory. The sciences of state and empire—mapping, navigation, mineral and botanical surveying, and early ethnography—did not rate highly according to traditional tastes. When LaFeber pointed to the work of Lucile Brockway and Lewis Pyenson on science, technology, and global imperialism, he was referencing important early contributions in what has become a burgeoning field in the two decades since.[31]

Questions about expertise, scientific knowledge production, alternative ways of knowing, and their interplay with systems of power now occupy center stage within the history of science, and they are also commonplace in histories of capitalism and of US foreign relations. Moreover, the old notion that innovations in scientific knowledge simply spread outward from metropolitan European centers in the early modern period and nineteenth century, or from the United States and other major powers in the twentieth century, has been replaced by decentering tendencies that emphasize the contact zones and cultural encounters in diverse parts of the world that reshaped scientific understandings.[32]

Postcolonial analyses, for example, have stressed that the forms of modern science associated with colonial rule did not emerge from self-proclaimed advanced societies introducing enlightened order to unruly nature and alien peoples; instead they grew from the cultural encounters in which novel mixtures of peoples and places coalesced to generate new ideas.[33] Historical studies of natural history, taxonomy, and empire have also shown how projects of classification inevitably relied upon local knowledge of species, particularly the traditional names and cultural markers attached to them, even as the creation of universalized knowledge through taxonomical practice demanded the erasure of vernacular understandings.[34] The much-vaunted internationalism of science itself, as one of us has written, arguably has less to do with an intrinsic universalism of scientific knowledge than it does with global geopolitical conditions that either facilitate or obstruct flows of knowledge.[35] As with culture, scientific knowledge, too, moves through intricately dispersed entanglements and crosscurrents of ideas, information, and constructions of meaning.

From the standpoint of more recent scholarship, LaFeber's depiction of a new global capitalism and US consumerist fantasies emanating outward from a US center of Jordanesque prowess and US corporate clout overlooked multiple sources of agency and myriad contestations at work. The rapidity with which the edifice of post–Cold War, US-driven capitalism and consumerism has crumbled perhaps suggests that its claims of power were no more than a façade in the first place. In 2019, in response to pressure from the Chinese government and business counterparts in China, the NBA hastily disavowed the tweets of the Houston Rockets' general manager in support of protests against a Chinese crackdown on political freedoms in Hong Kong.[36] China's twenty-first-century capacity to actively shape professional basketball, and not merely buy into it, was nowhere on the horizon in LaFeber's depiction of a Jordan-centered economic and cultural juggernaut twenty years earlier. The power to enter new markets, however, is also the power to be consumed by them.

Turning Outward and Returning Inward

Amid the decentering impulses of 1990s scholarship, LaFeber's account of capitalism and US cultural relations remained decidedly US-centric, as did almost all of his work. The most prominent exception came with *The Clash*, in which LaFeber relied on translators, including one of the coauthors here, in order to wrestle with Japanese-language sources and explore on level terms both countries' intertwined histories of engagement and imperial expansion within a complex, ever-shifting global order. As Anne L. Foster and Andrew Rotter have elaborated in chapter 7 in this book, the approach opened LaFeber to opprobrium from East Asia experts. His earlier studies of Latin America, by contrast, focused more exclusively on US power and the human suffering it inflicted. Consequently, as Lorena Oropeza and James F. Siekmeier have noted in chapter 6 in this book, Latin Americanists sometimes took issue with *Inevitable Revolutions* and *The Panama Canal* for denying agency to the peoples, societies, and governments of the region. One-way depictions of cultural expansionism also risk neglecting all of the ways in which individuals and societies do not act as passive recipients of popular culture, but instead create new meanings out of everyday cultural encounters. As one of us has shown in a study of baseball, for example, Japanese people made "America's game" into their own.[37] More recently, Japan's championship roster in the 2023 World Baseball Classic, which sported five "Japanese" US Major Leaguers, including half-Dutch American Lars Nootbaar and half-Iranian Darvish Yu, illustrates how attempting to engrave "nationality" into cultural formations is fundamentally a fool's errand.

One can therefore lament the limitations of US-centered approaches and take issue with how they overestimate the level of US power and control in shaping global structures, institutions, and processes. Yet as much as LaFeber acknowledged and admired the enlarged scope of US international history, its increasingly multi-archival, multilingual, globe-trotting source base, its willingness to engage race, gender, and culture in novel ways, and its openness to contemplating power from below, he also remained, at heart, a US historian.[38] As he unabashedly declared in the tenth edition of *America, Russia and the Cold War*, his work, "unlike part of some recent, so-called trans-national historical approaches . . . examines the United States not as part of larger trans-national movements. . . . [Instead] it sees the United States as the major world power which often unilaterally decides much else, including on a large scale, who lives and who dies."[39] LaFeber hewed to this line throughout his career because, at the end of the day, he believed that understanding capitalism and its imperatives was not an end in itself but instead a means for interrogating the basic viability of the United States as a political project.

Questions about the state of US democracy and society were never far from LaFeber's thoughts. They formed the heart and soul of his scholarly endeavors. In *The New Empire* (1963), US expansionism in the late nineteenth century emerged precisely from the economic dilemmas of an industrial society and the desperate hope that trade abroad could preserve political institutions at home. Four years later, the first edition of *America, Russia, and the Cold War* flagged the disturbing trend toward concentrated executive authority and expansion of presidential power.[40] At a raw moment on May 12, 1970, when LaFeber spoke at Cornell's Bailey Hall to advocate publicly on behalf of the Hatfield-McGovern Amendment just days after the Kent State killings, he led not with foreign policy disasters but with "the onrushing problems of racism and poverty in American society." Racism and poverty, he declared, were the first and foremost of the "historical forces . . . bearing down upon us" that together endangered the cohesiveness of US society and a better future in the United States. "Racism, poverty, inequality, and injustice," he warned, "threaten over the long-run to wound this society more deeply than the Indo-China War itself." Notably, when LaFeber updated the essay four days later, he referenced not Kent State, but the deaths of two Black students shot by the National Guard at Jackson State College in Mississippi on May 15.[41]

The inseparability of the nation's foreign policy from its domestic political trajectory became increasingly explicit in LaFeber's writings in the 1980s and 1990s. In response to "Marking Time," Charles Maier's famously critical analysis of the state of diplomatic history as a research field, LaFeber in 1981, instead of embracing Maier's call to internationalize the study of US foreign relations, doubled down on the need to focus on the United States. He pointed first to the reality of asymmetries of power and cautioned, "What he [Maier] terms 'international history' . . . will be misleading if all parts of the 'system' are considered to be roughly equal, or if the influence of that system on the United States is assumed to be as great as the American influence on the system."[42] That observation, however, was mere prologue to LaFeber's primary concern with understanding foreign relations in order to comprehend the US political system's prospects at home. US diplomatic historians rightly kept the United States at the center, he argued, because "the United States is the only nation in the twentieth century that continually exercises power globally while maintaining a liberal system at home. The parts cannot be separated, and Americans have increasingly believed that the exercise of their power overseas is necessary to keep their domestic system functioning."[43]

The need to reckon with the imbrication of foreign and domestic, moreover, constituted a political imperative and not a matter of mere intellectual interest. LaFeber contended that amid an already visible decline in US power, scholars faced "an additional responsibility"—namely, the need "to examine how a liberal domestic system arose within, and became an integral part of, the global empire, and how the liberalization and individual freedoms can be protected as national power suffers a relative, inevitable decline." This central problem, LaFeber concluded, was mission enough: "To trace the rise and relative decline of a three-century-old-empire, while relating its story to a unique political experiment in self-government, is a sufficient agenda for any discipline."[44]

This preoccupation with the meaning of empire abroad for democracy at home, which LaFeber explained so eloquently in his response to Maier, became increasingly urgent for LaFeber as the years went by. It drove his indignation and anger, in *Inevitable Revolutions*, over US coercion and hideous violence in Central America, and it expressed itself in more measured form in his textbook, *The American Age*, with the expansion of presidential power as one of the book's key themes. Hence, his 1999 SHAFR address hinted at the challenges the information revolution posed for political systems, while *Michael Jordan and the New Global Capitalism* concluded with an acute sense of uneasiness about what late 1990s capitalism would mean for political life in the United States and its democratic experiment.

In his SHAFR presidential lecture, LaFeber previewed what he called "the Tocqueville problem." As Eric Alterman and Richard H. Immerman discuss in chapter 9 of this book, LaFeber would explicate this conundrum more fully several years later in his final book, *The Deadly Bet*. In his preliminary examination, he concentrated on George Shultz's perspective to convey the sense that although the information revolution undermined states that sought tight control over the flow of ideas, its decentralizing tendencies also exacerbated the unwieldy free-for-all that characterized democratic societies. As Tocqueville observed, democracy's fractious nature militated against the political consensus necessary for a nation to pursue an effective foreign policy. But technology, LaFeber speculated, offered a potential end run around the restraints of a fickle and unruly citizenry that could be goaded by the unifying forces of warfare and national security crises but easily turn impatient in the longer term. "The Raytheon Doctrine"—that is, the ability to engage in asymmetric warfare by using air power rather than risking American lives on the ground—promised to "make fighting certain wars from thirty thousand feet sufficiently effective, and safe for the society deploying the weapons, that domestic politics are rendered less important."[45]

Meanwhile, in *Michael Jordan and the New Global Capitalism*, LaFeber closed his account of a first post–Cold War era that rode the giddy wave of global, basketball-fueled capitalism and other frenzied manifestations of US consumerism with a sober note about markets and politics. The end of the Cold War had allowed free-market ideology to run riot, but skepticism about the inherent symbiosis between liberal political institutions and market economies was already brewing in Russia and China. Americans, too, had qualms about the market as a basis of a viable social order. LaFeber quoted financier and philanthropist George Soros on this point: "We can have a market economy, but we cannot have a market society."[46] The limits of consumerism and the market as a way of life and a foundation for a cohesive, functional society would only become increasingly apparent over the next two decades. As LaFeber himself observed in a 2007 email to James F. Siekmeier that if he were to revise the book, he would "make the anti-globalization points sharper" and focus even more closely on the disruptive social and political effects of late twentieth- and early twenty-first-century globalization.[47]

Alongside profound and disturbing economic shifts, US militarism also loomed as an existential threat to US democracy. As LaFeber observed in the book's expanded edition, the terrorist attacks of 9/11 replaced post–Cold War complacency with novel opportunities for US misadventurism in the world and its attendant risks for domestic political order. The George W. Bush administration's global war on terror demanded that Americans accept heightened secrecy, broader governmental latitude, and reduced state accountability. By whipping up the politics of fear, LaFeber wrote, the White House "triggered a crisis for US democracy in the aftermath of September 11." He explained, "Having developed new technologies that had entranced much of the world, Americans had to begin surrendering a right to know what their soldiers were doing on battlefields, and what their government was doing in its policies. The new global capitalism that Americans had taken for granted as their fast-food, sports-obsessed culture penetrated other nations, had turned to threaten some fundamentals of American democracy itself."[48] Combined with the technological and organizational capacities of the new global capitalism, elevated state power now put democracy at further peril.

One can ask whether LaFeber overreached in trying to tie al-Qaeda's version of global terrorism to global capitalism and a struggle of "capital versus culture."[49] His more fundamental concern with the antidemocratic tendencies of US foreign relations, however, requires consideration. Insofar as we, the coauthors of this chapter, have chosen to decenter the United States in our own work, it is because we have sought to move away from US exceptionalism and explore the commonalities in states' navigation of globalized political, economic, and cultural relations. LaFeber, however, wanted to understand what was distinctive about the United States, particularly the struggles of a nation that from the beginning portrayed itself as a new kind of self-governing society, yet time and again pursued policies and ways of being in the world that empowered authoritarianism abroad and placed liberal democracy at home in jeopardy.

At one level this tension may be innate to a settler colonial nation that aspired to be an "empire of liberty" in the late eighteenth and early nineteenth centuries, or a United States that thought it could forestall political crisis at home by pursuing empire abroad in the late nineteenth and early twentieth centuries, only to discover that it could not have a liberal economic order without illiberal interventionism. The steadily accumulating tendency toward expanded executive authority and its resistance to oversight, especially when it came to foreign policy, further eroded democratic possibility and stymied democratic practices throughout the twentieth century. Yet the suspicion of centralized power at the heart of LaFeber's work is also characteristic of US political culture, especially for someone who grew up with the instinctive populism of the Midwest. He cautioned that despite the seductive manifestations of US soft power courtesy of Microsoft, Nike, and Michael Jordan, and the perennial appeal of economic and military hard power, Americans could not sustain a global empire without incurring its costs, both for themselves and for others. That, in the end, is the dilemma not just of Tocqueville but of US exceptionalism.

Notes

1. Sandy LaFeber email to Jessica Wang, February 13, 2023 (on LaFeber's basketball-playing days and her first visit to Walkerton); Anne L. Foster email to Jessica Wang, February 14, 2023, and Lloyd Gardner email to Jessica Wang, February 14, 2023 (on Cornell football); email, Richard Immerman email to Jessica Wang, February 13, 2023, and Lloyd Gardner email to Jessica Wang, February 14, 2023 (on the OAH baseball outing); email, Suzanne Kahl email to Jessica Wang, February 19, 2023 (on the 2015 playoff game). All these emails are in authors' possession.

2. Suzanne Kahl email to Jessica Wang, February 19, 2023, in authors' possession.

3. See, for example, Emily S. Rosenberg, *Spreading the American Dream: American Economic and Cultural Expansion, 1890–1945* (New York: Hill and Wang, 1982).

4. As Sayuri Guthrie-Shimizu has succinctly emphasized, historians need "to appraise the nature of American power in international relations in a less America-centric way," and to understand "'American expansionism' . . . as a local instantiation of global patterns and processes." Guthrie-Shimizu, *Transpacific Field of Dreams: How Baseball Linked the United States and Japan in Peace and War* (Chapel Hill: University of North Carolina Press, 2012), 4–5.

5. For a good introduction to the Anthropocene and its analytical counterpart, the Capitalocene, see Christophe Bonneuil and Jean-Baptiste Fressoz, *The Shock of the Anthropocene* (London: Verso, 2016); originally published as *L'événement Anthropocène: La terre, l'histoire et nous* (Paris: Éditions du Seuil, 2013).

6. Sven Beckert and Christine Desan, "Introduction," in *American Capitalism: New Histories* (New York: Columbia University Press, 2018), 1–32, esp. 6–9, 13, and 31n53 (quotation at 9).

7. Seth Rockman, "Review Essay: What Makes the History of Capitalism Newsworthy?," *Journal of the Early Republic* 34 (Fall 2014): 441–42.

8. Peter James Hudson in "Interchange: The History of Capitalism," *Journal of American History* 101 (September 2014): 535.

9. Paul A. Kramer, "Embedding Capital: Political-Economic History, the United States, and the World," *Journal of the Gilded Age and Progressive Era* 15 (2016): 331–62, quotations at 333.

10. Kramer, "Embedding Capital," 339–40.

11. Consider the opening chapter of *The Tragedy of American Diplomacy*, in which Williams mined the commercial and industrial press in order to reconstruct the economic anxieties of the 1890s and the search for foreign markets as a critically necessary outlet for US surplus production. William Appleman Williams, *The Tragedy of American Diplomacy*, 50th anniv. ed. (New York: W. W. Norton, 2009; orig. pub. Cleveland: World, 1959), chap. 1.

12. E. P. Thompson's magisterial study *The Making of the English Working Class* (New York: Vintage Books, 1966; orig. pub. 1963) was not just a pathbreaking work that helped launch the new social history, but also an incisive critique of neoclassical economics. Gabiel Kolko's *The Triumph of Conservatism: A Reinterpretation of American History, 1900–1916* (New York: Free Press of Glencoe, 1963) likewise attempted to denaturalize US industrial and finance capitalism by stressing the political circumstances, particularly a corporate liberal alliance between business and political elites, that undergirded the evolution of the US economy in the early twentieth century.

13. Kramer, "Embedding Capital," 333–34.

14. Williams, *Tragedy of American Diplomacy*, 93–94, 104–7.

15. Walter LaFeber, "Presidential Address: Technology and U.S. Foreign Relations," *Diplomatic History* 24 (January 2000): 1–19, quotation at 1; LaFeber, *The American Age: United States Foreign Policy at Home and Abroad since 1750* (New York: W. W. Norton, 1989), 18–21; George C. Herring, *From Colony to Superpower: U.S. Foreign Relations since 1776* (New York: Oxford University Press, 2008), 14–16.

16. LaFeber, "Technology and U.S. Foreign Relations," 3–7, quotation at 6.

17. LaFeber, "Technology and U.S. Foreign Relations," 8–12, quotation at 10.

18. For more on Shultz, see Philip Taubman, *In the Nation's Service: The Life and Times of George P. Shultz* (Stanford, CA: Stanford University Press, 2023).

19. LaFeber, "Technology and U.S. Foreign Relations," 12–17.

20. On the Theranos story, including both Shultz's and Henry Kissinger's enthusiasm for Holmes, see John Carreyou, *Bad Blood: Secrets and Lies in a Silicon Valley Startup* (New York: Knopf, 2018). Holmes was ultimately convicted on fraud charges, and in May 2023 she began serving an eleven-year prison sentence. Bobby Allyn, "Elizabeth Holmes Has Started Her 11-Year Prison Sentence," National Public Radio, May 30, 2023, https://www.npr.org/2023/05/30/1178728092/elizabeth-holmes-prison-sentence-theranos-fraud-silicon-valley.

21. Walter LaFeber, *Michael Jordan and the New Global Capitalism*, new and expanded ed. (New York: W. W. Norton, 2002), 13 (orig. pub. 1999).

22. LaFeber, *Michael Jordan*, 47–48, 54–74.

23. LaFeber, *Michael Jordan*, 50–51, 90–94, 144, 147–48.

24. LaFeber, *Michael Jordan*, 18, 19.

25. LaFeber, *Michael Jordan*, chap. 7.

26. Eugene D. Genovese, *Roll, Jordan, Roll: The World the Slaves Made* (New York: Pantheon Books, 1974).

27. James C. Scott, *Weapons of the Weak: Everyday Forms of Peasant Resistance* (New Haven, CT: Yale University Press, 1985).

28. Gilbert M. Joseph, "Close Encounters: Toward a New Cultural History of U.S.–Latin American Relations," in *Close Encounters of Empire: Writing the Cultural History of U.S.–Latin American Relations*, ed. Gilbert M. Joseph, Catherine C. LeGrand, and Ricardo D. Salvatore (Durham, NC: Duke University Press, 1998), 3–46, quotation at 15.

29. Lauren Derby, "Gringo Chicken with Worms: Food and Nationalism in the Dominican Republic," in Joseph et al., *Close Encounters of Empire*, 451–93.

30. Yunxiang Yan, "McDonald's in Beijing: The Localization of Americana," in *Golden Arches East: McDonald's in East Asia*, ed. James L. Watson (Stanford, CA: Stanford University Press, 1997), 39–76.

31. Here LaFeber cited Lucile Brockway, *Science and Colonial Expansion: The Role of the British Royal Botanic Gardens* (New York: Academic Press, 1979); Lewis Pyenson, *Cultural Imperialism and Exact Sciences: German Expansion Overseas, 1900–1930* (New York: Peter Lang, 1985); and Pyenson, *Civilizing Mission: Exact Sciences and French Overseas Expansion, 1830–1940* (Baltimore: Johns Hopkins University Press, 1993). Brockway's study was particularly ahead of its time and garnered mixed appraisals upon publication. In one of the few unreservedly positive reviews, Susan Sheets-Pyenson notably described the book as offering "an exciting alternative to studies of modern science that ignore the 'world system' of capitalism." Sheets-Pyenson, review of *Science and Colonial Expansion*, *Isis* 72 (September 1981): 495–96. The book experienced a second life after its republication by Yale University Press in 2002, and it is now recognized as a classic work on natural history, colonialism, and state power.

32. The classic and now much-maligned "diffusionist" argument comes from George Basalla, "The Spread of Western Science," *Science* 156 (May 5, 1967): 611–22.

33. See, for example, Kapil Raj, *Relocating Modern Science: Circulation and the Construction of Knowledge in South Asia and Europe, 1650–1900* (New York: Palgrave Macmillan, 2007), orig. pub. Ranikhet: Permanent Black, 2006.

34. Geoff Bil, "Indexing the Indigenous: Plants, Peoples and Empire in the Long Nineteenth Century" (PhD diss., University of British Columbia, 2018); Kathleen C. Gutierrez, "The Region of Imperial Strategy: Regino García, Sebastián Vidal, Mary Clemens, and the Consolidation of International Botany in the Philippines, 1858–1936" (PhD diss., University of California, Berkeley, 2020), chap. 5.

35. Jessica Wang, "Knowledge, State Power, and the Invention of International Science," in *Knowledge Flows in a Global Age: A Transnational Approach*, ed. John Krige (Chicago: University of Chicago Press, 2022), 31–73.

36. Daniel Victor, "Hong Kong Protests Put N.B.A. on Edge in China," *New York Times*, October 7, 2019, updated October 21, 2021, https://www.nytimes.com/2019/10/07/sports/basketball/nba-china-hong-kong.html; Jordan Valinsky, "How One Tweet Snowballed into the NBA's Worst Nightmare," CNN Business, October 11, 2019, https://www.cnn.com/2019/10/09/business/nba-china-hong-kong-explainer/index.html. On the intertwined history of the NBA and China, see Brook Larmer, *Operation Yao Ming: The Chinese Sports Empire, American Big Business, and the Making of an NBA Superstar* (New York: Gotham Books, 2005).

37. Guthrie-Shimizu, *Transpacific Field of Dreams*.

38. On his understanding of the state of the field, see, for example, Walter LaFeber, "The World and the United States," *American Historical Review* 100 (October 1995): 1027–31.

39. Walter LaFeber, *America, Russia, and the Cold War, 1945–2006* (New York: McGraw Hill, 2008), xii.

40. Walter LaFeber, *America, Russia, and the Cold War, 1945–1966* (New York: John Wiley, 1967), esp. 60, 77, 79, 92, 104, 168, 182, 197, 258.

41. Walter LaFeber, "The Indochina War," typescript, "Speech Delivered by Professor Walter LaFeber of Cornell University, May 12, 1970, at Bailey Hall (Revised and expanded, May 16)," www.smu.edu/cph/LaFeber.

42. Walter LaFeber in "Responses to Charles S. Maier, 'Marking Time: The Historiography of International Relations,'" *Diplomatic History* 5 (Fall 1981): 362. LaFeber made a similar point more than a quarter of a century later, when he warned, "A major problem with transnational history or, as many job descriptions now call a variation, international history, is that, in the effort to be inclusive, the realities of power are too often avoided. Those realities are sometimes sacrificed to the illusion of perspective." LaFeber, "Some Perspectives in U.S. Foreign Relations," *Diplomatic History* 31 (June 2007): 424.

43. "Responses to Charles S. Maier," 363.

44. "Responses to Charles S. Maier," 363, 364.

45. LaFeber, "Technology and U.S. Foreign Relations," 14, 18–19. Curiously, although LaFeber referred directly to "the Tocqueville problem" in his SHAFR address, and it constituted a through-line in his famous lectures in his survey course on US foreign relations, he did not use the phrase in *The Deadly Bet*.

46. LaFeber, *Michael Jordan*, 164.

47. Walter LaFeber email to James Siekmeier, November 18, 2007, in authors' possession.

48. LaFeber, *Michael Jordan*, 183.

49. LaFeber, *Michael Jordan*, 162. For an example of another perspective, Middle East historian James L. Gelvin has suggested that al-Qaeda had more in common with

anarchism than with any kind of ideology of civilizational struggle, and that its anti-globalization leanings appealed "to those alienated not only from the current global economic and state systems, but from non-anarchist alternatives to amending those systems as well." Those sources of alienation, he contended, were not primarily about the stultifying homogenization of an Americanized global culture of consumerism. Rather, they reflected the real material deprivations of late twentieth- and early twenty-first-century globalization. On this point, he also expressed regrets about some of his own earlier writings on globalization and al-Qaeda. Gelvin, "Al-Qaeda and Anarchism: A Historian's Reply to Terrorology," *Terrorism and Political Violence* 20 (2008): 563–581, quotation at 577.

CHAPTER 9

Confronting the Tocqueville Problem
The Deadly Bet

ERIC ALTERMAN AND RICHARD H. IMMERMAN

Walter LaFeber's final book, *The Deadly Bet: LBJ, Vietnam and the 1968 Election*, has received far less attention than *The New Empire, Inevitable Revolutions*, or his other monographs. He wrote it not to challenge historians and other scholars but to inform and stimulate undergraduates. This was appropriate. While LaFeber was an extraordinary scholar and mentor to many graduate students, his undergraduate teaching was legendary. For the two of us, he is best remembered as the greatest college teacher from whom we were fortunate enough to learn.[1] Yet anyone reading *The Deadly Bet* will quickly recognize that it is much more than a postmortem on a failed presidency or a tragic war. Instead it is a meditation on Alexis de Tocqueville's 1835 classic *Democracy in America* and a cautionary tale about the fate of "the American experiment" at the dawn of the new millennium. In this sense *The Deadly Bet* is a fitting capstone to his career.

Approaching the end of his more than forty-year tenure at Cornell University, LaFeber deployed his meticulous scholarly methods and captivating expository style to provide an insightful, provocative, and yet intelligible guide to the political events of one of the pivotal years in US history. With the benefit of more than a half a century of hindsight, it can now be seen that 1968 exposed a nexus of forces that today threaten the very survival of the United States as a democratic nation. LaFeber could not have anticipated all the dangers that bedevil our nation in the era of the attempted coup against the US Constitution by Donald Trump and his supporters. LaFeber's history, nevertheless, gives us the tools to understand better how we in the United States came to this perilous juncture in our history.

In this chapter we assess LaFeber's argument that the turmoil and tragedy that defined the United States in 1968 was a manifestation of a deep-seated problem in US democracy that Alexis de Tocqueville identified 150 years earlier. The upheaval that the United States experienced in 1968, LaFeber writes persuasively, reflected the convergence of internal and external forces that seriously threatened US values and institutions. We identify those forces and examine how LaFeber historicizes and contextualizes them. In addition, we explain why reading *The Deadly Bet* enhances our understanding of the precarious conditions the United States confronts today.

Alexis de Tocqueville observed long ago that in the conduct of foreign affairs, "democratic governments do appear decidedly inferior to others." Foreign policy, he lamented, requires none of the good qualities peculiar to democracy but instead demands the cultivation of those sorely lacking. Democracies find it "difficult to coordinate the details of a great undertaking and to fix on some plan and carry it through with determination," and have "little capacity for combining measures in secret and waiting patiently for the result."[2] LaFeber calls this phenomenon "the Tocqueville problem in American history." How, he wondered, can a "democratic republic, whose vitality rests on the pursuit of individual interests with a minimum of central governmental direction, create the necessary national consensus for the conduct of an effective, and necessarily long-term, foreign policy?"[3]

The Deadly Bet explicates, illustrates, and analyzes the United States' Tocqueville problem. Quick to compliment those few public intellectuals who "[took] Tocqueville seriously," most of whom he called "intelligent conservatives," like the Cornell-educated Francis Fukuyama, LaFeber spent his entire career wrestling with, and encouraging all Americans to wrestle with, the incompatibility between the United States' democratic ideals and the wars its elected leaders choose to fight.[4] It is a small book with a big story, and at first glance, a departure from the pattern of his publications during the previous two decades. Beginning with his history of the Panama Canal treaty, written when the nation was debating its merits during Jimmy Carter's presidency, LaFeber dedicated himself to offering readers deeply researched historical analysis of problems facing the nation at that moment in time.[5] His histories were not "presentist" in the sense that the term is often used; that is, they were not overly influenced and therefore distorted by "present" debates in the United States. Rather, his books provided pundits, policymakers, and the public alike opportunities to situate those debates in their appropriate historical context.

In *The Deadly Bet* this practice is there only by implication.[6] LaFeber sticks to the story that took place nearly four decades earlier. Yet he succeeds in providing helpful historical context not only for 2005, when the book was published and US soldiers were returning in body bags from Iraq, but also for 2023 and beyond. By doing so, as is appropriate for a book aimed at undergraduate students, *The Deadly Bet* reflects the pedagogical style and techniques that attracted thousands of students—and often their friends, parents, and siblings—to LaFeber's lectures. LaFeber was a storyteller par excellence. Writing in his characteristic fluid, accessible, and unpretentious style, his narratives, punctuated by deep dives into personalities and laced with anecdotes, irony, and humor, seize the readers' (and audience's) attention even as they inform, raise questions, and provoke thinking otherwise. *The Deadly Bet* makes learning, and critical analysis, both pleasurable and unavoidable.

Because of LaFeber's expertise in and devotion to pedagogy, the contemporary relevance of *The Deadly Bet* has increased over time. With racial unrest and violent crime, white supremacy, political polarization, and inequality on the rise; social and economic reform at a standstill; education and housing in crisis; the US public's confidence in their institutions and respect for their government leaders dangerously low and falling; deceit and misinformation accepted as standard and the media widely distrusted; and democracy under siege—*The Deadly Bet* provides readers with a "usable past" by locating the antecedents to the current crises in President Lyndon Johnson's failed response to the crises of his time.

Throughout the book LaFeber identifies and explores the United States' Tocqueville problem through the prism of the Vietnam War and the 1968 election. He uses the metaphor of a "hurricane" to capture the power and consequences of the war, with its protests and days of rage, carnage, and disillusionment; the theatrical and tragic presidential campaigns and election; and the explosive synergy of their juxtaposition. The year 1968 began with the Tet Offensive in Vietnam, during which the enemy briefly breached the walls of the US Embassy in Saigon and took over the South Vietnamese capital. As the year evolved, it was marked with riots, assassinations, two chaotic presidential conventions, and the death of the hope that liberal reform could cure what ailed the nation. These forces bore down on the United States, LaFeber writes, "until, like an overloaded electrical circuit, the society began to explode."[7] The denouement was the election of Richard Nixon, the notorious red-baiter and Dwight D. Eisenhower's former attack-dog, as US president. That outcome spelled doom for the Great Society and 1960s-style liberalism.⁸ "Resembling other such storms, this hurricane had causes that can be analyzed and continue to be instructive in the twenty-first century," reads the introduction.⁹

To frame the hurricane, LaFeber deploys the concept of betting. "[During the] 1960s US presidents made a life-or-death bet that Americans could fight a long war against a determined foe and, at the same time, maintain order and protect constitutional rights in their own society," *The Deadly Bet* begins. Johnson, albeit not alone in this, staked his future, and that of the United States, on the un-Tocquevillian belief that the people of the United States "had the patience, foresight, and willingness to sacrifice—and the necessary money and power to fight a vague, undeclared, unending war abroad while carrying out reforms at home." If that belief was wrong, US society "could be torn apart, and two hundred years of U.S. democracy endangered, by the war they had to fight."¹⁰ Johnson was wrong and lost the bet, wounding US society so deeply it has yet to recover. When it comes to the state of US democracy, that wound has metastasized to potentially fatal proportions.

War, observed Tocqueville after traveling across the United States a century earlier, had been chosen by President Andrew Jackson as an instrument for promoting expansion, prosperity, and democracy. LaFeber repeatedly emphasizes that Johnson was following Jackson's script, and at the same cost. The French aristocrat warned that "all those who seek to destroy the liberties of a democratic nation ought to know that war is the surest and shortest means to accomplish it." A nation, he cautioned, "couldn't put its strength into a war and keep its head level: it had never been done."¹¹

"Expand or die" became what LaFeber described in his must-read *The American Age* as the "shadowy underside of American thinking."¹² It was likewise a central theme of his lectures to thousands of Cornell undergraduates. And yet war also was the shortest and simplest way to continue the United States' historically unprecedented growth. This was possible—and especially tempting—because, as Tocqueville wrote, it was "chiefly in foreign relations that the executive power of the nation finds occasion to exert its skill and its strength." In foreign policy, the president "possesses almost royal prerogatives."¹³ And so Johnson had the tools at his disposal to make his "deadly bet."

Any number of Johnson's predecessors understood the dangers this power represented. Few, nevertheless, managed to avoid the trap. James Madison condemned war as the root of all evil—the precursor of taxes and armies and all other "instruments for hiring the many under the domination of the few."¹⁴ Still, he led the country into a potentially ruinous war in 1812.

Abraham Lincoln did virtually everything he could to avoid civil war. LaFeber quotes him in *The American Age* warning:

> The provision of the Constitution giving the war-making power to Congress was dictated, as I understand it, by the following reasons: Kings had always been involving and impoverishing their people in wars, pretending generally, if not always, that the good of the people was the object. This our [Constitutional] convention understood to be the most oppressive of all Kingly oppressions; and they resolved to so frame the Constitution but that no one man should hold the power of bringing this oppression upon us.

Yet Lincoln went to war to preserve the union, and in doing so shuttered newspapers, suspended habeas corpus, imprisoned dissidents, and otherwise wielded unprecedented executive power that challenged constitutional rule.[15]

Then there was Woodrow Wilson. LaFeber does not cite or quote Randolph Bourne in either *The Deadly Bet* or the *American Age*. Yet he was surely familiar with Bourne's writings, particularly his essay "War Is the Health of the State," which prior to his succumbing to the Spanish flu pandemic in 1918, Bourne intended for inclusion in his unfinished *The State*. The essayist, social critic, and public intellectual lamented that Wilson's decision to enter World War I predictably undermined US democracy. The "moment war is declared," Bourne wrote, the "mass of people" come to resemble a "herd." Through "some spiritual alchemy," they allow themselves "to be regimented, coerced, deranged in all the environments of their lives, and turned into a solid manufactory of destruction toward whatever other people may have, in the appointed scheme of things, come within the range of the Government's disapprobation." The "State" transforms into "a repository of force, determiner of law, arbiter of justice."[16]

Wilson, a scholar of the US Constitution and an avowed progressive, recognized the danger. He knew that by committing US forces and resources to a fight to make the world safe for democracy, he was putting US democracy at risk. "Once lead this people into war," Wilson famously said only hours before requesting a declaration from Congress, "and they'll forget there ever was such a thing as tolerance. To fight you must be brutal and ruthless, and the spirit of ruthless brutality will enter into the very fiber of our national life."[17] He too, nevertheless, chose war.

LaFeber labeled the perception of the separation between the foreign and domestic realms in US politics as "artificial and perilous."[18] Lyndon Johnson agreed. He felt that if he did not prove himself a strong leader in Vietnam and

CONFRONTING THE TOCQUEVILLE PROBLEM

face down the communists there, he could not expect to pass his ambitious domestic agenda on behalf of the poor whites and people of color, for whom he saw himself as savior. He knew full well before committing himself to war that his decision could jeopardize his grandiose hopes and dreams for his presidency. Fighting a land war 8,000 miles away in a country few people in the United States could locate on a map against an elusive enemy who never remained in one place and blended into the same civilian population US forces allegedly sought to protect was, almost by definition, a loser's bet. LBJ nonetheless felt powerless to avoid the commitment. Terrified of the future that lay before him, he confessed to his frequent confidant and future biographer, Doris Kearns Goodwin:

> All my programs. All my hopes to feed the hungry and shelter the homeless. All my dreams to provide education and medical care to the browns and the blacks and the lame and the poor. . . . History provided too many cases where the sound of the bugle put an immediate end to the hopes and dreams of the best reformers: the Spanish-American War drowned the populist spirit; W.W.I. ended WW's New Freedom; WWII brought the New Deal to a close. Once the war began, then all those conservatives in Congress would use it as a weapon against the Great Society. You see, they never wanted to help the poor or the Negroes in the first place. But they were having a hard time figuring out how to make their opposition sound noble in a time of great prosperity. But the war. Oh, they'd use it to say that they were against my programs not because they were against the poor—why, they were as generous and as charitable as the best of Americans—but because we had to beat those Godless Communists and then we could worry about the homeless Americans.[19]

Johnson felt boxed in. He had convinced himself that his most deeply felt yearnings for the country and for his own role in the history books would come to nothing if he showed weakness in Vietnam. "If I don't go in now," he admitted early on in the war, "they won't be talking about my civil rights bill, or education or beautification. No sir, they'll push Vietnam right up my ass every time. Vietnam. Vietnam. Vietnam. Right up my ass."[20]

Johnson predictably bet wrong and eventually found himself forced to forego running for a second full-term as president. LaFeber dissects the drivers of Johnson's decision to withdraw from the 1968 presidential campaign and seek an exit from Vietnam in a way that not only exposes the Tocqueville problem but also highlights the role of people, ideas, and the domestic underpinnings of US foreign policy. As with the lectures that the coauthors of this chapter recall so vividly, LaFeber organizes his narrative around portraits of bigger-than-life individuals, each of whom receives a full chapter. They are, in order, William Westmoreland, Eugene McCarthy, Lyndon Johnson, Martin Luther King Jr., Robert Kennedy, Richard Nixon, Hubert Humphrey, George Wallace, and the Vietnamese leader Nguyen Van Thieu. LaFeber could have chosen different subjects. Alternatives range from antiwar leaders such as Tom Hayden and Abby Hoffman to Black Panthers such as Huey Newton and Bobby Seale to feminists such as Carol Hanisch and Robin Morgan, who organized an iconic protest in 1968 against the Miss America pageant in Atlantic City. But he "read his room." LaFeber did not seek to resurrect Great Man history; he exploited biography as a strategy for making the history of US foreign relations appealing and intelligible to undergraduates.

What is more, just as he did in his celebrated *New Empire* and standing-room only lectures, LaFeber uses individuals to highlight and analyze the themes and dynamics he judges most vital to influencing the course of events that make up the historical moment that he sought to illuminate.[21] One of the most important of LaFeber's themes is the role those individual personalities play in shaping historical outcomes. He appreciated the constraints and opportunities generated by broad societal and international forces. Notwithstanding the evolution of the historiography on the history of US foreign relations during LaFeber's career, and his support of its many innovations, he remained comfortable featuring individuals in his narratives. The word "bet" in his title signals that individuals make choices, and the choices one individual makes are never identical to the choices another person would make in the same position or circumstance. Individuals, therefore, matter. Would John Kennedy have handled Vietnam as his successor did? Almost certainly not![22]

LaFeber positions Johnson's choice of war at the center of his narrative.[23] The choices of the other eight individuals featured in the book were to varying degrees reactions to or products of Johnson's choice. LaFeber's primary concern, however, as was Tocqueville's, is less with the choices themselves than with the consequences of those choices for US liberty, democracy, and cohesion. In different ways each of the individuals LaFeber writes about either reflected or contributed to the consequences of Johnson's choosing war, and those consequences were uniformly detrimental.

LaFeber's most constant and pervasive theme is the war's impact on the United States' historic problem with race. The issue was rarely absent in his scholarship; how could it be? The pursuit of white supremacy has never been far from the United States' simultaneous pursuit of empire. The theme emerges most prominently in his chapter on Martin Luther King Jr. Yet it suffuses the book as LaFeber shows the many ways that Johnson's losing bet in Vietnam exacerbated US racial fissures despite Johnson's sincere desire to improve the lives of Black and Hispanic populations in the United States.

The Tocqueville problem worked in reverse as well: the failure to conduct a foreign policy openly and honestly and thereby retain the democratic support of US citizens resulted in its subversion from within. Riots, counter-riots, police brutality, and a commitment to nihilist violence on almost every side of the political divide frustrated Johnson's grand dreams of a Great Society. Cities went up in flames. Across the world demonstrators burned American flags and declared their support for our enemies. The very people to whom Americans believed they were proving their "credibility" viewed the endeavor with a mixture of horror and disgust, while their adversaries found strength and opportunity in the United States' weakened, divided condition. By the time it was over, the war had caused many of the unhappy events it was designed to prevent, and then some. What's more, the period of unchallenged US economic supremacy—the astounding engine of prosperity upon which all dreams of social progress rested—was sputtering to the point of near collapse. Manufacturers were packing up and shipping jobs to places with plentiful supplies of cheap labor and few, if any, laws against creating pollution. These losses put additional pressure on the lives of those who saw their own dreams for their futures going up (literally) in smoke.

Johnson had recognized that as a southerner, appearing as a moderate on civil rights was crucial to his national aspirations. John F. Kennedy could never have selected a segregationist as his running mate. Having grown up and risen to power in a political culture that many historians call American apartheid, Johnson had to tread carefully in his support for the political rights of Black voters. As senate majority leader, he used all of his legendary political acumen to pass a civil rights bill that, despite its extreme modesty, few observers at the time thought possible. Johnson's commitment to civil rights grew over time, however, and soon became central to what he understood would be his legacy. Delivering his first State of the Union address on January 8, 1964, Johnson boldly declared, "This Administration today, here and now, declares unconditional war on poverty in America."[24]

With these words, the president became his own man, no longer merely carrying out his predecessor's agenda. Five months later, speaking to students at the University of Michigan, Johnson gave one of the landmark speeches in the history of US liberalism. "For in your time," he said to the young students gathered around him, "we have the opportunity to move not only towards the rich society and the powerful society, but upward to the Great Society."[25]

Here LBJ articulated a fundamental faith of 1960s liberalism: the United States had entered a potentially perpetual cycle of economic abundance, and that abundance could be deployed to ensure the creation of a fairer and more equal society without any segment of it being asked to endure significant sacrifice.[26] (This was yet another "bet" that was to go south on LBJ.) "Will you join in the battle to give every citizen the full equality which God enjoins and the law requires?," Johnson asked the nation. "Will you join in the battle to build the Great Society, to prove that our material progress is only the foundation on which we will build a richer life of mind and spirit?"[27]

This was liberalism as a Sunday sermon, and it perfectly captured Johnson's limitless aspirations for his presidency. His decisiveness was the expression of a boldness rare in liberalism, but at the same time the hubris of his ambition begged for trouble. Amid the soaring ideals and inspirational rhetoric, LBJ and his advisors paid little attention to the potential unintended consequences of what Johnson and his administration assumed to be noble purposes. Johnson believed that the United States' bounty, and his now nearly limitless power, gave him not just the opportunity but also the responsibility to try to right almost all of society's wrongs. He planned to do all this while fighting a land war in far-off Southeast Asia in a country alien to most people in the United States.

As Tocqueville had foreseen, however, war drained and then strangled the momentum for reform and social justice. Increased unrest and violence marked the interval between the 1957 and 1964 Civil Right Acts. LaFeber recounts that in 1963 white supremacist Byron De La Beckwith gunned down NAACP field officer Medgar Evers in his driveway outside Jackson, Mississippi. The same year Police Chief Theophilus Eugene "Bull" Connor turned fire hoses and snarling dogs on children marching for civil rights in Birmingham, Alabama, the same city where members of the Ku Klux Klan had bombed a Black church, murdering four young girls. Enacted in the wake of such violent and virulent racism, Johnson's Great Society civil rights legislation appeared to many Black activists as a mere band-aid, one that was further undermined by the fact that the federal government drafted a disproportionate number of young Black men to fight in Vietnam, even as wealthy and well-connected white parents sent their sons, armed with student deferments, off to college and graduate school.

On March 15, 1965, Johnson addressed the nation in language that shocked and delighted even his most liberal supporters. "Their cause must be our cause, too," he said of the marchers being beaten in Alabama, Mississippi, and elsewhere, "because it is not just Negroes, but really all of us who must overcome the crippling legacy of bigotry and injustice. And we shall overcome."[28] Yet just five days after the August 6 signing ceremony for the 1965 Voting Rights Act, massive riots broke out in Watts, an area of Los Angeles, when a Black driver was pulled over by a policeman for drunk driving. Violence there, televised across the land, continued for five more days, signaling that the United States was not about to "overcome" just yet. Liberalism was finding itself embattled on all sides—from angry Black Americans, leftists who thought not enough was being done (and who thought liberals were too often condescending toward those they wanted to "help"), and conservatives who resisted the growth of the federal government and who wanted a firmer and tougher reaction to the lawlessness and lack of respect for legitimate authority that they believed liberals had unleashed.

The president's contrite 1967 State of the Union address offered little to please liberals. Steven M. Gillon points out that "only once in his 1967 State of the Union Message, a thirteen-page single-spaced text, did he refer to the Great Society." James Reston in the *New York Times* called it a speech of "guns and margarine," a play on "guns and butter" that referred to the cost of the ever-expanding war in Vietnam and the reduced spending for domestic priorities that appeared to accompany it. (Johnson had committed nearly half a million US troops to the conflict by this time.) In LBJ's own language, that "bitch of a war" in Vietnam destroyed "the woman I really loved—the Great Society." It was Vietnam, not his support for civil rights or the Great Society, that ultimately did in Johnson. The historian Allen Matusow writes: "Vietnam cut short the rush to the Great Society, smashed his consensus, widened the credibility gap, and made him one of the most hated chief executives in a hundred years."[29]

Martin Luther King Jr., to whom LaFeber devotes chapter 4, had emerged from the 1955 Montgomery bus boycott as the leader and voice of an increasingly powerful nonviolent civil rights movement. Addressing a crowd of thousands at Montgomery's Holt Street Baptist Church as both the pastor of a neighboring church and president of the Montgomery Improvement Association, King, in his soon-to-be celebrated oratorical style, had put the United States on notice that African Americans had lost patience with the pace of reform. "[There] comes a time when people get tired of being trampled over by the iron feet of oppression," King had warned. "There comes a time . . . when people get tired of being plunged across the abyss of humiliation, where they experience the bleakness of nagging despair. . . . There comes a time."[30]

King struggled long and hard before finally speaking up against the war; Johnson had championed the cause of civil rights beyond anything King had imagined possible. Moreover, King, like Johnson, had more than enough to worry about at home. He hoped to bring his movement to the North with his Poor People's Campaign, but it was making little progress. Radical and violence-promoting challengers were growing in power and influence, and J. Edgar Hoover's FBI was serving him a daily diet of harassment and torment. By 1966, though, King decided that he could keep silent no longer. He directed the Southern Christian Leadership Conference (SCLC), established in 1957 with King as the first president, to draft a statement protesting that the "promises of the Great Society top the casualty list of the conflict [in Vietnam]."³¹

On April 4, 1967, exactly one year before the day of his assassination, King announced from the pulpit of Riverside Church in New York City that the war had left the US commitment to civil rights and social justice "broken and eviscerated as if it were some idle political plaything of a society gone mad on war." Johnson's policies were "taking the black young men who had been crippled by our society" and sending them "eight thousand miles away to guarantee liberties in Southeast Asia which they had not found in Southwest Georgia and East Harlem." The United States, he concluded, had become "the greatest purveyor of violence in the world today."³²

LaFeber notes that even as King gravitated toward a more radical critique of US society, embracing not only an antiracist agenda but also an "explosive" one based on class, young African Americans in ever-greater numbers were forsaking the reverend's commitment to nonviolence. Frustrated by broken promises and trapped in a cycle of poverty, they switched their allegiance to the proponents of Black Power. LaFeber highlights Stokely Carmichael, who as national chairperson of the Student Non-Violent Coordinating Committee (SNCC) in 1966 transformed the organization and made its name into a misnomer (in 1967 Carmichael quit SNCC and joined the Black Panthers, embracing antiwhite violence and antisemitism as well). Riots erupted in cities across the nation. Throughout *The Deadly Bet* LaFeber draws on insights provided by British ambassador Sir Patrick Dean in reports to London that chronicle the growing fissures in the African American community and US society as the Tocqueville problem festered and intensified. "Moderate Negro leaders such as King [have] lost control [of the young]," Dean reported. Then, after King's assassination, Dean quoted Carmichael's description of the assassination "as the biggest mistake white America had made, and as killing all reasonable hope for the future." Carmichael went on to warn, Dean continued, that the time had arrived "for the Negro to retaliate by getting guns and carrying out executions in the street."³³

LaFeber argues that the disaffection of so many African Americans with Johnson and his Great Society program of reform, for which the Vietnam War was pivotal, was fundamental to the unravelling of US society and democratic order in the 1960s. Still, another major theme of *The Deadly Bet* is that the white backlash, political polarization, and attendant violence produced by this rejection was most decisive in giving rise to Tocqueville's nightmarish scenario. LaFeber assigns a chapter to George Wallace, who, he makes clear, must be remembered by today's Americans as more than a historical footnote. By campaigning for the presidency in 1968, Wallace became the national standard bearer not just for segregationists and white supremacists but also for those who attributed their own struggles and insecurities to perceived advances by people of color and who identified the erosion of law and order as a greater concern than either civil rights or the Vietnam War. Wallace seized on "white anger to form a political base that made him a presidential contender in 1968."[34]

While few of Wallace's supporters appreciated the relationship between the war in Vietnam and the social upheaval that they judged so threatening, LaFeber maintains that Wallace did. To be sure, he does not claim that the Alabama governor, in contrast to the bookish Eugene McCarthy, read Tocqueville. Wallace was confident that faced with Black Power advocates and antiwar protestors, the people of the United States would sacrifice their civil liberties in exchange for security. Previewing Donald Trump's first presidential campaign almost a half century later, Wallace, according to LaFeber, posited that combining a populist program with police power was the most effective response to the Tocqueville problem. As Wallace saw it, "African Americans would probably have to surrender most of their recent gains and antiwar protesters would have to be quieted," but that was an "acceptable price to pay."[35]

That millions of Americans agreed is essential to LaFeber's narrative. Especially but not exclusively in the southern states, exacerbating Wallace voters' frustrated search for security was a concomitant belief in a zero-sum outcome that defined Black advances as white defeats. For this they blamed Johnson, LaFeber maintains. "[Many] whites, especially those who had less education and made low wages, believed Johnson's administration was unfairly trying to help people of color, often at the expense of whites," he writes. The perception grew progressively more pervasive, he continues, that "the riots, black nationalist demands, and growing violence in the cities had been shaped by Johnson's attempts to protect the civil rights of minorities, especially African Americans." The politically astute Johnson recognized the power and danger of this growing "white backlash." Fueled and fanned by Wallace's campaign in 1968, white fear and anger were "splitting the nation at a very critical time."[36]

In Wallace's success LaFeber located a dystopian thread in US history presaged by the 1968 presidential campaign. Richard Nixon and his advisers, most prominently the young conservatives Kevin Phillips and Patrick Buchanan, saw in Wallace's campaign the seeds of a "Southern strategy" that exploited racial animosity on both sides to turn the South Republican. After losing the 1958 governor's race to a more rabid segregationist, Wallace vowed to put his racist and white supremacist credentials on full public display. He told an aide that he would never to be "out-n[——]" again.[37] But the Republican political consultant Lee Atwater would later argue that to be effective, rhetoric needed to change with the times. "You start out in 1954 by saying, 'N[——], n[——], n[——].' By 1968 you can't say 'n[——]'—that hurts you, backfires. So you say stuff like, uh, forced busing, states' rights, and all that stuff, and you're getting so abstract."[38]

Richard Nixon understood the need to use code words to provoke racism, so he stuck mostly to the language of "law and order." Ronald Reagan, Newt Gingrich, Mitch McConnell, and almost all nationally ambitious Republican politicians adopted this language in coded appeals to racist and racially motivated voters. Over time, the sheet dropped from their faces, and they spoke their truths. Surely Donald Trump never read *The Deadly Bet*. Still, he built on Wallace's racist rhetoric and preyed on white grievance; the Alabama segregationist and his 1968 campaign can now be seen as a prophecy of his presidency. Trump praised a murderous mob made up of neo-Nazis and Klan members and other proto-fascist "alt-right" leaders marching in Charlottesville as "very fine people," helping to lay the groundwork for the most violent attacks on police and others during Trump's coup attempt on January 6, 2021.

These themes are central to US history, albeit sometimes only as undercurrents to the more visible parts. The intense and destructive polarization, which Tocqueville had anticipated in the nineteenth century, and which previewed the United States of the twenty-first century, framed the 1968 election. There are no heroes in LaFeber's account of it; he is critical of all the candidates. Yet he is sympathetic to the Democrats because of the analytic framework he constructs. All were, to use LaFeber's word, "trapped" by the forces unleashed by the war and exploited by their Republican opponents. Johnson had bet that he could manage the war at a cost sufficiently low for him to continue to build a Great Society. Losing the bet cost him Black and white support for both the Great Society and for the war—and what's more, left no money in the budget for the enormously expensive domestic agenda he had in mind. Eventually he just gave up, defeated by his own hubris, and walked away from the presidency.[39]

Eugene McCarthy, the most consistent opponent of the war among those covered in *The Deadly Bet* and conventionally portrayed as a loser, is to LaFeber the most conscious of and sensitive to the Tocqueville problem. "Like Tocqueville a century before, McCarthy had come to the conclusion that a long conflict undermined the nation's democratic principles—and . . . thus American freedom itself—by creating an all-powerful presidency," LaFeber explains. To McCarthy, Vietnam had turned into an "endless war that would allow that president to have even more power, while student movements took out their frustration by turning either dangerously to the left or opting out through a drug-infested counterculture." His overriding concern was Tocqueville's (and

Bourne's): Finding a way to avert a long war's corruption of US democracy. His emphasis was on saving democracy, not winning the war. A decade later McCarthy published a book comparing the state of US democracy at that time to what Tocqueville observed.[40]

McCarthy perceived Vietnam as integral to the United States' growing racial divide and inner-city rioting. The centralization of power in the executive branch and the "militarization" of US life—manifest in "rising vigilantism," a "preoccupation" with "weapons of destruction," and the spread of "rifle clubs urging all civilians to be armed"—were byproducts of the war. So was the proliferating drug culture. McCarthy judged "turn on, tune in, and drop out" as a threat to democracy equal to that of the imperial presidency and the outsized influence of the military-industrial complex. LaFeber quotes extensively from McCarthy's 1968 campaign book: "For the first time since the Depression, Americans are asking whether our republic, as we know it, can survive its present course. We are not threatened with imminent attack, economic collapse, or sectional dismemberment. There is no single danger that can be precisely pinpointed. Yet all around us are signs that something is wrong." For this reason, the "peace candidate" went on, the "most important struggle for the future welfare of America is not in the jungles of Vietnam; it is in the streets and schools and tenements of our cities."[41]

McCarthy's diagnosis resonated with Americans, especially young Americans. The latter were fundamental to McCarthy's surprising showing in the New Hampshire primary, where he came within a hair of upsetting Johnson. McCarthy was better at diagnosing the Tocqueville problem than prescribing an antidote to it, however, and what he achieved in New Hampshire was not to drive Johnson from the race but to help convince Robert Kennedy to enter it. By this point Kennedy had converted to full-throated opposition to the war and defined the "root" of the upheaval that it generated as a battle for the national soul.[42]

When he lost his older brother in November 1963, Robert Kennedy went on a personal journey unlike that of any other known US politician. He studied Greek tragedy and existential philosophy. He opened his eyes to the inner-city poor trapped in places like New York's Bedford-Stuyvesant slum, the striking farmworkers organized by César Chávez, the poverty of families in Appalachia. He became fascinated with the debates of intellectuals regarding Vietnam, civil rights, and the urban crises, and began a series of seminars in his home for himself and his political allies.[43]

It was this openness—the raising of the curtain of his otherwise sheltered world to the voices of the poor and downcast—combined with the flashes he showed of his brother's charisma that led many liberals to believe that Kennedy alone had the potential to save the country from spinning off its axis into an abyss of nihilistic violence, social anarchy, and political reaction. Antiwar activists had been desperate for him to challenge Johnson, but he dithered, certain he'd have a better chance of winning in 1972 and concerned for his own safety. But as McCarthy was making his run for president known, RFK appeared on *Face the Nation* and ramped up his antiwar rhetoric: "Do we have the right here in the United States to say that we're going to kill tens of thousands, make millions of people, as we have, refugees, [and] kill women and children, as we have? I very seriously question whether we have the right."[44]

This period proved a kind of custom-made torture for Lyndon Johnson. He had done his utmost to live up to the promises and potential of John Kennedy's presidency, doing a better job than Kennedy himself in bringing his legislation to fruition. And now, here was Bobby Kennedy, returning not only to defeat him but also to destroy him personally and politically and taking the president's most trusted advisers with him.

Ironically, the very presence of Robert Kennedy had contributed to Johnson's conviction that he had no choice but to go full force into Vietnam. He told Doris Kearns Goodwin of his fear of what would have happened had he chosen withdrawal back in 1964: he dreamed of crowds coming at him crying, "Coward. Weakling. Traitor. . . . There would be Robert Kennedy out in front leading the fight against me, telling everyone that I had betrayed John Kennedy's commitment to South Vietnam. That I had let a democracy fall into the hands of the Communists. That I was a coward. An unmanly man. A man without a spine."[45]

Bobby heaped piles of scorn and abuse on Johnson, all to great applause. Who was responsible for the war, the riots, the dropouts, the drugs?, Kennedy asked. It was not "those who were calling for change," he cried to thunderous applause, his fists in the air. "They are the ones, the President of this United States, President Johnson, they are ones who divide us"[46] Now came Johnson's new nightmare, in which he was again being chased by "a giant stampede" and "forced over the edge by rioting blacks, demonstrating students, marching welfare mothers, squawking professors and hysterical reporters." Next came "[the] final straw: The thing I feared from the first day of my presidency was actually coming true. Robert Kennedy had openly announced his intention to reclaim the throne in the memory of his brother. And the American people, swayed by the magic of his name, were dancing in the streets."[47]

To an extent far beyond McCarthy, moreover, Kennedy appealed to African Americans because of what he said and who he was. For this reason, Kennedy, although forced to play catch-up with McCarthy, understood that his primary rival for the nomination was Hubert H. Humphrey, who had amassed a large lead in rounding up convention votes from individual state party bosses and organizations. Kennedy's plan, LaFeber informs his undergraduate readers, was to unite African Americans and white blue-collar workers, both of whom "knew their sons and daughters were dying in Vietnam in disproportionate numbers to the whole population," into a reconstituted New Deal coalition.[48]

Nothing demonstrates the importance of Bobby Kennedy's campaign to US liberalism—and to the United States itself—more than his performance on the awful night of the assassination of Martin Luther King, when he gave the country perhaps its most hopeful glimpse of his potential to heal the nation as its president. Speaking to a largely Black audience in Indianapolis that had not yet heard the horrible news, Kennedy gave it to them straight. Then, in a voice cracking from emotion, he spoke extemporaneously, not only from his own broken heart but also from what felt like the broken hearts of much of humanity:

> For those of you who are black and are tempted to be filled with hatred and mistrust of the injustice of such an act, against all white people, I would only say that I can also feel in my own heart the same kind of feeling. I had a member of my family killed, but he was killed by a white man. But we have to make an effort in the United States, we have to make an effort to understand, to get beyond these rather difficult times. My favorite poet was Aeschylus. He once wrote: "Even in our sleep, pain which cannot forget falls drop by drop upon the heart, until, in our own despair, against our will, comes wisdom through the awful grace of God."
>
> What we need in the United States is not division; what we need in the United States is not hatred; what we need in the United States is not violence and lawlessness, but is love and wisdom, and compassion toward one another, and a feeling of justice toward those who still suffer within our country, whether they be white or whether they be black.[49]

Indianapolis was peaceful that night; few American cities were.

Kennedy's crusade could travel only so far. LaFeber writes that the "reasons why Kennedy failed to create such a coalition goes to the heart of US politics and, indeed, the nation's history." The cost of the war in Vietnam drained the resources from the populist social and economic programs that would be required to fulfill the needs and aspirations of both Black and white Americans. In what middle- and working-class Americans perceived as a zero-sum society, Kennedy's coalition fractured along racial lines. White Americans in urban areas also tended to associate Kennedy with the antiwar protests and rioting, which they saw as menacing. It is possible, of course, that LaFeber's verdict was premature. Given enough time, Kennedy might have succeeded in "pull[ing] off a truly radical reform in both military and corporate policies." His assassin, Sirhan Sirhan, deprived the United States and the world of that chance and maybe its last, best hope.[50]

The candidate who did emerge victorious from the raucous 1968 Democratic Convention in Chicago and the subject of *The Deadly Bet*'s chapter 7 was Hubert Humphrey, the very embodiment of a US post–World War II liberalism that promoted government as the corrective to corporate greed, a job creator, and a provider of essential infrastructure. LaFeber labeled Humphrey a "national star." As a Minneapolis mayor running for the Senate twenty years earlier, Humphrey had given one of US liberalism's most consequential speeches. Addressing the attendees of that year's Democratic Convention, he thundered, his voice pitched, his fist raised: "To those who say that we are rushing this issue of civil rights, I say to them, we are 172 years too late. To those who say that this civil rights program is an infringement of states' rights, the time has arrived in America for the Democratic Party to get out of the shadow of states' rights and walk forthrightly into the sunshine of human rights."[51] At barely more than eight minutes, it was one of the shortest speeches of Humphrey's famously long-winded career—which eventually included twenty-six years in the Senate and four unsuccessful runs at the presidency—but it would transform the politics of civil rights in the Democratic Party forever. One would have to go as far back as William Jennings Bryan's 1896 "Cross of Gold" oration to find a single speech in the party's history that had galvanized so many people so powerfully on so central a political principle. And Humphrey's principle, unlike Bryan's, was a winner. The Democrats included the civil rights plank in the party's 1948 platform, leading to the departure of Strom Thurmond and the "Dixiecrats" who remained committed to white supremacy in the South and elsewhere.

But as Lyndon Johnson's vice president, Humphrey in 1968 was caught in a vice grip of his boss's making. "I don't want loyalty," Johnson once told an aide. "I want him to kiss my ass in Macy's window at high noon and tell me it smells like roses."[52] Humphrey understood this, and as vice president and presumed successor, he did his best to live up to Johnson's impossible demands. A diehard Cold Warrior, Humphrey had resolutely stood by Johnson's side in waging war in Vietnam. Not only had Humphrey's anticommunism and loyalty to everything Johnson said and did wear thin by 1968, but the president's refusal to go all in or all out on the war made Humphrey a target of the political left and as well as the right. LaFeber explains, liberals "were not used to strong, organized opposition on the left. . . . Now, under the impact of a growing antiwar movement and its belief that the Great Society program was inadequate, the left launched all-out attacks on Humphrey's liberalism on the streets and in university teach-ins." Caught in the throes of the Tocqueville problem, "Humphrey's lifelong political identity was under blistering attack."[53]

Unable to count on a shrinking liberal constituency, anathema to conservatives, and in almost all respects the odd man out in the Johnson administration, Humphrey had no choice but to suppress his doubts and support his president—as ardently on Vietnam as on the Great Society. The thousands of antiwar protesters who flooded the streets surrounding Grant Park across from the convention hall in Chicago therefore saw his first-ballot nomination as a bull sees a red flag. "All hell broke loose," LaFeber writes with typical understatement. "In his hotel room," he goes on, Humphrey watched the "Battle of Chicago, as it has been called, . . . with horror, no doubt a premonition that he was watching his chances for the presidency disappear among the clouds of tear gas." Chicago caught Humphrey in the nexus between the protracted war in Vietnam and the breakdown of US societal order. The Minnesotan has become "a symbol for antiwar riots on the streets."[54]

Humphrey's brand of liberalism played no better after Chicago. He was hoisted on the petard of an endless war that he had promoted. The belief in equality and opportunity with which he identified seemed progressively more out of reach, particularly to the African Americans and other minorities Humphrey had championed. And a safe, secure, and prosperous future was under siege by core elements of his own political party. The long odds Humphrey faced in the competition for the presidency became longer still because he faced off against Richard Nixon.

Nixon, whom LaFeber examines in chapter 6, also benefited from Wallace's candidacy. Wallace's choice of Curtis LeMay as a running mate allowed Nixon to portray himself as the moderate alternative to Humphrey's allegedly defeatist policy. When asked at his first press conference as a candidate for vice president whether he would consider using nuclear weapons in Vietnam, LeMay, as quoted by LaFeber, replied, "I would use anything we could dream up . . . including nuclear weapons if it was necessary." Once president Nixon cultivated the image of a madman with his finger on the nuclear trigger as a negotiating tactic. During the campaign, however, it was Wallace and LeMay whom journalists dubbed the "bombsy twins."[55]

Nixon, counterintuitively with an assist from Wallace, adroitly exploited Humphrey's vulnerabilities. He did not need to disclose his "secret plan" to achieve a "peace with honor" in Vietnam because Humphrey could propose no plan that could avoid bringing down upon him the wrath of Lyndon Johnson. LaFeber points out that Humphrey's motivation for supporting the war so enthusiastically in 1968 was to "return to Johnson's good graces" after angering him earlier by "gently" suggesting the administration pursue a negotiated settlement—which became Johnson's policy only after he withdrew from the race himself. Making matters worse, Nixon was able to turn the tables on Humphrey's effort to "smoke out" his secret plan. In September Humphrey pledged that once elected he would "move toward a systematic reduction in American forces" whether or not Nguyen Van Thieu's South Vietnamese government consented to join the Paris peace negotiations. Nixon immediately scored political points by labeling Humphrey's pledge a "turn and tail policy" that would preclude achieving the honorable peace that polls showed most Americans wanted. Johnson could have offered Humphrey cover; he did not.[56]

Despite all this, Humphrey had a strong chance to win at the end. Nixon had been polling comfortably ahead Humphrey, but the gap was closing, from fifteen points in September down to just two right before the election. The announcement of a Vietnam peace deal would likely have sealed Humphrey's election. Johnson had already announced a partial halt to the bombing of North Vietnam and was aggressively pursuing peace talks in Paris. Henry Kissinger sabotaged his effort. Nixon's future secretary of state, whom the Johnson team had trusted as an adviser to the talks, secretly leaked their contents to the Nixon campaign. Seeking, in Nixon's words, to "monkey wrench" any potential deal, the Nixon campaign enlisted Anna Chennault, a well-connected Republican socialite and fundraiser, to pass a message to Bui Diem, South Vietnam's ambassador to the United States. Chennault told the South Vietnamese, "Hold on. We are gonna win." When Johnson learned of Chennault's efforts via surveillance by the FBI and the National Security Agency, he called Senator Minority Leader Everett Dirksen in a fury: "It's despicable," he said. "We could stop the killing out there. . . . But they've got this . . . new formula put in there—namely, wait on Nixon. And they're killing four or five hundred every day waiting on Nixon." He then added, "I'm reading their hand, Everett. . . . This is treason." The Republican Dirksen agreed.[57]

The day before the election, Johnson called in the members of his national security team to help him decide whether to go public with Nixon's subterfuge. Just as Barack Obama would choose to keep quiet about Russian interference in the presidential election of 2016, LBJ and his advisers chose not to risk appearing to throw the election. What's more, Johnson was hardly eager to reveal his own illegal domestic spying. Finally, it is far from clear that Johnson preferred a Humphrey victory, because, ironically, he thought Nixon, the "peace candidate," would be less likely than his own vice president to give up on Vietnam. So the plot worked: South Vietnam boycotted the talks, which killed Humphrey's momentum and ensured Nixon's paper-thin electoral victory.[58]

LaFeber, accordingly, makes it explicit that while Tocqueville may not have predicted Nixon's victory, he would not have been surprised by it.[59] Nor would the French aristocrat have been shocked by the fallout from the 9/11 attacks thirty-three years later. Not long after al-Qaeda terrorists blasted the Pentagon and destroyed Manhattan's Twin Towers, the master historian returned to his time-honored theme of the US confrontation with the Tocqueville problem in order to make sense of where the nation stood as its leaders chose a path for its military response. "The trade-off of military needs, if this New War is to be successfully waged, against the requirement that Americans become associated with highly undemocratic, militaristic, even medieval, regimes," LaFeber insisted, "will have to be explained and debated." Likewise, the "tradeoff of internal security against the restriction of civil liberties (that panoply of liberties for which the war is allegedly being fought) will have to be explained and debated." And finally, the "simultaneous waging of the war against terrorism while carefully considering how Americans should think about other foreign policy problems, such as a rapidly changing China and an increasingly unstable Latin America, has to be explained and debated." LaFeber concluded with elegant simplicity: "Doing all this simultaneously challenges the Tocqueville problem with a dangerous overload."[60]

Under George W. Bush's presidency, the United States failed LaFeber's Tocqueville test no less spectacularly than it had under Lyndon Johnson and Richard Nixon in Vietnam—even more shamefully, perhaps, because it should have heeded the lessons of its previous misadventure. Then again, learning from the mistakes of the past, and applying appropriate lessons in the future, occurs with far greater frequency in the work of scholars—particularly careful, meticulous historians like Walter LaFeber—than in the policymaking of US politicians. For that reason, sadly, had he authored *The Deadly Bet* in the aftermath of Donald Trump's 2016 election, his update of the original would have demanded only minor revisions. As he so aptly notes in the final sentence of this short, masterful study: "The Ghosts survived."[61]

Notes

1. Andrew J. Rotter and Frank Costigliola, "Walter LaFeber: Scholar, Teacher, Intellectual," *Diplomatic History* 28 (November 2004): 625–35.

2. Alexis De Tocqueville, *Democracy in America* (Garden City, NY: Doubleday, 1969), 228–29.

3. Walter LaFeber, "Jefferson and American Foreign Policy," in *Jeffersonian Legacies*, ed. Peter S. Onuf (Charlottesville: University of Virginia Press, 1993), 376–77.

4. Walter LaFeber to David Maisel, August 22, 1995. We thank David Maisel for providing us with a copy of his personal correspondence.

5. Walter LaFeber, *The Panama Canal: The Crisis in Historical Perspective* (New York: Oxford University Press, 1978). LaFeber followed *The Panama Canal* with *Inevitable Revolutions: The United States in Central America* (New York: W. W. Norton, 1983).

6. Depending on the context and platform, LaFeber could be more direct. In a speech delivered in 1970 at Cornell University's Bailey Hall, where for years he taught a survey of the history of US foreign policy to many hundreds of undergraduates, LaFeber explicitly applied Tocqueville's warning to support the (George) McGovern-(Mark) Hatfield Amendment that called for the withdrawal of all US troops from Vietnam. Walter LaFeber, "The Indochina War," typescript, "Speech Delivered by Professor Walter LaFeber of Cornell University, May 12, 1970, at Bailey Hall (Revised and expanded, May 16)," www.smu.edu/cph/LaFeber.

7. Walter LaFeber, *The Deadly Bet: LBJ, Vietnam, and the 1968 Election* (Lanham, MD: Rowman and Littlefield, 2005), 7. See also David Farber, *Chicago '68* (Chicago: University of Chicago Press, 1988); Todd Gitlin, *Years of Hope, Days of Rage*, rev. ed. (New York: Bantam, 1993).

8. Eric Alterman, *The Cause: The Fight for American Liberalism from Franklin Roosevelt to Barack Obama* (New York: Viking, 2012), 59–61.

9. LaFeber, *The Deadly Bet*, 1.

10. LaFeber, *The Deadly Bet*, 1, 5.

11. Henry Steele Commager, *Commager on Tocqueville* (Columbia: University of Missouri Press, 1993), 56; LaFeber, *The Deadly Bet*, 15.

12. Walter LaFeber, *The American Age: United States Foreign Policy at Home and Abroad since 1750* (New York: W. W. Norton, 1989), 92. See also chapter 4 in this book.

13. Tocqueville, *Democracy in America*, 126; LaFeber, *The Deadly Bet*, 15.

14. LaFeber, *The American Age*, 58.

15. Daniel Farber, *Lincoln's Constitution* (Chicago: University of Chicago Press, 2003).

16. Randolph Bourne, "War Is the Health of the State," unfinished 1918 manuscript, http://fair-use.org/randolph-bourne/the-state/. See also Eric Alterman, *Who Speaks for America: Why Democracy Matters in Foreign Policy* (Ithaca, NY: Cornell University Press, 1998), 112–13.

17. Robert C. Hilderbrand, *Power and the People: Executive Management of Public Opinion in Foreign Affairs, 1897–1921* (Chapel Hill: University of North Carolina Press, 1981), 141.

18. Walter LaFeber, "The Constitution and United States Foreign Policy: An Interpretation," *Journal of American History* 74 (December 1987): 696.

19. Doris Kearns [Goodwin], *Lyndon Johnson and the American Dream* (New York: New American Library, 1976), 264.

20. David Halberstam, "LBJ and Presidential Machismo," in Jeffrey Kimball, *To Reason Why: The Debate about the Causes of U.S. Involvement in the Vietnam War* (Philadelphia: Temple University Press, 1990), 201.

21. Walter F. LaFeber, *The New Empire: An Interpretation of American Expansion, 1860–1898*, 35th anniv. ed. (Ithaca, NY: Cornell University Press, 1998).

22. Fred I. Greenstein and Richard H. Immerman, "What Did Eisenhower Tell Kennedy about Indochina? The Politics of Misperception," *Journal of American History* 79 (September 1992): 583–87.

23. Johnson was not exclusively responsible for choosing war. But as Frederik Logevall demonstrates, he could have chosen differently when he succeeded to the presidency following Kennedy's assassination. Frederik Logevall, *Choosing War: The Lost Chance for Peace and the Escalation of the War in Vietnam* (Berkeley: University of California Press, 2001).

24. Robert A. Caro, *The Years of Lyndon Johnson*, vol. 3, *Master of the Senate* (New York: Vintage, 2002), 910–89; quoted in Nicholas Lemann, *The Promised Land: The Great Black Migration and How It Changed America* (New York: Vintage, 1991), 144.

25. Quoted in Robert Dallek, *Flawed Giant: Lyndon Johnson and His Times, 1961–1973* (New York: Oxford University Press, 1998) 82.

26. Ira Katznelson, "Was the Great Society a Lost Opportunity?," in *The Rise and Fall of the New Deal Order*, ed. Steven Fraser and Gary Gerstle (Princeton, NJ: Princeton University Press, 1989), 199–200.

27. Quoted in Richard Goodwin, *Remembering America: A Voice from the Sixties* (Boston: Little Brown, 1988), 280.

28. Quoted in James Patterson, *Grand Expectations: The United States, 1945–1974* (New York: Oxford University Press, 1996), 582.

29. Steven Gillon, *Politics and Vision: The ADA and American Liberalism, 1947–1985* (New York: Oxford University Press, 1987), 190; Martin Binkin and William W. Kaufmann, *U.S. Army Guard and Reserve: Rhetoric, Realities, Risks* (Washington, DC: Brookings Institution Press, 1989) 52; quoted in George C. Herring, *America's Longest War: The United States and Vietnam, 1950–1975* (New York: Knopf, 1986), 133; Allen J. Matusow, *The Unraveling of America: A History of Liberalism in the 1960s* (New York: Harper and Row, 1984) 155.

30. Martin Luther King Jr., "The Montgomery Bus Boycott," *BlackPast*, January 12, 2012, https://www.blackpast.org/african-american-history/1955-martin-luther-king-jr-montgomery-bus-boycott/.

31. David Garrow, *Bearing the Cross: Martin Luther King, Jr., and the Southern Christian Leadership Conference* (New York: Vintage, 1986), 470. King's harassment by the FBI and outspoken criticism of the Vietnam War despite the objections of most of the SCLC leadership are major themes of Jonathan Eig's masterful *King: A Life* (New York: Farrar, Straus and Giroux, 2023).

32. Quoted in Robert Buzzanco, *Vietnam and the Transformation of American Life* (Malden, MA: Blackwell, 1999), 2.

33. LaFeber, *The Deadly Bet*, 70, 77. On Carmichael, see Perneil E. Joseph, *Stokely Carmichael: A Life* (New York: Basic Books, 2014).

34. LaFeber, *The Deadly Bet*, 94–95. See also Dan T. Carter, *The Politics of Rage: George Wallace, the Origins of the New Conservatism, and the Transformation of American Politics* (New York: Simon and Schuster, 1995).

35. LaFeber, *The Deadly Bet*, 145–46.

36. LaFeber, *The Deadly Bet*, 10, 53.

37. Peter Baker, "A Half-Century after Wallace, Trump Echoes the Politics of Division," *New York Times*, July 30, 2020, https://www.nytimes.com/2020/07/30/us/politics/trump-wallace.html.

38. *The Nation*, "Exclusive: Lee Atwater's Infamous 1981 Interview on the Southern Strategy," November 13, 2012, https://www.youtube.com/watch?v=X_8E3ENrKrQ&ab_channel=TheNation.

39. LaFeber, *The Deadly Bet*, 12, 132.

40. LaFeber, *The Deadly Bet*, 38; Eugene J. McCarthy, *American Revisited: 150 Years after Tocqueville* (Garden City, NY: Doubleday, 1978).

41. LaFeber, *The Deadly Bet*, 31–43; Eugene J. McCarthy, *First Things First: New Priorities for America* (New York: New American Library, 1968), 18–19, 21, quoted in LaFeber, *The Deadly Bet*, 42–43.

42. LaFeber, *The Deadly Bet*, 89–90.

43. Arthur Schlesinger Jr., *Robert Kennedy and His Times* (New York: Ballantine, 1978), 638–39.

44. Thurston Clarke, "The Last Good Campaign," *Vanity Fair*, June 2008, https://archive.vanityfair.com/article/2008/6/the-last-good-campaign.

45. Kearns, *Lyndon Johnson*, 264–65.

46. Jeff Shesol, *Mutual Contempt: Lyndon Johnson, Robert Kennedy, and the Feud That Defined a Decade* (New York: Norton, 1997), 425.

47. Kearns, *Lyndon Johnson*, 359.

48. LaFeber, *The Deadly Bet*, 175.

49. "Robert Kennedy on the Death of Martin Luther King," April 4, 1968, http://www.historyplace.com/speeches/rfk.htm.

50. LaFeber, *The Deadly Bet*, 93–95.

51. LaFeber, *The Deadly Bet*, 117; Hubert H. Humphrey, "1948 Democratic Convention Address," July 14, 1948, *American Rhetoric*, https://www.americanrhetoric.com/speeches/huberthumphey1948dnc.html. Humphrey has finally received the biographies he warrants, and their titles are telling. See Arnold A. Offner, *Humbert Humphrey: The Conscience of the Country* (New Haven, CT: Yale University Press, 2018); Samuel G. Freedman, *Into the Bright Sunshine: Young Hubert Humphrey and the Fight for Civil Rights* (New York: Oxford University Press, 2023); and *James Traub: True Believer: Hubert Humphrey's Quest for a More Just America* (New York: Basic Books, 2024).

52. Quoted in David Halberstam, *The Best and the Brightest* (New York: Fawcett, 1972), 434.

53. LaFeber, *The Deadly Bet*, 120–21.

54. LaFeber, *The Deadly Bet*, 128–30.

55. LaFeber, *The Deadly Bet*, 140–41; on Nixon's effort to convince the North Vietnamese to accept US terms for a settlement in Vietnam or confront a madman in control of America's nuclear arsenal, see 110; also see Zachary Jonathan Jacobson, *On Nixon's Madness: An Emotional History* (Baltimore: Johns Hopkins University Press, 2023).

56. LaFeber, *The Deadly Bet*, 122, 131. LaFeber covers Thieu's efforts to sabotage the peace negotiations in his chapter on Thieu in *The Deadly Bet*, 155–65.

57. John A. Farrell, "Nixon's Vietnam Treachery," *New York Times*, December 31, 2016, https://www.nytimes.com/2016/12/31/opinion/sunday/nixons-vietnam-treachery.html; Peter Baker, "Nixon Tried to Spoil Johnson's Vietnam Peace Talks in '68, Notes Show," *New York Times*, January 2, 2017, https://www.nytimes.com/2017/01/02/us/politics/nixon-tried-to-spoil-johnsons-vietnam-peace-talks-in-68-notes-show.html; and Farrell, "When a Candidate Conspired with a Foreign Power to Win an Election," *Politico*, August 6, 2017, https://www.politico.com/magazine/story/2017/08/06/nixon-vietnam-candidate-conspired-with-foreign-power-win-election-215461.

58. Offner, *Hubert Humphrey*, 315–36.
59. LaFeber, *The Deadly Bet*, 13.
60. Walter LaFeber, "Tocqueville, Powell, Miller, and September 11," *Historically Speaking* 3 (November 2001): 9–10.
61. LaFeber, *The Deadly Bet*, 179.

Coda

With a Bow to Walter LaFeber, "What Then Can We Say in Conclusion?"

SUSAN A. BREWER, RICHARD H. IMMERMAN, AND DOUGLAS LITTLE

The constancy of America's Tocqueville problem described by Walter LaFeber continues to haunt the makers of US foreign policy. The chapters dedicated to him in this volume illustrate the degree to which his teaching and scholarship provided both students and readers with the essential tools needed to historicize—and thereby better understand—the present. As his tough-minded, thoughtful, and accessible scholarship consistently demonstrated, the present echoes the past even if it does not repeat it. Moreover, the past informs the present even if it does not predetermine it.

Central to LaFeber's understanding of the Tocqueville problem was the viability and sustainability of the US experiment in what has proven to be an uneasy combination of liberalism, democracy, republicanism, and of course, capitalism. Writing early in the 1800s, Tocqueville was not pessimistic about the United States' future, and neither was Walter LaFeber writing 150 years later. Both men, however, understood that reconciling the individualism and the decentralization that were foundational to the birth of the United States posed a severe challenge to fashioning and conducting successful foreign policies.

As LaFeber would repeatedly note, James Madison's *Federalist No. 10* foreshadowed the degree to which effective and coherent foreign policies would be crucial to meeting the challenge of America's Tocqueville problem. By "extending the sphere," the United States could best accommodate the multiplicity of individual interests and thereby bolster a pluralistic society even as it mitigated against the tyranny of the majority and the excessive centralization of political, economic, and cultural power. "Extending the sphere" need not demand either continental or overseas expansion, but in the United States' case, it could—and did—lead to both.

The chapters of *Thinking Otherwise* fit together to produce a troubling record of US involvement in world affairs. Wars with Britain and Mexico pushed the boundaries of the continental United States to the Caribbean Sea, the Gulf of Mexico, and the Pacific Ocean. This expansion provided opportunities for the incorporation of large swaths of territory in Central and South America and Mexico to the south and Asia and the Pacific to the west into the US sphere. By the end of the nineteenth century, the United States had risen to global prominence. By the middle of the twentieth, prominence had become predominance. At the dawn of the new millennium, the United States had become the liberal global order's foremost advocate and greatest beneficiary. Once the United States emerged as a world power, US policymakers subordinated territorial conquest to increasing trade and investment, securing access to natural resources, and cultivating acquiescent foreign leadership. To achieve their goals, they preferred diplomacy, economic pressure, or the threat of force to actual armed intervention.

Even so, US presidents found numerous occasions to deploy force to serve what they believed, often incorrectly, to be in America's global interest. The war with Britain in 1812, the war with Mexico in 1848, and most notably the war with Spain in 1898 and its corollary in the Philippines, would prove pivotal to LaFeber's conception of the "New Empire." His subsequent books encompassed World War I, World War II, the Korean War, and the Vietnam War. He is most renowned for writing about a different kind of war, the Cold War, a fifty-year ideological conflict. Integral to that war were shadow wars, covert and paramilitary operations that the United States initiated across the globe; Iran, Guatemala, Cuba, Laos, Congo, Chile, El Salvador, Nicaragua, and most recently Afghanistan are among the best known, but the list continues well beyond these examples. Whether cold or hot, shadow or overt, these wars required ever increasing appropriations for defense that over time contributed to a bloated federal budget and an ever more powerful executive branch.

The root of the Tocqueville problem was the undeniable connection between the high cost—whether measured in blood or treasure—of US foreign adventures and the existential damage those adventures inflicted on America's domestic institutions, its unity of purpose, its impulses for reform, and, eventually, its democratic bona fides. This "cruel paradox" explains why the quest for security produced greater insecurity, and why Tocqueville's dilemma suffused LaFeber's lectures and his scholarship.[1] That is evident in the texts and the titles of the chapters in *Thinking Otherwise*: "Extending the Sphere," "Reconstructing the Backstory," "Thinking about Democracy," "Turning to Asia," "Demystifying Global Capitalism and US Power," and most explicitly, "Confronting the Tocqueville Problem."

In his final book, LaFeber observed that 1968's political protests, racial upheaval and violence, white backlash and polarization, political assassinations, and the demagoguery, disillusion, and despair that attended the escalation of the Vietnam War manifested not only the United States' inability to resolve the Tocqueville problem but also its refusal to acknowledge it. When *The Deadly Bet* came out in 2005, it was not as common to refer to "endless war" as it would be a decade later, yet LaFeber used the phrase early in the book.[2] There can be little doubt that the wars in Afghanistan and Iraq were very much on his mind, because he wrote and spoke about both.[3]

LaFeber spelled out the catastrophic consequences of the Iraq War in an email to Andrew Tisch in August 2008, four months before President George W. Bush announced his timetable for US withdrawal. "In my view, the invasion of Iraq turned out to be the greatest disaster in U.S. diplomacy and warfare in the last half-century, at least. It was worse than Vietnam because when we went in and pulled out of Vietnam, it made little difference in the balance of power." Regime change in Iraq, LaFeber concluded grimly, "has allowed the rise of a nuclearized Iran" and "weakened the US military to the point that Putin can humiliate both Georgia and the United States with impunity" while making Bush and his national security team "significantly less effective in handling problems in Latin America, Central Asia," and even with "our one-time allies in Western Europe."[4]

By the time that President Joe Biden finally withdrew US forces from Afghanistan thirteen years later, Russia had gone to war with Georgia and conquered Crimea. Then, two years into Biden's presidency, Russia launched a full-fledged invasion of Ukraine. Ukraine's reliance on the United States for support—for arms, munitions, missiles, tanks, aircraft, intelligence, lots and lots of money, and more—is so extensive that its war with Russia threatens to turn into another endless war. Moreover, as Sino-US competition steadily intensifies, the United States risks being drawn into a direct military conflict with China over Taiwan and the South China Sea. A similar and perhaps even greater risk is presented by Israel's assault on Gaza in retaliation for Hamas's attack on Israel in 2023. Even as the United States upholds its longstanding commitment to safeguard Israel, regional states and non-state actors threaten to drag the United States into an expanded war. The nuclear arms race and nuclear blackmail have both resurfaced. Yet even these worrisome challenges pale in comparison to that of climate change. For this the "great powers," none more so than the United States, are primarily responsible. They are, however, loathe to take more than palliative measures as we march, Zombie-like, toward climate-led catastrophe.

For the United States, the domestic repercussions of these external shocks could eclipse those of 1968. With inequality having reached such historic proportions that it now mirrors the "gilded age" that LaFeber exposed in *The Search for Opportunity*, avenues for social mobility—the backbone of the so-called American Dream—disappear into the ether. The US middle-class is shrinking. Meanwhile, white supremacist and neo-Nazi organizations with names such as the Proud Boys and Oath Keepers, supported and enabled by mainstream leaders of a Republican Party refashioned in the image of Donald Trump, roam the land, threatening people of color, LGBTQ folk, immigrants, Jews and Muslims—anyone, really, whom they deem insufficiently white, Christian, and conservative.

Lies and disinformation up to and including incitements to mass violence proliferate across countless media platforms as profitability and hyper-partisanship define the so-called MAGA movement to the point where honest debate over means and ends becomes impossible and historic trade-offs go not merely unresolved but also undiscussed. The massive US defense budget—which surpasses the combined total of the next ten largest countries in rank order—remains sacrosanct. Meanwhile, opioid addiction at home has destroyed entire communities, Black and white. That Americans have understandably lost faith—and patience—in once-hallowed institutions like the US Supreme Court as well as the other branches of government demonstrates what may prove to be an irreversible deterioration of political culture. Transparency and openness have given way to purloining classified documents, book banning, censorship, and naked bribery. Military officers become paid lobbyists for US adversaries, elected officials fabricate their entire biographies, and Supreme Court justices accept extravagant vacations as gifts. Polarization and the venality of US elected officials has consigned the adage "politics stops at the water's edge" to the ash heap of history.[5]

Defeated in his campaign for reelection in 2020, former president Donald J. Trump incited an insurrection aimed at subverting the US Constitution and denying the presidency to the victorious Joe Biden. As Trump—despite facing legal jeopardy, including federal indictments, far more severe than that of any previous president in US history—prepares to square off against Biden again in 2024, believers in his "Big Lie" remain his core constituency and the media continue to fear holding him and his supporters accountable. If elected, will Trump make an even deadlier bet than LBJ made in 1968 or than he himself made on January 6, 2021? Win or lose, the man in the red MAGA baseball cap and his tens of millions of devoted followers are a threat to US democracy more serious than any it has faced since the South started pounding Fort Sumter.

In the immediate aftermath of the 9/11 attacks, LaFeber had a premonition that the deadly bet that George W. Bush had made with his "global war on terrorism" might eventually make Tocqueville's ghost shudder. Always attentive to the irony of American history and the tragedy of American diplomacy yet appreciative of the potential humor in the story, LaFeber was a lifelong theatergoer. Following the Taliban's defeat by US forces in late 2001, he recalled the

LaFeber spent his entire career as a teacher and scholar thinking otherwise and challenging his students and colleagues to follow suit. Photo by Charles Harrington. Cornell University Library Division of Rare and Manuscript Collections.

prophetic words of one of the greatest US playwrights: "Arthur Miller once reformulated the Tocqueville problem by remarking that Americans respond to a call for righteousness if they mistake it for a call to lunch," LaFeber quipped. "The New War will be an ultimate test of Miller's skepticism, and one hopes he is wrong. Meanwhile, it might also be remembered that in the hard power world of international affairs and terrorism, there is no free lunch."[6]

Walter LaFeber was a gentle soul and a mild-mannered teacher-scholar, but he possessed a contrarian streak. During his valedictory lecture at the Beacon Theatre in April 2006, he recalled a story about the nineteenth-century British philosopher Samuel Butler. At a London dinner party, a wealthy dowager asked Butler: "Why does God tolerate historians?" Butler thought for a moment and then replied: "Well, you see Madam, it is because since God himself cannot change the past, he is obliged to tolerate historians who can."[7]

Our mentor devoted his entire career to seeking, uncovering, and disseminating new insights into the past. Over and over again, he encouraged us to challenge conventional wisdom and to think otherwise. He taught us to recognize the signs of the Tocqueville problem and to utilize our historical sensibilities to address it. He showed us that scholarship is a powerful tool with the potential to contribute to the public good. Most important, he reminded us that while there is no free lunch, there is also no giving up. That is Walter LaFeber's legacy to us, the contributors to this volume, and, we hope, to its readers as well.

Notes

1. On LaFeber's identification of the cruel paradox, see chapter 4.
2. Walter LaFeber, *The Deadly Bet: LBJ, Vietnam, and the 1968 Election* (Lanham, MD: Rowman and Littlefield, 2005), 38.
3. Examples include Walter LaFeber, "The Bush Doctrine," *Diplomatic History* 26 (Fall 2002): 543–58; and LaFeber, "The Rise and Fall of Colin Powell and the Powell Doctrine," *Political Science Quarterly* 124 (Spring 2009): 71–93.
4. LaFeber email to Andrew Tisch, August 20, 2008, in authors' possession.
5. Paul R. Pillar, *Beyond the Water's Edge: How Partisanship Corrupts U.S. Foreign Policy* (New York: Columbia University Press, 2023).
6. Walter LaFeber, "Tocqueville, Powell, Miller, and September 11," *Historically Speaking* 3 (November 2001): 10.
7. Walter LaFeber, "A Half-Century of Friends, Foreign Policy, and Great Losers," April 26, 2006, https://www.cornell.edu/video/walter-lafeber-beacon-theatre-2006.

Bibliography of Walter LaFeber's Works: How Did He Ever Find the Time?

Books

America, Russia, and the Cold War, 10 editions. New York: McGraw-Hill, 1966–2006.

The American Age: U.S. Foreign Policy Abroad and at Home since 1750. New York: W. W. Norton, 1989. 2nd edition, 1994.

The American Search for Opportunity, 1865–1913. Volume 2 in *The Cambridge History of American Foreign Relations.* Edited by Warren I. Cohen. New York: Cambridge University Press, 1993.

The Clash: U.S. Relations with Japan throughout History. New York: W. W. Norton, 1997.

The Deadly Bet: LBJ, Vietnam, and the 1968 Election. Lanham, MD: Rowman and Littlefield, 2005.

Inevitable Revolutions: The United States in Central America. New York: W. W. Norton, 1983. Expanded edition, 1984. 2nd edition, 1994.

Michael Jordan and the New Global Capitalism. New York: W. W. Norton, 1999. New and expanded edition, 2002.

The New Empire: An Interpretation of American Expansion, 1860–1898. Ithaca, NY: Cornell University Press, 1963. Thirty-fifth anniversary edition, with a new preface, 1998.

The Panama Canal: The Crisis in Historical Perspective. New York: Oxford University Press, 1978. Expanded edition, 1979. 2nd edition, 1989.

The Third Cold War. The Edmundson Lectures. Waco, TX: Baylor University Press, 1981.

Edited and Coauthored Books

America and the Cold War, 1947–1967. Editor. New York: John Wiley, 1969.

America and the Origins of the Cold War. Editor. New York: John Wiley, 1971.

America in Vietnam. Coauthor with William Appleman Williams, Lloyd Gardner, and Thomas McCormick. New York: Anchor-Doubleday, 1985; New York: W. W. Norton, 1989.

The American Century: The United States since 1890. Coauthor with Richard Polenberg and Nancy Woloch. New York: Alfred Knopf, 1973. 5th edition, 1997.

Behind the Throne: Essays in Honor of Fred Harvey Harrington. Coeditor with Thomas McCormick. Madison: University of Wisconsin Press, 1993.

The Creation of the American Empire. Coauthor with Lloyd Gardner and Thomas McCormick. Chicago: Rand McNally, 1973. 2nd edition, 1979.

Eastern Europe and the Soviet Union. Editor. Volume 2 in *Dynamics of World Power*, edited by Arthur Schlesinger Jr. New York: McGraw-Hill, 1973.

The Impact of War upon America in the Twentieth Century. Coauthor with Ernest May. B. K. Smith History Lecture. Houston: The University of St. Thomas, 1974.

John Quincy Adams and American Continental Empire: Letters, Speeches and Papers. Editor. Chicago: Quadrangle Books, 1965.

Essays

"The 1900 Election." In *History of American Presidential Elections*, edited by Arthur Schlesinger Jr. and Fred Israel. New York: Chelsea House, 1971.

"Acheson," "Kennan," "Mahan," and "Hay." In *Encyclopedia of American Biography*, edited by John Garraty. New York, 1974.

"Afterward." In *Fire from the Mountain*, by Omar Cabezas. New York: Crown, 1985. Paperback 1986.

"American Policymakers, Public Opinion, and the Cold War, 1945–1950." In *The Origins of the Cold War in Asia*, edited by V. Nagai and A. Iriye. Tokyo: University of Tokyo Press; New York: Columbia University Press, 1977.

"Burdens of the Past." In *Central America: Anatomy of Conflict*, edited by Robert Leiken for the Carnegie Endowment. Oxford: Pergamon Press, 1984.

"Congress, the Executive, and Foreign Policy (1770–1990)." In *Encyclopedia of the American Legislative System*, edited by Joel H. Silbey. New York: Scribner's, 1994.

"The Constitution and U.S. Foreign Policy: An Interpretation." In *The Constitution and American Life*, edited by David Thelen. Ithaca, NY: Cornell University Press, 1988.

"Crossing the 38th: The Cold War in Microcosm." In *Reflections on the Cold War*, edited by Stanley Hoffman et. al. Philadelphia: Temple University Press, 1974.

"Decline of Relations during the Vietnam War." In *U.S. and Japan in the Postwar World*, edited by Akira Iriye and Warren Cohen. Lexington: University of Kentucky Press, 1989.

"The Evolution of the Monroe Doctrine." In *Redefining the Past: Essays in Honor of William Appleman Williams*, edited by Lloyd Gardner. Corvallis: Oregon State University Press, 1986.

"Foreign Policies of a New Nation, 1750–1804." In *From Colony to Empire: Essays on American Foreign Policy*, edited by William Appleman Williams. New York: John Wiley, 1972.

"Foreword." In *The Virginius Affair*, by Richard Bradford. Boulder: University of Colorado Press, 1980.

"Four Essays on the Bicentennial and U.S. Foreign Policy." In *American Issues Forum*, vol. 2. Syndicated in 300 US newspapers. 1976.

"From Détente to the Gulf (1973–1992)." In *American Foreign Policy, Reconsidered*, edited by Gordon Martel. Milton Park, UK: Routledge, 1993.

"Jimmy Carter and the Iranian Hostage Crisis." In *True Stories*, edited by William Graebner. New York: McGraw Hill, 1992. 2nd edition, 1996.

"Johnson, Vietnam, and Tocqueville." In *Lyndon Johnson Confronts the World*, edited by Warren Cohen and Nancy Tucker. New York: Cambridge University Press, 1994.
"Kennedy to Carter." In *American History Reference Series*. Milwaukee, WI: MacDonald, Raintree, 1980.
"Latin American Policy." In *The Johnson Years*, edited by Robert Divine. Austin: University of Texas Press, 1982.
"Liberty and Power: U.S. Diplomatic History, 1750–1945." In *The New American History*, edited by Eric Foner. Philadelphia: Temple University Press, 1990. 2nd edition, 1997.
"NATO and the Korean War: A Context." In *American Historians and the Atlantic Alliance*, edited by Lawrence Kaplan. Kent, OH: Kent State University Press, 1991.
"The Reagan Policy in Historical Perspective." In *The Central American Crisis*, edited by Kenneth M. Coleman and George C. Herring. Wilmington, DE: Scholarly Resources Press, 1985. 2nd edition, 1991.
"Rethinking the Cold War and After." In *Rethinking the Cold War*, edited by Allen Hunter. Philadelphia: Temple University Press, 1997.
"Thomas Mann and Latin America." In *Behind the Throne: Essays in Honor of Fred Harvey Harrington*, ed. Walter LaFeber and Thomas McCormick. Madison: University of Wisconsin Press, 1993.
"The Truman Doctrine." In *The Course of U.S. History*, edited by David Nasaw. Belmont, CA: Dorsey Press, 1986.
"The Truman Doctrine." In *Encyclopedia of American Foreign Policy*, edited by Alexander DeConde. New York: Scribner's, 1987.
"The U.S. and Central America: The Perspective in History." In *Central America, Human Rights, and U.S. Foreign Policy*, edited by Dermot Keogh. Cork, Ireland: Cork University Press, 1985.

Articles

"Ah, If We Had Studied It More Carefully": The Fortunes of American Diplomacy." *Prologue*, Summer 1979, 121–31.
"The American Business Community and Cleveland's Venezuelan Message." *Business History Review* 34, no. 4 (Winter, 1960): 393–402, https://www.jstor.org/stable/3111426.
"The Background of Cleveland's Venezuelan Policy: A Reinterpretation." *American Historical Review* 66, no. 4 (July 1961): 947–67, https://www.jstor.org/stable/1845865.
"Before Pearl Harbor." *Current History* 57, no. 336 (August 1969): 65–70, 114.
"Betrayal in Tokyo." *Constitution* 6, no. 2 (Fall 1994): 4–11.
"The Bush Doctrine." *Diplomatic History* 26, no. 4 (Fall 2002): 543–58, https://www.jstor.org/stable/24914277.
"Carl Becker's Histories and the American Present." *Ezra Magazine*, Fall 2011, 8–9.
"China and Japan: A Matter of Options." *Current History* 55, no. 325 (September 1968): 153–58, 179–80, https://www.jstor.org/stable/45311964.

"China and Japan: Different Beds, Different Dreams." *Current History* 59, no. 349 (September 1970): 142–46, 178–79, https://www.jstor.org/stable/45312352.

"Comments" on "American Imperialism: The Worst Chapter in Almost Any Book." With Robert L. Beisner. *American Historical Review* 83, no. 3 (June 1978): 669–78, https://www.jstor.org/stable/1861843.

"Communication." Coauthor with David L. T. Knudson. *Pacific Historical Review* 41, no. 4 (November 1972): 568–72, https://www.jstor.org/stable/3638426.

"The Constitution and United States Foreign Policy: An Interpretation." *Journal of American History* 74, no. 3 (December 1987): 695–717, https://www.jstor.org/stable/1902149.

"The Creation of the Republican King." *Constitution* 3, no. 3 (Fall 1991): 43–53.

"An End to Which Cold War?" *Diplomatic History* 16, no. 1 (Winter 1992): 61–65, https://www.jstor.org.stable/24912175.

"An Expansionist's Dilemma." *Constitution* 5, no. 3 (Fall 1993): 4–12.

"Fred Harvey Harrington." *Diplomatic History* 9, no. 4 (Fall 1985): 311–19, https://www.jstor.org/stable/24911691.

"Inevitable Revolutions." *The Atlantic* (June 1982): 74–83, https://www.theatlantic.com/magazine/archive/1982/06/inevitable-revolutions/666196/.

"Internationalism as a Current in the Peace Movement: A Symposium." Coauthor with Sondra Herman, Manfred Jonas, Robert A. Divine, Richard D. McKinzie, and Theodore A. Wilson. *American Studies* 13, no. 1 (Spring 1972): 189–209, https://www.jstor.org/stable /40641070.

"Kissinger and Acheson: The Secretary of State and the Cold War." *Political Science Quarterly* 92, no. 2 (Summer 1977): 189–97, https://www.jstor.org/stable /2148349.

"The Last War, the Next War, and the New Revisionists." *Democracy* 1, no. 1 (January 1981): 93–103.

"The 'Lion in the Path': The U.S. Emergence as a World Power." *Political Science Quarterly* 101, no. 5 (1986): 705–18, https://www.jstor.org/stable/2150973.

"NATO and the Korean War: A Context." *Diplomatic History* 13, no. 4 (Fall 1989): 461–77, https://www.jstor.org/stable/24911792.

"A Note on the 'Mercantilistic Imperialism' of Alfred Thayer Mahan." *Mississippi Valley Historical Review* 48, no. 4 (March 1962): 674–85, https://jstor.org/stable /1893248.

"The Post September 11 Debate over Empire, Globalization, and Fragmentation." *Political Science Quarterly* 111, no. 1 (2002): 1–17.

"The Reagan Administration and Revolutions in Central America." *Political Science Quarterly* 99, no.1 (Spring 1984): 1–25, https://www.jstor.org/stable/2150256.

"The Rise and Fall of Colin Powell and the Powell Doctrine." *Political Science Quarterly* 124, no. 1 (2009): 71–93.

"Roosevelt, Churchill, and Indochina, 1942–1945." *American Historical Review* 80, no. 5 (December 1975): 1277–95, https://doi.org/10/1086/ahr/80.5.1277.

"Some Perspectives in U.S. Foreign Relations." *Diplomatic History* 31, no. 3 (June 2007): 423–26, https://www.jstor.org/stable/24916082.

"Technology and U.S. Foreign Relations." *Diplomatic History* 24, no. 1 (Winter 2000): 1–19, https://www.jstor.org/stable/249141153.

"The Tension between Democracy and Capitalism during the American Century." *Diplomatic History* 23, no. 2 (Spring 1999): 263–84, https://www.jstor.org/stable/24913741.

"Tocqueville, Powell, Miller, and September 11." *Historically Speaking* 3, no. 2 (November 2001): 9–10.

"United States Depression Diplomacy and the Brazilian Revolution, 1893–1894." *Hispanic American Historical Review* 40, no. 1 (February 1960): 107–18, https://www.jstor.org/stable/2509803.

"The World and the United States." *American Historical Review* 100, no. 4 (October 1995): 1015–33, https://doi.org/10.1086/ahr/100.4.1015.

Book Reviews

The Atlantic, American Historical Review, Business History Review, Diplomatic History, Hispanic American Historical Review, The Historian, International History Review, Journal of American History, Journal of Asian Studies, Journal of the Illinois State Historical Society, New York Times, Pacific Historical Review, Political Science Quarterly, Slavic Review, Washington Post, Wisconsin Magazine of History.

Op-Ed Essays and Articles

The Atlantic, Baltimore Sun, Boston Globe, Bulletin of Atomic Scientists, Chicago Sun-Times, Chronicle of Higher Education, Colloquium, Columbia University Human Rights Law Review, The Nation, New York Times, Newsday, Texas Quarterly, Times Literary Supplement, Washington Post.

Index

Acton, Lord John Dalberg, 15
Adams, Brooks, 18, 68
Adams, Henry, 14, 18, 91
Adams, John, 71, 96
Adams, John Quincy ("JQA"), 28, 39, 40, 53, 63, 68, 78, 133, 135, 159; and Latin America, 26, 113; and Monroe Doctrine, 7; and US continental empire, 67, 72–73
Addams, Jane, 19
Afghanistan, 100, 201, 202
Africa, 7
African Americans, 76, 183–88, 191, 193; at Cornell, 23, 124
Alaska, 68
Albany Congress (1754), 70
Alexander I, Czar, 78
Ali, Muhammad, 162
Alliance for Progress, 104, 105, 112, 113, 115, 116, 121
al-Qaeda, 163, 171, 174–75n49, 195
Alsop, Joseph, 223
Alterman, Eric, 10, 20, 223
Altschuler, Glenn, 22–23
America, Russia, and the Cold War, 7–8, 43–44, 47, 48, 82–101, 149, 168, 229
America in Vietnam: A Documentary History, 42
The American Age, 1, 19, 43, 75, 89, 120, 169, 179–80, 236
American Civil War, 63, 74
American Expansionism, 6–7, 18, 62–63, 64–67; commercial, 67–69, 73–79; territorial, 70–73, 75, 78
American Historical Association (AHA), 6, 13, 16, 29, 47, 53, 64, 91
American Revolution, 70–71, 108, 158
The American Search for Opportunity, 1865–1913, 43, 75–78, 136, 137, 203
Anti-Comintern Pact (1936), 138–39
Antifederalists, 36, 71

Arabs, 27
Arbenz, Jacobo, 114–15
Arbogast, Stephen, xiii
Argentina, 111
Aruga, Tadashi, 229
Ashe, Arthur, 162
Asia, 9, 11, 53, 135, 136, 139, 165, 167; and Cold War, 6, 7, 140; US expansionism in, 68, 77, 137, 162, 201. *See also* individual countries
Association of Southeast Asian Nations (ASEAN), 144
Atomic Bomb, 140
Atwater, Lee, 187–88

Bailey, Thomas A.: as LaFeber's teacher, 58, 61n31, 63, 132–33, 145; as popular historian, 33, 90
Baker, James A., 97
Balboa, Vasco Nuñez, 105
Balkans, 9
Banks, Ernie, 20
Baseball, 2, 9, 22, 95, 134, 141, 146, 153, 155, 167, 231
Basie, Count, 39
Basketball, 9, 153–55, 161–63, 165, 167, 170
Beacon Theatre, 12, 25–28, 29, 89, 205
Beale, Howard K., 33, 40
Beard, Charles, 34, 39, 95, 133, 149; influence on LaFeber, 13–14; and Wisconsin School, 5, 33, 85, 86
Bechtel Group, 161
Becker, Carl, 7, 14, 119; at Cornell, 13, 83, 91, 119; and *Everyman His Own Historian*, 91–93; influence on LaFeber, 13–14, 84, 101n3
Beckert, Sven, 156–57
Beeson, Mark, 142
Behind the Throne: Servants of Power to Imperial Presidents, 42

INDEX

Bemis, Samuel Flagg, 26, 65
Berger, Samuel ("Sandy"), 21, 28, 98–99
Bermuda, 70
Bernstein, Barton J., 89–90
Bethe, Hans, 4
Beveridge, Albert J., 76
Bialos, Jeffrey, xiii
Biden, Joseph R., 10, 202, 203
Billias, George, 233
Bin Laden, Osama, 163
Black Panthers, 182, 186
Black Power, 124, 186, 187
Blaine, James G., 68, 73
Blair, William D., Jr., 47
Bloom, Allan, 17, 24
Blumin, Stuart, 13
Bolshevism, 26, 87, 88–89
Bonaparte, Napoleon, 72
Borstelmann, Thomas ("Tim"), 23, 131n89
Bourne, Randolph, 180, 189
Bowers, Robert E., 63, 134–35
Brazil, 111
Brewer, Susan, 6, 19, 21, 224
British Empire, 40, 106
British Guiana, 69
Brockway, Lucile, 166, 173n31
Brown, Davis S., 133
Bryan, William Jennings, 78, 192
Buchanan, Patrick, 187
Buckley, Thomas, 118
Bullitt, William C., 27
Burr, Aaron, 17, 72
Bush, George H. W., 7–8; and end of Cold War, 90, 97
Bush, George W., 21, 91, 195; global war on terrorism, 99, 170, 204; war in Iraq, 27–28, 98, 202
Butler, Samuel, 205

Canada, 70
Capitalism, 83, 120, 133, 148–49, 200; in 19th century, 39, 108; and globalization, 9, 10, 11, 154–56, 161–63, 166–67, 170–71; history of, 156–58
Capone, Al, 27
Caraley, Demetrios James ("Jim"), 232
Caribbean Basin, 6, 8, 43, 65, 68, 69, 77, 107, 108, 111, 118, 119, 157, 201
Carmichael, Stokely, 186
Carr, E. H., 37
Carter, James Earl ("Jimmy"), 17, 116, 177
Castro, Fidel, 104

Central America, 1, 75, 135, 136, 143, 169, 201; and Cold War, 122–23; and Reagan administration, 8–9, 11, 43, 104–19, 125–26. *See also* individual countries
Central Asia, 202
Central Intelligence Agency (CIA), 21, 47, 48, 125, 131n93; in Guatemala, 115, 231
Chanler, Winthrop Astor, 74
Chávez, César, 124, 189
Cheney, Richard ("Dick"), 21, 97
Chennault, Anna, 194
Chicago Cubs, 2, 20, 22, 134, 153–54, 155, 231
Chile, 8, 111, 201
China, 11, 26, 43, 75, 135, 136, 137, 139, 140, 142, 143, 148, 202; and global capitalism, 165, 167, 170, 195; and McKinley administration, 69, 74; and Open Door Policy, 77, 138; People's Republic (PRC), 32, 141
Christianity, 94, 95–96, 100, 149
Churchill, Winston, 101
Civil Rights Act (1957), 184
Civil Rights Act (1964), 184
The Clash: US Relations with Japan throughout History, 9, 43, 46, 132, 136–49, 167
Cleveland, Grover, 17, 43, 64, 69, 73
Clinton, William ("Bill"), 9, 21, 97, 98–99
Cohen, Warren, 75
Colby, Bainbridge, 35
Cold War, 7–8, 14–15, 24, 37, 48, 63, 74, 82–83, 106, 135, 145; end of, 11, 97, 99, 100–01, 154, 161, 167, 170; origins of, 86–91, 93–94, 95–96, 158; in 1960s, 94–95; in 1980s, 44
Cole, G. D. H., 37
Cole, Wayne, 132
Colombia, 110
Combs, Jerald, 120
Committee in Solidarity with the People of El Salvador (CISPES), 121
Congo, 201
Connor, Theophilus Eugene ("Bull"), 184
Contras, 105
The Cornell Review, 18
Cornell University, 1, 3–4, 6, 136; History Department, 12–13, 83; and Willard Straight Hall takeover (1969), 23–24, 25, 94–95
Corson, Dale, 4, 23–24
Costa Rica, 105, 107, 114, 115, 117
Costigliola, Frank, 1, 7, 29, 225
Cott, Nancy, 16

Coulter, Ann, 18–19
Crapol, Edward, 66
The Creation of the American Empire, 42
Crichton, Michael, 136
Cronon, William, 157
Cuba, 66, 73, 74, 75, 77, 108, 135, 201, 231; and Bay of Pigs Invasion, 22; and Castro's revolution, 104, 115; and McKinley administration, 69, 74; and Reagan administration, 8
Cuban Missile Crisis, 48
Current Documents (State Department publication), 48, 49, 59n5
Curti, Merle, 33, 40, 133
Curtin, Philip, 40
Czechoslovakia, 115

Darvish, Yu, 167
The Deadly Bet, 10, 14, 169, 176–95, 202
Dean, Patrick, 186
De La Beckwith, Byron, 184
Democratic Party, 192–94
Desan, Christine, 157
Deutscher, Isaac, 37
Dewey, George, 66
Diem, Bui, 194
Dilthey, Wilhelm, 37
Dirksen, Everett, 194
Dollar Diplomacy, 77
Dominican Republic, 77, 165
Dos Passos, John, 44
Dos Santos, Theotonio, 111
Doub, James, 16
Downs, Donald, 24
Drea, Edward, 142
Dreizen, Alison, xiii, 29
Dulles, John Foster, 90, 115
Dunne, Finley Peter, 147

Eastern Europe, 87–88
Economic Determinism, 16–17, 35, 158
Edelman, Eric, xiii, 21
Edwards, Jonathan, 28, 93, 95–96
Einhorn, Robert, xiii
Eisen, LizAnn Rogovoy, xiii
Eisenhower, Dwight, 5, 13, 87, 115, 179
Eisenhower Doctrine, 41
The Elements of Style (book by Strunk and White), 53–54
Ellington, Duke, 39
El Salvador, 8, 104, 105, 118, 126, 201
Emerson, Rupert, 110
Engel, Jeffrey, 7, 20, 226

ESPN, 9
Evers, Medgar, 184

Falcoff, Mark, 120
Faulkner, William, 39
Federal Bureau of Investigation (FBI), 185
Federalist No. 10, 62, 71, 93, 200
Federalists, 36
Fels, Anthony, 16
Field, James A., Jr., 65
First World War. *See* World War I
Fitzgerald, F. Scott, 84
Florida, 70
Ford, Gerald R., 5, 97
Ford Foundation, 34
Foreign Relations of the United States (FRUS), 5, 37, 47, 48, 49, 50–52, 57, 59n2
Foster, Anne, 9, 21, 227
Fox, Richard Wightman, 93
France, 135, 136
Franklin, Benjamin, 63, 70, 78
Freedom of Information Act, 51, 57
Freeman, Adm. Rowland G., 52–53
Freud, Sigmund, 39
Fried, Daniel, 21, 98
From Colony to Empire: Essays in the History of American Foreign Relations, 70
Fromm, Eric, 37
Frost, Robert, 70
Fukuyama, Francis, 177

Gaddis, John Lewis, 60n19, 133
Gallagher, John, 64
Gandhi, Mohandas K., 124
Gantt, Harvey, 162
Gardner, Lloyd C., 4, 22, 63, 90, 225, 228; friendship with LaFeber, 5, 13, 86, 153, 231, 233; midwestern background of, 132–33
Gardner, Nancy, 36, 41
Gaza, 202
Geertz, Clifford, 147–48
Gelvin, James l., 174–75n49
General Services Administration (GSA), 52
Genovese, Eugene, 13, 164
Gentleman's Agreement (1906), 138
Georgia (nation in Caucasus), 202
Germany, 89, 96, 136, 138
Gillon, Steven M., 185
Gingrich, Newt, 188
Globalization. *See* Capitalism
Gluck, Carol, 142
Good Neighbor Policy, 114

INDEX

Gorbachev, Mikhail, 7, 90, 97, 100–01
Grandin, Greg, 78
Grant, Ulysses S., 17
Great Britain, 5, 27, 74, 78, 135, 138, 140, 201
Great Society, 179, 183–84, 185, 186, 188, 193
Green, David, 3, 228
Gresham, Walter Q., 73
Guam, 69
Guatemala, 8, 105, 119, 201; and Eisenhower administration, 114–15; and Reagan administration, 104, 118
Guthrie-Shimizu, Sayuri, 9, 21, 136, 142, 229

Hacker, Andrew, 21
Hadley, Stephen, xiii, 21, 28
Haiti, 8, 78
Halle, Louis, 88
Hamas, 202
Hamilton, Alexander, 39, 72, 159
Hanisch, Carol, 182
Hanna, Mark, 39
Hannigan, Robert, 6, 230
Hanover College, 3, 12, 63, 134, 153, 155
Harriman, Averell, 88
Harrington, Fred Harvey, 40, 42, 44, 91, 120–21, 133, 228; and George F. Kennan, 89; as LaFeber's mentor, 13, 15, 32, 33–37, 58, 63–64, 83, 84–86, 90, 119, 149
Harris, Townsend, 146
Harrison, Benjamin, 68, 73
Harvard University, 14, 21, 85, 100
Hatfield-McGovern Amendment, 168, 196n6
Hawaii, 73, 75
Hawthorne, Nathaniel, 39
Hay, John, 74, 77, 78
Hayden, Tom, 182
Healy, David, 34
Hearn, Lafcadio, 146
Hearst, William Randolph, 66
Hegel, G. W. F., 44
Helms, Jesse, 162
Hemingway, Ernest, 36, 39
Henry, Patrick, 71
Herring, George C., 89
Hesseltine, William B., 33, 133
Hicks, John, 133
Historical Advisory Committee ("HAC"). See US Department of State
Hitler, Adolf, 119
Hoffman, Abby, 182
Hoganson, Kristin, 123, 134
Holloway, Thomas, 111, 124

Holmes, Elizabeth, 161, 173n20
Honduras, 105
Hoover, Herbert, 39
Hoover, J. Edgar, 185
House, Edward M., 17
Hubble, Jackie, 230
Hudson, Peter James, 157
Human Rights, 116
Humphrey, Hubert, 182, 192–94
Hunt, Michael, 148
Hussein, Saddam, 99

Immerman, Richard, 10, 16, 52, 153, 231
India, 34
Indochina, 55, 135. See also Vietnam War
Inevitable Revolutions: The United States in Central America, 8, 43, 46, 104–07, 110–16, 118–22, 125–26, 143, 167, 169, 176, 234
Informal Colonialism. See Neodependency
Institute for Advanced Study (Princeton, New Jersey), 225
Iran, 121, 201, 202
Iran-Contra Scandal, 121–22
Iraq, 25, 27, 28, 98, 99, 100, 124, 178, 202
Iriye, Akira, 60n19, 146
Islamic Extremism, 8
Israel, 202
Italy, 138
Iwakura, Tomomi, 146

Jackson, Andrew, 18, 179
Jackson State College, 168
Japan, 1, 5, 11, 43, 53, 56, 135; and Cold War, 136, 141; and Kennedy administration, 148; in 19th century, 137, 146; and Theodore Roosevelt administration, 138, 146, 147; in 1920s, 138; in 1930s, 138–39; and Wilson administration, 143–44, 147; and World War II, 9, 14, 139–40, 147, 149
Japanese Americans, 138, 139, 147
Jay, John, 71
Jefferson, Thomas, 14, 17, 39; and US continental expansion, 67, 71–72, 113
Jensen, Merrill, 33, 40
John, James, 230
John Quincy Adams and American Continental Empire, 72–73
Johnson, Andrew, 68
Johnson, Chalmers, 125
Johnson, Lyndon B. ("LBJ"), 22, 111, 203; and 1968 election, 192; and civil rights, 182–86, 187; and Vietnam War, 98, 115, 178–79, 180–82, 189–90, 194, 195

INDEX

Jones, Paul xiii
Jones, Thomas W., 23
Jordan, Michael, 9–10, 154, 161, 162–63, 164, 166–67, 171

Kagan, Donald, 40
Kahin, George, 21, 230
Kahl, Suzanne (LaFeber), 1
Kahn, Alfred, 24–25
Kammen, Michael, 13
Kearns Goodwin, Doris, 181, 190
Kennan, George F., 7, 18, 32, 34, 82; and Bolshevik Revolution, 89; influence on LaFeber, 83–84, 225; and Niebuhr, 94, 96
Kennedy, John F. ("JFK"), 83, 111, 183; and Alliance for Progress, 104, 112, 116, 121; and Bay of Pigs, 22; and Japan, 148; and Vietnam, 190
Kennedy, Paul, 94
Kennedy, Robert ("RFK"), 23, 182, 189–92, 225
Kent State University, 168
Kerry, John, 100
Khrushchev, Nikita, 5
King, Martin Luther, Jr., 23, 182, 185–86
Kishi, Nobusuke, 144
Kissinger, Henry, 50, 51, 90, 144, 194
Kolko, Gabriel, 13, 172n12
Korean immigrants, 138
Korean War, 48, 83, 96, 140, 201
Kosovo, 98
Kramer, Paul, 157
Kristof, Nicholas, 141, 142
Ku Klux Klan, 184
Kurds, 27
Kurosawa, Akira, 146
Kushner, Howard, 230

LaCapra, Dominick, 230
LaFeber, Sandra ("Sandy"), 1, 36, 82, 86, 153, 228
LaFeber, Scott, 1, 146
LaFeber, Walter: and academic freedom, 24, 27–28; as chair of State Department Historical Advisory Committee ("HAC"), 46, 47–53; childhood and adolescence, 12, 36, 84, 132–35; as Cornell commencement speaker (1976), 24–25; and the cultural turn in diplomatic history, 9, 10, 145, 148–49, 168, 171; as faculty colleague at Cornell, 13, 22–24, 25; and gender, 21, 123, 124, 130n81, 159, 168; at Hanover College, 3, 12, 36, 63, 134–35, 153, 155; and international history, 123, 143, 145–46, 168–69; and Latinx occupation of Day Hall (1993), 124–25; love of sports, 9, 153–55, 231; and the 9/11 attacks, 25; in retirement, 28–29; and race, 6, 8, 9, 23, 75, 117, 123, 124, 139, 145, 146–47, 148–49, 159, 168, 182, 187; SHAFR presidential address of (1999), 154, 159–61, 165, 169; at Stanford University, 4, 12, 33, 61n31, 63, 90, 132, 135, 228; as teacher at Cornell, 1–4, 15–21, 29, 40, 46, 53–54, 56, 62, 84–85, 98, 176, 178, 179; and the transnational approach to diplomatic history, 123–24, 155–56, 174n42; trip to Asia (1975), 5–6, 53–56; valedictory lecture at the Beacon Theatre (2006), 12, 25–28, 29, 89, 205; at the University of Wisconsin, 4–5, 12–13, 32–43, 63–64, 83–86, 90–91, 112, 119, 132, 135, 149; and Vietnam War, 22, 95, 96, 98, 144; and Willard Straight Hall takeover (1969), 23–24, 25, 94–95, 124; and the Wisconsin School, 5, 9, 13, 14, 21, 32, 44, 120–21, 156
LaFollette, Robert, 4, 35
Laise, Carol, 50, 51
Lake, Anthony ("Tony"), 97
Landau, Saul, 40
Langbart, David, 5, 232
Lansing, Robert, 27
Laos, 201
Latin America, 7, 40, 55, 68, 74, 109, 111, 116, 165, 195; and Cleveland administration, 43, 64; and George W. Bush administration, 202; and John Quincy Adams, 26, 113; and Kennedy administration, 112; and Reagan administration, 18; and Theodore Roosevelt administration, 117–18. *See also* individual countries
Latinx Students, 124
League of Nations, 147
Lebanon, 27, 41, 48
Lehrer, Jim, 99
LeMay, Curtis, 193
Lenin, Vladimir, 88–89, 112, 120
Liberalism, 14, 92, 158, 179, 183–85, 192–93, 200
Liliuokalani, Queen, 75
Lincoln, Abraham, 68, 78, 180
Linowitz, Sol, 17
Lippmann, Walter, 223
Little, Douglas, 4, 232, 234
Lodge, Henry Cabot, 18, 66, 74
Logevall, Fredrik, 23, 197n23

INDEX

The Lord of the Rings (trilogy by J. R. Tolkien), 88
Louisiana Purchase, 72
Lytle, Mark, 16

Madison, James, 39, 67, 70, 74, 78, 93, 94, 101, 159; and *Federalist #10*, 62, 71, 200; and US continental expansion, 6–7, 17, 63, 72; and War of 1812, 179
Mahan, Alfred Thayer, 68–69, 75
Mahoney, James, 113
Maier, Charles, 61n33, 168–69
Maisel, David, xiii, 3, 16, 98
Manchuria, 137
Manifest Destiny, 75
Mao Zedong, 9
Marshall Plan, 83, 97, 99
Marx, Karl, 5, 13, 39
Marxism, 8, 16, 111, 120, 125, 158
Massachusetts Institute of Technology (MIT), 20
Matusow, Allen, 185
May, Ernest R., 60n19, 66
McCarthy, Eugene, 182, 187, 188–89, 190
McCarthy, Joseph, 4, 16, 18
McConnell, Mitch, 188
McCormick, Jeri, 36, 39
McCormick, Thomas J., 4, 13, 63, 135, 226, 228; and friendship with LaFeber, 86, 132, 233; and Midwest, 133
McCoy, Drew, 16
McDonald's, 165
McKinley, William, 66, 69, 74
Melville, Herman, 19, 39
Mexican Revolution, 26, 77
Mexican War (1846–48), 73, 113, 201
Mexico, 72, 75, 78, 107, 117, 126, 201
Michael Jordan and the New Global Capitalism, 9–10, 43, 153–54, 159, 161–64, 169–71
Microsoft, 10, 171
Middle East, 7, 9, 18, 27, 29
Midwest, 4, 9, 13, 36, 132–35, 171, 233
Miller, Arthur, 205
Monroe, James, 72
Monroe Doctrine, 7, 13, 19, 41, 72–73; Roosevelt Corollary, 77, 117–18
Moore, R. Laurence, 13
Morgan, Robin, 182
Morgenthau, Hans, 34
Morison, Samuel Elliot, 14, 85
MS-13 (Salvadoran gang), 126
Munro, Dana G., 119
Myrdal, Gunnar, 37

Nabokov, Vladimir, 4
National Archives and Records Administration (NARA), 5, 46, 50, 52, 54, 57, 61n30, 232
National Basketball Association (NBA), 162–63, 165, 167
National Security Agency (NSA), 21
National Security Council (NSC), 21, 47, 48, 50, 51, 98, 121–22
Native Americans, 70, 75, 76, 78
Neodependency, 8, 105, 109, 110–13, 116–17, 125, 127n14
Netherlands, 78
Neu, Charles, 141
New Deal, 32, 39, 181, 191
The New Empire, 6–7, 10, 14, 18, 34, 43, 46, 56, 64–70, 73–75, 77–79, 135, 137, 154, 168, 176, 182
New Left, 47, 83, 86, 90, 157
Newman, Skip, 31n41
Newton, Huey P., 182
Nicaragua, 8, 201; and 1979 revolution in, 109; National Guard in, 114; and Reagan administration, 43, 104, 105, 118, 121–22; and Somoza regime, 117; and Taft administration, 119. *See also* Sandinistas
Niebuhr, Reinhold, 7, 33, 40, 101; influence on LaFeber, 14–15, 28, 83, 84, 92–96, 99, 100, 149; and *The Irony of American History*, 14, 93
Nike Corporation, 10, 154, 161, 162, 163, 165, 171
9/11 attacks, 10, 18, 25, 43, 99, 123, 163, 170, 195, 204
Nixon, Richard, 5, 182, 225; and 1968 election, 178–79, 187–88; and Japan, 144; and Vietnam, 98, 193–94, 195
Nootbaar, Lars, 167
Noriega, Manuel, 105
North Atlantic Treaty Organization (NATO), 8, 97
Norton, Mary Beth, 13, 23

Oath Keepers, 203
Obama, Barack, 194
Olney, Richard, 69
Open Door Policy, 37, 74–75, 77, 85, 96, 137, 138, 144, 158
Organization of American Historians (OAH), 153, 231
Organization of American States (OAS), 117
Oropeza, Lorena, 8, 21, 234
Ortega, Daniel, 119
Osgood, Robert, 34, 80n18

INDEX 219

Palestine, 27
Panama, 17, 109, 110, 111, 115, 117–18
Panama Canal, 17, 24, 105, 108, 135, 177
The Panama Canal: The Crisis in Historical Perspective, 43, 105, 109–11, 117, 119, 167
Paris Peace Conference. *See* Versailles Conference
Parrini, Carl, 34, 40
Paterson, Thomas, 231
Peabody, O. H., 135
Peñalver, Eduardo, 131n90
Pepinsky, Thomas, xii–xiii
Perkins, Dexter, 13, 23, 41
Perkins, James, 23
Pershing, Gen. John J. ("Black Jack"), 26
Persian Gulf, 17, 28, 99
Philippines, 66, 69, 74, 75, 76, 135, 201
Phillips, Kevin, 187
Platt Amendment, 108
Plummer, Brenda Gayle, 130n79
Polenberg, Richard, 13, 236
Polk, James K., 18, 113
Princeton University, 26
Pringle, Henry F., 66
Progressive Era, 113
Progressive Historians, 63, 64, 79n6, 85, 119–20
Proud Boys, 203
Prussia, 78
Puerto Rico, 73, 74, 108
Pulitzer, Joseph, 66
Putin, Vladimir, 8, 100, 202
Pyenson, Lewis, 166
Pyle, Ernie, 147

Race and racism, 6, 68, 124, 130n79, 159, 168, 191; in the 1960s, 182–85; and the 1968 election, 186–88; and Central America, 110, 117, 123; at Cornell, 23; and Japan, 137, 139, 146–47, 148–49
Rambo (1981 film), 90
Rawlings, Hunter, 24, 25
Raytheon Doctrine, 170
Reagan, Ronald, 133, 188; and Central America, 8, 11, 18, 104–06, 109, 110, 118, 121, 125; and Cold War, 90, 116
Relativism, 92
Republican Party, 73, 160, 187–88, 203
Reston, James, 185
Revisionism, 7, 9, 13, 16, 32, 47, 121, 132, 149, 156
Reynolds, E. Bruce, 142
Rhodes, Frank H. T., 24

Robins, Raymond, 88–89, 102n19
Robinson, Jackie, 162
Robinson, Ronald, 64
Rockman, Seth, 157
Rodriguez-Franco, Diana, 113
Rogers, William, 17
Roosevelt, Franklin D. ("FDR"), 139; and the Good Neighbor Policy, 114; and the Soviet Union, 87, 88, 90; and World War II, 14, 35, 147
Roosevelt, Theodore, 18, 40, 66, 136, 160; and Central America, 113; and Gentleman's Agreement (1906), 138; and Japan, 146; and Panama, 110; and Roosevelt Corollary, 77, 117–18
Root, Elihu, 76, 154, 159–60
Rosenberg, Emily, 154
Rossiter, Clinton, 4, 21, 24, 30n3
Rostow, Walt, 111
Rotter, Andrew, 9, 29, 235
Russia, 1, 17, 78, 86–87, 94, 136; in 19th century, 69, 91; Bolshevik Revolution, 26, 88–89; and Cold War, 7–8, 82, 90, 96; post-Cold War, 11, 100, 101, 170, 202. *See also* Soviet Union

Sandinistas, 43, 118, 119, 122
Santayana, George, 20
Schaller, Michael, 141
Schlesinger, Arthur M., Jr., 22, 39, 112, 121, 225
School for the Americas, 115
Schuck, Peter, xiii
Schumpeter, Joseph, 43
Schurman, Jacob Gould, 17
Schurz, Carl, 73
Scott, James C., 164
Scowcroft, Brent, 97
Scully, Eileen, 142
Seale, Bobby, 182
Second World War. *See* World War II
Serbia, 98
Seward, William Henry, 17, 68, 154, 159–60
Shultz, George, 57, 122, 154, 159, 160–61, 169
Siekmeier, James F., 8, 170, 235
Silbey, Joel, 13, 22, 57
Singapore, 5, 46, 55–56
Sirhan, Sirhan, 192
Sklar, Martin, 40
Smith, Robert Freeman, 35, 112, 120–21
Smith, Shannon, xiii, 21
Smoot-Hawley Tariff, 135
Social Darwinism, 66

220 INDEX

Society for Historians of American Foreign Relations (SHAFR), 1, 10, 154, 159, 161, 165
Somalia, 8
Somoza, Anastasio, 117, 129n51
Soros, George, 170
South America, 136, 201. *See also* Latin America
Southeast Asia, 18, 54, 55, 74, 141, 186
Southern Christian Leadership Conference (SCLC), 185–86
Soviet Union, 1, 11, 63, 82, 100, 145; and end of the Cold War, 8, 94, 97; and origins of the Cold War, 7, 14, 96, 140; and Reagan administration, 116, 161; and World War II, 88. *See also* Russia
Spain, 7, 108, 135
Spanish-American War (1898), 6, 65–67, 135, 181, 201
Spanish Empire, 18, 108
Stalin, Josef, 87, 88, 90, 140
Stanford University, 4, 12, 33, 63, 90, 132, 135, 228–29
Starr, Steven, 23
Steel, Ronald, 233–34
Stevenson, Adlai, 36
Stewart, C. Evan, xiii
Straight, Willard, 17, 53, 77
Strong, Josiah, 68
Student Nonviolent Coordinating Committee (SNCC), 186
Syria, 27

Taft, William Howard, 77, 119
Taiwan, 202
Taliban, 204
Tannenbaum, Frank, 34
Teagle, Walter, 17
Technology, 6, 154, 159–61, 170–71
Terrorism, 44, 163, 171, 195, 204, 205
Tet Offensive (1968), 178
Texas, 73
Thailand, 5, 46, 54–55
Thieu, Nguyen Van, 182, 194
Thurmond, Strom, 192
Tillich, Paul, 95
Tisch, Andrew, xiii, 3, 16, 26, 202
Tisch, James, 26
Tocqueville, Alexis de, 169–70, 171, 176, 177, 179, 204; and Eugene McCarthy, 187, 188–89; influence on LaFeber, 10, 15, 149, 186, 195
Tocqueville Problem, 74, 169, 176–77, 181–83, 200, 201–02, 205

Transcontinental Treaty (1821), 72
Transjordan, 27
Trotsky, Leon, 89
Truman, Harry, 7, 18, 32, 87, 90, 97, 99, 140
Truman Doctrine, 83, 97, 99
Trump, Donald, 10, 78, 177, 187, 188, 195, 203
Turner, Frederick Jackson, 13, 33, 68, 91, 133
Twain, Mark, 10, 75

Ukraine, 202
Unabomber, 100
United Fruit Company, 114
University of Michigan, 183
University of Wisconsin-Madison, 13, 24, 33, 35, 91, 158, 233; LaFeber at, 3, 4, 6, 12, 15, 32, 42, 63, 83, 112
Urbana-Champaign, Illinois, 134
US Constitution, 85, 122, 177, 180, 203
US Department of Defense ("Pentagon"), 21, 47, 48
US Department of State, 21, 32, 50, 58; Historical Advisory Committee ("HAC"), 5, 46, 47–53; Office of the Historian ("HO" and later "OH"), 48, 49, 51, 59n2
US Information Agency (USIA), 5, 46, 53–56
US Information Service (USIS), 54, 55, 56

Vandenberg, Arthur S., 35
Venezuela, 69, 117
Versailles Conference (1919), 17, 27, 143, 147
Vietnam War, 5, 10, 15, 44, 54, 55, 100, 105, 115, 119, 126, 136, 141, 178, 186, 187, 201, 202, 223, 225, 230, 231; and Eugene McCarthy, 188–89; and Humphrey, 192–93; and LaFeber, 22, 95, 96, 98, 144; and LBJ, 180–81, 182, 184–85, 190–91; and Nixon, 193–94, 195
Vinson, J. C, 65
Vogel, Erza, 136
Voice of America, 56
Voting Rights Act (1965), 184

Walker, James, 132
Walkerton, Indiana, 3, 9, 12, 36, 132–35, 143, 153
Wallace, George, 182, 186–87, 188, 193, 225
Wallace, Henry, 18
Wall Street Journal, 120
Wang, Jessica, 9, 20, 236
War of 1812, 179, 201
Washington, George, 159
Washington Naval Conference (1921), 138
Watson, James L., 165

Wax, Bernie, 34
Wayne, John, 19
Webster, Daniel, 18
Welk, Lawrence, 233, 234
Welter, Barbara, 34
Western Europe, 96, 202. *See also* individual countries
Westmoreland, William, 182
White, Andrew Dickson, 17
Whitman, Walt, 81n50, 146
Willard Straight Hall ("The Straight"), 22; African American takeover of, 23–24, 25, 94–95, 124
Williams, Billy, 153
Williams, William Appleman, 16, 34, 70, 142–43, 149; and Bolshevik Revolution, 88–89; influence on LaFeber, 4–5, 63–64, 83, 85–86, 91, 225; midwestern background of, 132, 133; and *The Tragedy of American Diplomacy*, 39, 64, 86, 172n11; and Wisconsin School, 37–42, 44, 157–58
Wilson, Woodrow, 17, 18, 26–27, 32, 39, 88, 89, 99, 113, 116, 138, 143, 147, 180

Wisconsin School, 16, 32–35, 80n9, 133, 135, 157; and LaFeber, 5, 9, 13, 14, 21, 32, 44, 120–21, 156; and revisionism, 5, 9, 16, 21, 32
Wisconsin State Historical Society, 36
Wolff, John, 21
Wolfowitz, Paul, 17, 21
World Baseball Classic (2023), 167
World War I, 17, 26, 63, 134, 180, 181, 201; and Russia, 88–89; and US economic interests, 40, 54, 157
World War II, 35, 53, 74, 85, 91, 95, 114, 181, 201; and Japan, 136, 137, 140, 148–49; and Russia, 87–88

Yale University, 14, 21, 26, 27, 65, 100
Yalta Conference, 19
Yamagata, Aritomo, 143
Yeltsin, Boris, 97
Yoshida, Shigeru, 140

Zalaznick, David, xiii
Zinn, Howard, 13

About the Contributors

Tribute volumes like this one usually begin with an "About the Contributors" section in which the authors impress readers with their own scholarly accomplishments. Walter LaFeber was not a fan of that sort of thing, nor are we. What follows, with a bow to Walt, are our favorite stories about our friendship with a teacher, scholar, and mentor unlike any other. Some are funny and some are serious, but all of them reveal what a remarkable human being he was.

Three Cheers for AP History

I'm sorry I don't remember my first encounter with Walter LaFeber. What I do remember is that I had a terrific team-taught AP history class in high school. And the teacher who played the conservative—who was a bit conservative—Werner Feig—had a real bee in his metaphorical bonnet about this Cornell professor named "Walter LaFeber," whom he considered, for debating purposes, to be a Communist. The more I heard Mr. Feig attack him, the more I thought it made sense for me to search out the guy and maybe study with him.

I married the girl who was my girlfriend in that AP history class and she followed me to Cornell, transferring from Oberlin, but did so the semester I spent abroad at Tel Aviv University. It was the second semester of my sophomore year, and so even though I had taken 313 in Bailey Hall, I would not be able to take 314 until the spring semester of the year when I returned. This wonderful woman, now my ex-wife, went to every lecture that semester lugging a cassette tape recorder and saved them all for me to listen to upon my return, which of course I did. I was that much of a nerd.

I took an independent study with Walt upon my return about the arguments that the pundits Walter Lippmann and Joseph Alsop had about Vietnam. I chose this topic because my now ex-wife bought me Ronald Steel's *Walter Lippmann and the American Century* for my birthday that year. The next year Walt wrote me a recommendation to be Cornell's nominee for the Carnegie Endowment internship in Washington, which I got, and I became friends with Ron, who was a fellow there (he passed away in early 2023). Walt and he were friends, and Walt had told him about my paper, but I refused to show it to Ron when I got to Carnegie because in the comments, Walt said he thought I leaned a little too heavily on Steel's research and could have done more of my own. I wrote my first book, a history of punditry called *Sound & Fury: The Making of the Punditocracy* published in 1992, based in part on that paper. I published my twelfth book, *We Are Not One: A History of America's Fight over Israel*, thirty years later, using some of the research I did for the senior honors thesis I did for Walt. I hope he would have felt by then I had learned how to do my own research, but I can't say I'm confident that, at least in terms of the example of his scholarship, it would be true.

Eric Alterman
Professor of English
CUNY–Brooklyn College
Cornell BA 1982

★   ★   ★   ★   ★

On Training

After completing a master's degree in international history at the London School of Economics, I knew I wanted to learn more about how Americans saw themselves in the world and why, but not what to do about it. In London, I had been exposed to the attitude that the British had done a decent job of running the world and now the Americans were messing it up. Although I saw some justification for this point of view, when I, as "the American," was asked to explain the Reagan administration's claim that the United States could fight and win a nuclear war, I felt I still had more questions than answers.

I returned without funds to Ithaca and because my mother worked at Cornell, I was eligible for tuition coverage. I got jobs at J. C. Penney and the YMCA and audited two classes, one on US cultural history and one on the history of US foreign relations. When I heard Professor LaFeber discuss Walt Whitman and Reinhold Niebuhr as well as American clipper ships sailing the Pacific and Cold War strategies, I thought here was a place for me.

So, I presented myself to Professor LaFeber after waiting in line on the fourth floor of McGraw Hall during his office hours. He politely made it clear he did not want me. He was not taking graduate students, he said. Looking back, I realize I probably resembled a stray puppy gazing hopefully at him. He bent a little. He said, "You will have to be retrained." I nodded. It was worse than he knew because I had no idea what he was talking about. I did not know what it meant to be trained and certainly did not feel I had been. He put me on trial. I had to do a research paper for him, ace the GREs, and be accepted into the graduate school. I undertook these tasks, which was my way of refusing to go away. In the end, he gave me an academic home. It wasn't always a good fit, because I was difficult to train, but he was kind as well as demanding.

When I was offered a job at the University of Wisconsin–Stevens Point, Walt was pleased, pronounced it "a return to Wisconsin," and then said, "You will defend your dissertation before you go." Although my dissertation was far from finished, I scrambled to pull my research together and defend it, but it wasn't pretty. In the years that followed, he remained a generous mentor who took his pencil to my manuscripts of *To Win the Peace* and *Why America Fights*. In his correspondence, Walt often mentioned the activities and accomplishments of his students, but rarely his own. Instead, a package would arrive with an inscribed copy of his latest book. I see now how he was connecting us, his strays and stars, into a community of scholars, who, each in his or her own way, had joined the quest to discover what this American experiment is all about.

Susan A. Brewer
Professor of History Emerita
University of Wisconsin–Stevens Point
Cornell PhD 1991

★   ★   ★   ★   ★

The Summer of '68

Walt LaFeber rejected my application to graduate school—and with good reason. As a senior history major at nearby Hamilton College, I had ventured to Ithaca for an interview with Professor LaFeber on March 15, 1968. Coincidentally, that was a month to the day after Walt and Lloyd Gardner had bested Arthur M. Schlesinger Jr., George F. Kennan, and other skeptics of revisionist Cold War history at a seminar held at the Institute for Advanced Study in Princeton. Understandably, I knew nothing about Walt's and Lloyd's achievement. Nor would I necessarily have been impressed, since I had only vague notions about who Schlesinger and Kennan were. And if someone at that point had asked me what I thought of "William Appleman Williams," I might have replied that while I had no idea who he was, his name seemed rather redundant. Maybe Walt did ask me about Williams in that interview; I do not recall. In any case, he turned down my application.

There followed the bleak summer of 1968. Bobby Kennedy was assassinated. Fervent hopes for political change yielded only the grim choice of presidential candidates Hubert Humphrey, Richard Nixon, and George Wallace. The meat grinder in Vietnam was chewing up GIs my age. Draft calls were rising. My local draft board had turned down my application for conscientious objector (CO) status. Though I had appealed to the state draft board, I had little reason for optimism. I was determined to refuse induction into the military even if that meant going to prison. Amid these dire prospects, I ventured a Hail Mary pass. In late August I wrote to Walt, asking if perhaps the draft had thinned the ranks of the incoming graduate class and, if so, might there now be an opening. My life then changed. Walt wrote back to say I could come to Cornell, but without any funding. I would have to pay tuition and all living expenses. I grabbed this life line.

That first semester was intense. My seminar with Walt had just one other student and met at his house. Every two weeks we read five to eight books plus primary sources and wrote a paper. I began to grasp the magnitude of what I did not know. Amid this discovery, Walt never made me feel stupid. I got an A in the seminar. He then used his pull so that I received full, indeed generous, funding for my remaining three and a half years at Cornell. I finished my PhD with money in the bank. Meanwhile, the state draft board approved my CO application.

In the fifty-three years between that first year at Cornell and Walt's death, Walt remained a central figure in my life. He enabled my career as a scholar and teacher. He remained an inspiration. Our relationship was symbolized by our periodic five- or six-hour luncheons, fueled by coffee and wine, at which we would discuss people, history, and politics. I wish that he could have read my book on Kennan. Going forward, trying to understand what made Walt the person he was has become my intellectual focus.

Frank Costigliola
Professor of History
University of Connecticut
Cornell PhD 1972

* * * * *

God Called

In the premodern days before voice mail, roommates took messages. Whenever Walter LaFeber phoned, mine would write: "God called." Such was his campus-wide reputation. None of the engineers and hotellies who also lived at 214 College Avenue in the summer of 1993 ever took his courses. But even those obsessed with formulas and recipes knew this professor was different, as was his role in my life, which extended beyond directing my honors thesis to selecting each semester's courses. History wasn't the only thing Walt thought worth studying, though his ecumenism had limits. I only won his grudging consent for taking the Hotel School's wines course my senior year by giving him two American literature courses in exchange.

The Walt I knew was at the tail end of his career, experienced enough to excel at what an adviser does most: he gave great advice. Thirty years after I first walked into his office as a Cornell freshman, his words echo throughout my own conversations with students. "If you get 5% of what you apply for, you'll have a brilliant academic career," he once consoled when an application failed. Similar advice kept me in graduate school, when temporary insanity prompted by frustration with American politics prompted a brief enthusiasm for coupling my PhD in history with a concurrent law degree. I shudder at the thought today, but Walt rode to the rescue. "Doing multiple things at once rarely produces the best results," he advised. "Go to law school if you must, but only after finishing what you've started." I imagine he already knew that years of dissertation work would extinguish any short-term enthusiasm for the law.

So, I stayed. At the University of Wisconsin, a school chosen in brazen hope of joining Madison's long line of distinguished historians and, frankly, because Walt said it was the place to go (and Tom McCormick the man to work with next). Graduation's approach nonetheless prompted second thoughts. "Was Wisconsin good enough?" I asked. Cursory review of prestigious departments, Cornell's included, suggested most faculty came from prestigious private universities. Walt paused, the gleam in his eye signaling that he was about to enjoy the advice to come next. "Well," he said. "It worked for me."

I never regretted the choice, nor doubted that the most important decision of my academic career was that freshman visit to his office. In which, in retrospect, he showed not only how an adviser should be selected, but something of equal importance yet far less frequently discussed: how a mentor should choose a mentee.

Because I was Cold War curious and wielded rudimentary French, he told me to read five or six books on Franco-American relations (including some guy with a weird Italian name: "Costigli"-something?), and return to discuss. Few overly zealous undergraduates ever returned for a second conversation, I later learned, but his method imparted another piece of advice I try to follow to this day: give everyone a chance, and spend time with those who come back for more. I'm so glad he did both.

Jeffrey A. Engel
Professor of History
Southern Methodist University
Cornell BA 1995

★ ★ ★ ★ ★

It's the Little Things

As I think about all the Walt stories I could tell, I remember more the passing comments, brief bits of advice, and habits he had rather than any single anecdote. At our very first meeting, after I had arrived at Cornell in the fall of 1988 to do my PhD under his direction, he asked me what I wanted to write my dissertation on! He said then (and many times subsequently), "You are only in graduate school to get out of graduate school." A healthy reminder that the PhD is training to allow you to be a historian, not an end in itself. Shortly after that first meeting, he also began asking me at nearly every meeting, to state my argument in one sentence. I tried to comply, initially using spoken semicolons in a desperate bid to include all my unruly thoughts. Today, I ask my graduate students to do the same thing nearly every time we meet.

I remember that he (im)patiently edited every split infinitive and dangling participle. I learned better how to edit my own work in a bid to not see those circles on the page. Even though Walt taught hundreds of students each semester in the US foreign relations survey, he taught the voluntary section meeting rather than assigning that to us, his graduate assistants. I remember that we were all amazed that only a couple dozen showed up to meet with him. As his graduate assistants, our main responsibility was to grade. Whenever a student had a complaint, if the student wanted Walt to look over our work, Walt asked the student to write about what they thought we had gotten wrong. Then Walt typed, on a page from a yellow legal pad, an explanation for why that student was fortunate to have gotten as good a grade as they did. But at the end of the semester, when we met to assign final grades, Walt was often the one arguing to raise students' grades.

As I prepared my first attempt at an article for submission, I included caveats about languages I didn't speak, archives I hadn't visited. Walt advised me to boldly claim the value of what I had done rather than allow people to think about what I had not. I hear his voice in my head all the time when writing. When I finished my PhD, and was interviewing for jobs, Walt gave only as much advice as I asked for, which wasn't much. I do remember that he was more consistently supportive than any other Cornell faculty of my desire to find a job that fit with how I wanted to live my life rather than the most prestigious job. Each of these little comments, observations, bits of advice lives on in how I teach, write, and navigate my career.

Anne L. Foster
Professor of History
Indiana State University
Cornell PhD 1995

★ ★ ★ ★ ★

A Night to Remember

Walt LaFeber, Tom McCormick, and I became lifelong friends while in graduate school at the University of Wisconsin, "Ground Zero" for Cold War revisionism during the late 1950s. Our second year at Madison was the first year of Bill Williams's long tenure in the history department. It may have been Fred Harrington's hand behind the scenes, I don't know. But Walt and Tom and I were all assigned to be his teaching assistants. Tom was an assistant in his seminar course and Walt and I were assigned to the foreign policy survey. The principal textbook was *The Shaping of American Diplomacy*. Very soon, attending these lectures with our own notepads open as we wrote furiously, we found students coming up after class to ask us to explain what they were hearing. It was pretty embarrassing to admit we did not know.

Talking together, we decided on a bold step: We would ask Bill and his wife, Corrine, to dinner at Walt and Sandy's apartment in downtown Madison. It turned out to be, as they say, a night to remember. We talked about that experience for the rest of our lives. Bill gave an evening seminar like none other. It drew on so many threads to put American foreign policy into a coherent picture. It was an exploration of how policymakers made sense out of the world, not determinism, and beyond the action–reaction interpretations that had reigned supreme until those years. Over the course of my talking with colleagues, I have never met anyone whose graduate school experience included such an event. But more important, we no longer felt unable to answer our students' questions! We had a framework, what Bill always called a *Weltanschauung*!

Lloyd C. Gardner
Professor of History Emeritus
Rutgers University
University of Wisconsin-Madison PhD 1960

★ ★ ★ ★ ★

Walt Takes the Long View

In June 1962, having successfully defended my honors thesis, which I wrote under Walt's superb guidance, I went up to his West Sibley office to say goodbye. At his suggestion, and following in his footsteps, I was leaving to begin graduate work at

Stanford with Thomas A. Bailey. As always, Walt sat behind his desk while I sat across from him. We chatted, and suddenly I said, "I don't know any history." Walt smiled and said, "That's okay. Wait until you get to graduate school; you'll have lots of time."

Though not initially intending to, I again followed in his footsteps by leaving Stanford (and Bailey) after my MA. After taking a year off from graduate work, I happily accepted Walt's invitation to return to Cornell to become his first PhD student.

Fast-forward to June 1967. Having successfully defended my dissertation, I again went up to West Sibley to say goodbye. Largely on the strength of his letter of reference, I was leaving to take up my first teaching position, at Ohio State. He sat behind the desk while I sat across from him. We chatted, and suddenly I said, "I don't know any history." Walt smiled and said, "That's okay. Wait until you start teaching; you'll have lots of time."

Fast-forward again to August 1969. At Walt's initiative, I had been invited to teach summer session at Cornell prior to taking up my new position at the University of Saskatchewan. Since he was not teaching in the summer, he graciously invited me to use his West Sibley office while he used his Olin Library carrel. I had just finished entering final grades and was packing my books when suddenly there he was. I got up to offer him his chair, but he waved me to sit down while he sat across from me. So now I was sitting where he usually sat, while he was sitting where I usually sat. We chatted, and suddenly I said, "I don't know any history." Walt just smiled and said, "That's okay. Wait until you retire; you'll have all the time in the world."

More than half a century later, as I once again prepare (at age 81) to teach summer session at our beloved Cornell, I think to myself, "I don't know any history." And I can hear Walt laughing and saying, "What do you expect? You haven't retired yet."

David Green
Visiting Professor of History
Cornell University
Cornell BA 1962, Cornell PhD 1967

* * * * *

Rock Star

I "met" Walt through reading *America, Russia, and the Cold War* as a college student in Tokyo in 1981 or 1982. His book was assigned in my "American Foreign Policy History" seminar, and I immediately became enthralled by his scholarship. As I began my graduate studies, I slowly began to fantasize about someday meeting him and telling him in person how much I admired his work. My thesis adviser in Japan, the late Dr. Tadashi Aruga, had worked with Walt through international collaborative publishing projects and conferences. He would tell us how nice and unassuming Walt was to everybody. By 1985, I could not suppress the urge to "go to America" and work with this legendary figure. Yes, I was adoring Walt almost like the way I was adoring my then-favorite American rock star, Billy Joel.

I was fortunate enough to receive a Fulbright scholarship to study in the US and was quickly admitted to all the graduate programs I applied to *except* Cornell. Come

April 1986, still no word from Cornell, but I had to tell the Japanese Fulbright Commission which school I had chosen to attend. I was so desperate that I placed an international call (it was still very expensive) from my home in Tokyo at 2:00 a.m. My $20-per-minute call was first directed to the history department office. After speaking with Jackie Hubble (the department secretary) and then Dr. James John (the director of graduate studies at the time), I was informed that there had been some bureaucratic mixup, that I had been accepted into the program, and that a formal acceptance letter would be sent shortly. As I breathed a big sigh of relief, Jim John mentioned that he had just seen Walt pass by in the hallway and he would go get him and put him on the phone. The next thirty seconds were the most heart-throbbing moment of my life up to that moment. Walt said hello and kind words of welcome to Cornell to this Japanese graduate student. I may never be able to speak with Billy Joel (which has turned out to be true), but I was now speaking with THAT Walter LaFeber!

Thirty-seven years, a PhD, and three academic jobs spanning Japan and the US later, Walt remains the brightly shining star in my universe. He was so patient with this international student whose previous academic training in a different culture had never prepared her to engage in critical thinking and formulating her own questions. He was so generous with his time going through this former student's book manuscripts and offered detailed and insightful feedback. Come to think of it, I am now older than Walt was when I arrived at Cornell. Never a day goes by without me asking myself if I am treating my students and colleagues the same way Walt always did his. I try to do my best, but he is truly a tough act to follow. Thank you, Professor LaFeber (that's what I persisted in calling him until 2001 or 2002), for everything you've taught me through your own life and work.

Sayuri Guthrie-Shimizu
Professor of History
Rice University
Cornell PhD 1991

* * * * *

Hey LaFeber!

It was 1971. I had just graduated and was staying in Ithaca for the summer before heading off to grad school that fall. Before entering Olin Library one afternoon, I heard a female student hollering irately: "LaFeber! Hey LaFeber!" I was rather appalled by this rudeness, but then a second later understood when I saw a small furry dog running hurriedly in her direction.

As this recollection suggests, Walter LaFeber had a big impact on Cornell in my day, as I know he did for many years thereafter. Hundreds of students were taking his survey course on US foreign relations, desperately hoping it might help them make sense of what the United States was doing in Vietnam. Never had the study of history, taught by such masters as Walt, George McT. Kahin (of the government department), and Dominick LaCapra, among many others, seemed more important.

Speaking for myself, the results were life-changing. A pretty conservative young man, hailing from suburban Long Island, I entered college intending to prepare for law school and then, eventually, go into politics. (I recall describing myself as a "Nixon Republican" in one of my college interviews.)

Those goals came under serious review pretty quickly. The teaching assistant I had in the American survey course, Howard Kushner, one of Walt's grad students, made me wonder if I really knew as much about the world as I'd thought. On his advice, I signed up for Walt's US foreign relations survey for my sophomore year, and from then on took as many courses with him, and others in the history department, as I possibly could. I'd always loved the subject, but now I was also beginning to understand the discipline's immeasurable value as a "way of learning." I then followed a career of teaching, research, and writing in the field that has lasted for more than fifty years.

In every way, Walt was key to this. He provided a model of what a true teacher/scholar should be. Respectful and generous toward all, he presented his ideas clearly and courageously, welcomed reasoned debate, asked challenging questions, and insisted on intellectual rigor and integrity. Above all, as I learned over many years, he cared greatly about his students.

Robert E. Hannigan
Suffolk University (retired)
Cornell BA 1971

* * * * *

Rain Delay

I arrived at Cornell in 1967. The Vietnam War had already reached a level of intensity that generated a growing protest movement on campus, and by the end of my first semester that movement became the focal point of virtually all my activities. I took Walt's course because his lectures were already legendary and because of its connection to my focal point. But I spent more time trying to end the war than on my studies.

Walt nevertheless wrote a letter recommending me for graduate school. And unlike my PhD advisors, he urged me not to be discouraged by the challenge of writing a dissertation on the 1954 intervention in Guatemala. Then, after completing my degree, I organized a session on the CIA operations in Guatemala and Cuba for the 1980 OAH meeting in California. Walt agreed to chair it. The session turned into chaos; many in the audience used the forum to denounce US imperialism in every corner of the globe. Walt told me afterward that he was done with academic meetings. I feared that he was also done with me.

It took baseball for our relationship to recover—and to blossom. Again, the stage was a meeting of the OAH, this time in Cincinnati three years later. What prompted Walt to attend remains for me a mystery. I was there to receive an award for my revised dissertation. Of more significance, the Reds were at home playing the Cubs. Both teams were mediocre, and the weather was raw and damp. But it was the Cubs, and hence for Walt, attending was a must. He put together a small group that included Tom Paterson, Lloyd Gardner, myself, and a few others.

The temperature dropped, the rain intensified, and the Cubs fell farther and farther behind. Lloyd especially complained about how miserable he was and kept asking out loud to whomever was listening why we were there. Yet Walt remained riveted to the game, and he recognized that I was a kindred spirit. While Lloyd grumbled, we dissected and analyzed. Once again, I was Walt's student, and this time I was all in.

I recalled that game when, as a chaired professor decades later, I received an invitation to serve on the board of *Political Science Quarterly*. *PSQ*'s editor, Jim Caraley, made explicit that I would replace Walter LaFeber. We really did share a history, I thought to myself as I accepted, although knowing full well that Walt was irreplaceable.

Richard H. Immerman
Professor of History Emeritus
Temple University
Cornell BA 1971

★   ★   ★   ★   ★

Call Me Walt

Walter LaFeber's reputation preceded him. It was the time of detente, Watergate, and the imperial presidency and I had grown interested in US foreign policy. A high school classmate had taken part in a summer program at Cornell and spoke very highly of LaFeber, so when I found out that LaFeber was teaching a freshman seminar, I wanted in. This led to our first encounter. It was during freshman registration on August 29, 1975, at about 8:15 in the morning. I was in Uris Library signing up for that class and needed his signature on the registration form. In looking back, I can truly say that getting Walt to sign my form at this brief early-morning encounter was a life-altering moment. Much of the direction of my academic and professional careers stemmed from the relationship I had with him, and it all began in that meeting and in that class.

When I began corresponding with LaFeber after I graduated from Cornell in 1979, I addressed my letters to "Mr. LaFeber" and sometimes "Professor LaFeber." He signed his "Walter LaFeber." Over time, his signature morphed into "Walt LaFeber" and then to just plain "Walt." I continued with "Mr. LaFeber" and "Professor LaFeber" until he finally ordered me to change my ways, writing "Note: Not 'Mr. LaFeber'—Hell, David, you're nearly middle aged (like me!)." I wasn't yet, but I certainly felt like I had hit the big time.

Walt was not all about history. After one memorable dinner in Washington, during which we discussed a wide variety of topics, including music—another of his loves—and I extolled the attributes of a new modern classical recording (Henryk Gorecki's Symphony No. 3 with Dawn Upshaw), we walked past a local record store. He motioned that we should go in and for the next little while we shared our thoughts on a variety of musical styles. Walt purchased the recording I had recommended and later indicated that he liked it.

While the author's professional affiliation is the National Archives and Records Administration, his contribution to this volume is a personal statement written on his own time and reflecting his personal views and opinions.

David A. Langbart
Archivist
National Archives and Records Administration
Cornell BA 1979

★   ★   ★   ★   ★

A Shaggy Dog Story

I first met Walt LaFeber in August 1972 upon my arrival in Ithaca to start graduate school after completing my BA at the University of Wisconsin, where I had studied with Tom McCormick. It was awe at first sight. Walt was a fabulous lecturer and an extraordinary scholar, of course, but it was his mentorship that made him truly unique. He slogged through my 500-page PhD thesis on the Spanish Civil War without complaint, he ran interference with Cornell University Press so that my dissertation could become a book, and he provided constant encouragement and cogent advice for my later work on US policy in the Middle East. I landed my job at Clark University thanks largely to Walt's friendship with George Billias, who chaired the search committee.

There was not a kinder or wiser historian on the face of the planet, but I think I miss Walt's sense of humor most. My absolute favorite memory was back in the late 1970s when I was a TA in his survey of US foreign relations. Walt was teaching in Ives 120, a dual-level lecture hall that seated about 300 people on the ILR quad. There were two doors up front, one that exited outside onto Tower Road and the other that faced this weird interior courtyard.

It was a sunny morning in late April. Both doors were wide open, and in wandered two dogs. Not a problem. Walt liked dogs. And then the dogs started to become amorous. We TAs were always supposed to ride shotgun, so I got up, shooed the dogs outside, and closed the door. Walt quipped, "That's the open-door policy in action" and brought down the house. I took my seat, Walt resumed his lecture, and then we heard the sound of barking dogs getting closer and closer. The next thing we knew, the same two dogs burst back into Ives 120 from the courtyard. Walt deadpanned: "And that's just about how well the open-door policy usually works." Even more uproarious laughter erupted.

Douglas Little
Professor of History Emeritus
Clark University
Cornell PhD 1978

Tiny Bubbles and Prune Whip

Because Tom McCormick passed away on July 25, 2020, he could not participate in this project honoring Walt. Nevertheless, he co-authored with Lloyd Gardner chapter 2, which was originally published in *Diplomatic History*, and dating to their graduate school days together at the University of Wisconsin, he, Walt, and Lloyd remained life-long friends. In the spirit of this section "About the Contributors," we therefore asked Lloyd to tell us a story about Tom, Walt and himself.

Lloyd told us two. The first took place early in their relationship when Tom made an important, if disquieting, discovery about Walt: his favorite band leader was Lawrence Welk, whose "champagne music" was a staple on Saturday night television across the Midwest during the 1950s. "And a one-ah, and a two ah!"

The second story concerned tastes in food. Walt and Lloyd soon discovered Tom's secret. He did not eat any food that was green: no salads, no peas, or anything of the kind. Nor did he—or Walt—like prunes. That discovery came about the hard way, when Lloyd's wife Nancy prepared prune whip for dessert at an early dinner. Neither Tom nor Walt would touch it.

Yet their relationship overcame Lawrence Welk, prunes, and all other similar dividing points.

Thomas J. McCormick
Professor of History Emeritus
University of Wisconsin-Madison
University of Wisconsin-Madison PhD 1960

* * * * *

A Multifaceted Man

I first met Walt LaFeber through his scholarship. In the fall of 1987, I was an *Orlando Sentinel* journalist contemplating pursuing a graduate degree in history at Cornell University. I had only to read a few pages of *Inevitable Revolutions: The United States in Central America* before I knew that I had found the person with whom I wished to work. The persuasive prose, the damning evidence, the sheer timeliness of the book, captivated me.

The following spring, I met Professor LaFeber in person. All business, he immediately asked me what my dissertation was about. Although I had been accepted into the program, as a journalism major I was minimally prepared for graduate school. I barely understood what a dissertation was! Sensing that I had some catching up to do, Walt suggested that I move to Ithaca early. I spent the summer of 1988 taking two history courses (one taught by a visiting Doug Little) and plowing through a massive reading list that Walt provided.

I am just realizing now that I never paid for those courses. Walt arranged that. So along with maintaining impeccably high standards and high expectations, Walt acted on behalf of others. They were interconnected facets of the same man. Over the next two years, "W.L.," as he signed all his notes ("Walt" emerged only after graduation) kept asking me about my dissertation topic until I had a viable answer. His constant encouragement toward the finish line was embedded in the asking.

If Walt nonetheless appeared intimidating on occasion, he also paid careful attention to power relations between himself and his students, as one of my favorite memories of him attests: One day I had dropped by his cubbyhole of an office in Olin Library before heading to the history department in McGraw Hall. He had a letter he wished to mail from the department. Yet he appeared to squirm at the prospect of asking me to drop off the letter for him. I was a woman. I was a graduate student. This was an administrative task. His midwestern politeness no doubt added to his hesitation. I had to tell him to just give me the letter.

Powerful yet powerfully aware, demanding yet generous, Walt could be tender as well as tough. One final recollection: the genuine happiness he expressed when I told him that I was getting married. John Byrd, then a doctoral student in physics, was the reason I had started looking at graduate studies at Cornell in the first place. Instead of taking me less seriously (my worry all along), Walt was glad that I had found a life partner. Clearly speaking from experience, and a love of Sandra, he considered marriage a definitive advantage in life. Of course, he told me that before I drifted to thoughts of a December wedding, I had better turn in my final paper for him!

Lorena Oropeza
Professor of Ethnic Studies
University of California, Berkeley
Cornell PhD, 1996

* * * * *

The Best Advice I Never Expected

I became a historian because of Walt LaFeber, and I nearly didn't because of him. I never imagined myself doing what LaFeber did. No one else—certainly not I—could be that intellectually powerful, that polished a stage performer, that brilliant a scholar, that committed politically (while nevertheless remaining subtle and unpredictable in his politics), that kind and generous and decent despite his justified fame. Since I couldn't come close to him in any of these things, I saw no point in entering his field.

I did like the idea of teaching. In the fall of my junior year at Cornell, I took an education course, and in the spring I became a student teacher in a Western Civilization class at Ithaca High School. (One of my students was Walt's son, Scott, who perhaps unsurprisingly did very well.) It was a lot of work, but I enjoyed it, and when my apprenticeship ended, I went to see Walt and tell him that I thought I might like to teach secondary school history. He heard me out, then said—I'll never forget it—"An honorable profession. But you don't want to do that. Go get a PhD in history and teach at a university. Here's where you should apply." He listed off six places, really good ones. I wrote them down, nodding mutely, and walked out of his office feeling stunned and elated that he actually thought I could get into any of them and go on to do what he did.

It would later seem to me that Walt's advice, given to me during one of the profession's periodic job crises, was akin to one of Steve Martin's best bits. *"You*

[Martin declared] can be a millionaire! Here's how. First: [rapid fire] get a million dollars. Then . . . !" It turned out that Walt's seemingly matter-of-fact advice was no guarantee of my success. Graduate school wasn't easy. But Walt's confidence in me kept me at it, made me determined to fulfill whatever promise he had seen in me. I didn't have to be him. No one could be. But I could be me, and still find something to say, to my students and my fellow historians.

Andrew Rotter
Professor of History Emeritus
Colgate University
Cornell BA 1975

★ ★ ★ ★ ★

Letter of Recommendation

Others have said it; it's in this volume in multiple places but bears repeating. Walt LaFeber was one of the most intelligent, and decent, people any of us have ever met. He also gave his time selflessly to his students. One example of his giving of his time was that when I applied for jobs, he would write a second letter of recommendation (LOR), in addition to the letter that was sent with my job application. During one job interview, the chair of the history department told me specifically that he was impressed that LaFeber sent a second LOR (and I got the job).

And the content of LORs? Of course, they are anonymous. However, I did manage to see an LOR that he wrote for me. LaFeber's gifts were on display in that letter of recommendation. My last year of graduate school, I applied for a fellowship. The application required that he give me a sealed LOR, which I was to submit with my application to the granting agency. For some reason I cannot remember, I ended up not applying for the fellowship. So I opened the LOR. There I was, summed up perfectly, in that clear, crisp LaFeberian prose. I was flattered that he gave me such a positive evaluation. But in typical LaFeber fashion, he did not go overboard in his praise—and tactfully omitted criticisms he could have made. That LOR was the gift that kept on giving—because I used it as a model for the many LORs I've written for students over the years.

James F. Siekmeier
Professor of History
West Virginia University
Cornell PhD 1993

★ ★ ★ ★ ★

Faceoff at the Statler

I enjoyed the tremendous good fortune of not just one but two great undergraduate mentors. Richard Polenberg hired me as a research assistant when he was finishing

Fighting Faiths in the summer of 1986, and he supervised my research on an NEH-funded summer project a year later. Dick (I of course addressed him as Professor Polenberg at the time) wisely insisted I gain wider exposure, so he sent me to Walt LaFeber. I then happily spent my senior year writing my honors thesis under Walt's direction and reading page proofs of *The American Age* with him as one of his undergraduate RAs.

My favorite Walt story comes much later, during an archival trip to Cornell in October 2003, when Walt took me out to lunch at the Statler Hotel. We chatted happily and easily about all manner of topics, and then our salads arrived. I dredged up a dim memory from my Chinese immigrant upbringing that I should wait for the honored elder to start before digging in myself. Walt did not touch his plate, however. I knew he had had heart surgery recently and worried that he seemingly had no appetite. I nattered merrily away to cover up my growing sense of alarm, when finally, unable to stand it any longer, I picked up my fork and took the tiniest nibble.

Walt immediately tucked in, and I remembered: Walt was a gentleman. He had manners, he was raised right, and a gentleman never breaks bread before a lady. Walt was old school in the best sense of the term, with an insistence on civility and respect as fundamental to personal and professional relationships. I like to think that had I only possessed a more rigid devotion to filial duty, Walt and I would still be seated and facing off at the Statler to the present day.

Jessica Wang
Professor of History and Geography
University of British Columbia
Cornell BA 1988

www.ingramcontent.com/pod-product-compliance
Lightning Source LLC
Chambersburg PA
CBHW031316160426
43196CB00007B/551